A Body of Individuals

A Body of Individuals

The Paradox of Community in
Contemporary Fiction

SUE-IM LEE

 THE OHIO STATE UNIVERSITY PRESS / COLUMBUS

Library of Congress Cataloging-in-Publication Data
Lee, Sue-Im, 1969–
A body of individuals : the paradox of community in contemporary fiction / Sue-Im Lee.
   p. cm.
Includes bibliographical references and index.
ISBN 978-0-8142-0407-8 (alk. paper)
1. American fiction—20th century—History and criticism. 2. Communities in literature. I. Title.
PS374.C586L44 2009
813'.5409353—dc22
                    2008048781

This book is available in the following editions:
Cloth (ISBN 978-0-8142-0407-8)
CD-ROM (ISBN 978-0-8142-9181-8)

Cover design by James Baumann
Cover photo by Bohnchang Koo, Ocean 6, 2002. Courtesy of the artist.
Text design and typesetting by Jennifer Shoffey Forsythe. Type set in Adobe Sabon.
Printed by Thomson-Shore, Inc.

♾ The paper used in this publication meets the minimum requirements of the American National
Standard for Information Sciences—Permanence of Paper for Printed Library Materials. ANSI
Z39.48-1992.

9 8 7 6 5 4 3 2 1

To My Parents

CONTENTS

ACKNOWLEDGMENTS

This project has been through many incarnations. I wish to thank those whose involvement enabled this final one. I am grateful to Christian Messenger, Judith Kegan Gardiner, and Joseph Tabbi at the University of Illinois at Chicago for their dedicated involvement in my thinking and writing. I thank those colleagues at Temple University who kindly read and responded to portions and earlier versions of this book: Rachel Blau DuPlessis, Suzanne Gauch, Shannon Miller, Dan O'Hara, James Salazar, Alan Singer, and Susan Wells. An invaluable friend to this manuscript has been Josephine Park, who provided the discerning eye crucial in its final stages.

This project has been supported by Temple University's Research Study Leave and Summer Fellowship. A portion of chapter 4 appeared in *Symploke* as "Recognition as a Depleted Resource in Lynne Tillman's *Motion Sickness*"; an earlier version of chapter 2 appeared in *Modern Fiction Studies* as "We Are Not the World: Universalism and Global Village in *Tropic of Orange*." I thank the editors of The Ohio State University Press for their wonderful support and the external readers for their most useful responses. I am grateful to Mr. Bohnchang Koo for allowing me to use his artwork, *Ocean 6,* for the cover of this book; I could not have envisioned more fitting art for this project.

Finally, I thank my family here and elsewhere, especially those who lived through this book's disorderly growth—Mike, Snow S, and Lucia.

The Paradox of Community

T his book argues that community is a perennial source of contention because it holds a self-contradictory proposition in its most
basic definition—that multiple individuals become "a body of
individuals." "A body," after all, indicates a person, an individual,
a singleness of being. So how can community be a condition of multiple,
disparate, and distinct individuals as well as of a single body of being?
Two vastly different responses to this paradox circulate in contemporary literary criticism, philosophy, and cultural criticism, and these two
conflicting responses, I suggest, represent the competing discourses of
community that dominate current debates over community.

In one response, community functions as an aspiration and an ideal.
This idealized discourse of community argues that the paradox of community is superseded when multiple individuals are bound by forces of
commonality, sharing, belonging, connection, and attachment. As these
forces perform the seemingly impossible task of transforming many into
one, the enormity of the feat explains why community functions as the
ultimate expression of human unity. Indeed, there are numerous other
terms to describe unity—for example, organization, association, membership, collectivity, union, affiliation, group. Yet none of these terms
approaches the cultural prevalence, emotional appeal, and political heft
of the term community. The reason, this book ventures, rests squarely
on the paradoxical proposition of community: that many can become

1

one through *fusion*. While other terms of unity describe an aggregate number of individuals and particular modes of relationship between them, community as an ideal promises a fusion of multiple individuals into one subject position. Promising a degree of oneness that no other term of unity delivers, community becomes the seat of the most desirable human relationality—a unity that is convivial, productive, safe, familiar, comforting, intimate, and healing. Enacting what Raymond Williams calls the "warmly persuasive" connotation surrounding the word community (76), the many expressions of *idealized community* emerge from divergent sources—from ordinary speech, political discussions, communitarianism, feminist criticism, ethnic minority discourse, and, most importantly for the argument of this book, literary criticism of contemporary fiction.[1]

Conversely, no other term for unity provokes as much criticism and dismay as does the term community. *Because* community functions as the ultimate expression of fusion, community becomes the bearer of *totality*. In this response, the proposition of transforming many individuals into one body becomes the ultimate logic of totalitarianism. Rather than being the seat of conviviality and health, community's promise of oneness becomes the seat of all human organizations that are exclusionary, coercive, and oppressive, as found in historical evidences of nationalism, regionalism, racism, ethnicism, sexism, and heterosexism.[2] Relatedly, concepts that are valorized for their ability to fuse many into one, such as commonality, sharedness, belonging, and attachment, become synonymous with forces that demand homogeneity, regulation, and obedience. In its fundamental negation of the idealized community, this response may be called the discourse of *dissenting community*—a dissent from the assumptions, values, and goals of idealized community. To the paradox of community, then, dissenting community offers an antithetical answer. No, there cannot be a single body of individuals, and to aspire to one ignores the vital fact that heterogeneity, conflict, difference, and unbreachable singularity of being are inextricable ingredients of any unity. This negation of idealized community foregrounds postmodernist inquiry into power, identity, difference, and hegemony, as well as feminist and cosmopolitanist revisions of community.

This book examines contemporary American fiction that offers a third response to the paradox of community: to simultaneously believe and disbelieve in the proposition of "a body of individuals." As these novelists simultaneously pursue and critique the alchemy of community, they intervene in the debate over community in a unique manner.

They highlight the fact that the two competing discourses of community share a commonality: both of them remove the paradoxical nature of its proposition. Idealized community supersedes the paradox by arguing the transformative power of commonality, sharing, belonging, and attachment to fuse many into one. Dissenting community dismisses the paradox as a dangerous delusion. In profoundly different ways, then, the two competing discourses conceive of community only by excising the paradoxical nature of "a body of individuals."

In contrast, the fictions examined in this study conceive of community as full of paradoxes, impossibilities, and contradictions. Their conflicted movement between the values, assumptions, and ideals of community means that they invoke the two competing discourses of community in a dialectic manner. They idealize the proposition of community and pursue the transformative powers of commonality; in the next breath, they interrogate the nature of that commonality and even the very *category* of commonality. They expound the impossibility of many becoming one and follow that dismissal with the thought: but how nice it would be if it were possible. What these novels offer us, then, is a dialectic community without synthesis. While they richly illustrate the pulse points of idealized community and dissenting community, they do not arrive at a stable vision of community by legitimatizing one vision over the other. I suggest that the concept of ambivalence becomes an important theoretical category for understanding their dialectic community without synthesis. To be ambivalent is to be undecided between two contrary values, pursuits, or entities, to appreciate the desirability of one while still heeding the pull of the other. The state of ambivalence, then, attains a rich epistemological value in this study of community, affording a unique vantage point from which to intervene in debates over community, commonality, and fusion. As Dennis Foster eloquently describes, the state of ambivalence is a characteristic feature of American literary and cultural expression of community:

> [W]e express an ambivalence about community that is part of a fundamental American tension; fleeing compulsory society, we find some way to light out for the territories, where people unite freely. But once there, we again draw around us the strictures that had previously driven us from civilization. 'Community,' it turns out, refers both to a fantasy of a place we lost and hope to regain, and to the real, often agonizing condition of living in proximity with the separate bodies and minds of the others. (20)

Ambivalence about community certainly shows no abatement in contemporary American fiction. If anything, the philosophical, cultural, and
political implications of imagining community present one of the greatest
challenges to contemporary fiction. This book demonstrates the continuing challenge of community by tracing the ambivalent community in
vastly different areas of contemporary American fiction—through a multicultural spectrum of writers, ranging from canonical to avant-gardist,
whose works engage a wide range of social locations and topical issues.

In addition to demonstrating the ambivalence over community as
a central tension in contemporary fiction, the unusual combination of
writers examined in this book—Toni Morrison, Karen Tei Yamashita,
Richard Powers, Lydia Davis, Lynne Tillman, and David Markson—
uniquely contributes to the two aims of this book: to expand the critical
framework for discussing community in literary criticism, and to have
the two competing discourses of community talk to each other in a way
that is missing in contemporary scholarship of community. First, aside
from Toni Morrison, none of the other writers represents a familiar face
in literary discussions of community. While Morrison's novels anchor
discussions of community in contemporary fiction, and her presence
in this study seems self-explanatory, the array of other writers requires
some explanation. What does Yamashita, an Asian American writer
whose works centrally explore global migration, have to do with considerations of community? What does Powers, a leading writer of science
and technology in contemporary fiction, have to do with concerns over
community? What do Lydia Davis and Lynne Tillman, whose works
are better known for their epistemological quests, have to say about
community? What does David Markson, one of the most avant-gardist
writers of contemporary fiction, have to show about community?

Although it may sound quixotic, precisely the seeming irrelevance
of these writers to discussions of community is the point—to expand
the critical framework of community beyond the idealized vision. These
writers seem unrelated to the concerns of community, I suggest, because
their literary visions of community *diverge* from the idealized community dominating contemporary literary criticism. The rich topical concerns, diverse social locations, and different ideals brought into play
by these writers challenge the established discursive pathways by which
"community" as such is discussed in contemporary literary criticism.
Furthermore, the ambivalence these writers evince towards notions such
as commonality, unity, and fusion brings the two competing discourses
of community into dialogue.

In order to fully encompass these novels' unique intervention in discussion of community, this study does not begin with a fixed definition of community. Instead, it approaches the paradox of community through a study of the literary manifestation of first-person plural "we." As a pronoun that proposes to be singular and plural at the same time, the paradox of the pronoun "we" is metonymic of the paradox of "a body of individuals." What forces endow a single subject with the heft of the multiple? How does a single "I" presume to be a plural "we"? What needs and desires are met in this transformation into a single "we"? When we move beyond the prevailing understanding of community as the most benevolent, ultimate expression of unity, we can see that Yamashita's interest in global migration is an attempt to formulate a global "we"; that Powers's defense of human uniqueness is an attempt to say "we, the human" and make it *mean* something special in the face of virtual reality and simulation technology; that Davis's and Tillman's treatment of intersubjective transparency is an exploration of "we" as intersubjective continuity; and that Markson's philosophical treatment of language games is a dramatization of the biggest "we," the fact of coexistence. Through their complex arrival at a first-person plural "we," these works invoke a multifaceted vision of community that expands the critical framework for discussing community.

Furthermore, each of these literary manifestations of "we" calls up various ideals central to the community debate—the ideal of identification, universalism, humanism, universalism, communion, and coexistence. As familiar rationale for transforming multiple individuals into a unity, each of these concepts is thoroughly embedded in the philosophical, political, and cultural valence of community. Like community, every one of these concepts is subject to political contestation as rationale for unity, and, like community, each is under suspicion as a rationale for totality. Thus the literary drama of asserting a "we" becomes the drama of negotiating a whole host of contested ideals surrounding the very notion of unity. Finally, each of these literary instances of "we" articulates a need, a desire, or an expectation—that "we" are alike, that "we" are connected, that "we" are unique, that "we" fully know each other, or even that there *is* a "we." Addressing the work of "we" in contemporary fiction allows me to address the issue of *functionality* at the heart of the community debate. What does community do? At a more fundamental level, should community *do* anything? The answer to this question has severe repercussions in the debate over community.

In order to contextualize the significance of ambivalent community, let me begin with an overview of what I am calling the competing discourses of idealized community and dissenting community.

Idealized Community

"Community Is like Family, Sisterhood,
Brotherhood, Village, Neighborhood, Friendship"

In the discourse of idealized community, community as an ideal fundamentally relies on the kindness of analogies. In the familiar similes of community as family, kinship, village, and friendship, there is a direct transfer of affect between community and the particular relationship made analogous to that concept. That is, community becomes as natural, as primary, as normal, and as essential as family, kinship, neighborhood, village, or friendship. From such analogies, furthermore, community attains the benevolent relationality among its members (of sharing, support, understanding, warmth) as well as the consensual logic of operation (governed by common aims, consensus, and shared fate).

In using community as an aspiration, contemporary discourse of idealized community performs a revolutionary maneuver between Ferdinand Tönnies's *Gemeinschaft* (community) and *Gesellschaft* (society). The enormity of this maneuver lies in the fact that while Tönnies theorizes Gemeinschaft and Gesellschaft as contrasting models of human organization, contemporary discourse of idealized community utilizes the two in seamless conjunction, incorporating aspects of both in a strategic manner to generate a brand-new theory of community. As the most influential theory of community not only in sociology but in any consideration of community in the twentieth century, Tönnies's *Gemeinschaft Und Gesellschaft* (1887), translated as *Community & Society* (1957), offers a nostalgic description—and prescription—for what he sees as a way of life fast disappearing in the urbanization, industrialization, and fragmentation of late-nineteenth-century Europe. Tönnies theorizes the benevolent and consensual nature of community informed by "natural will" ("*Wesenville*"). This natural will expresses itself through the kinship group, the neighborhood, and friendship as relationships of intimacy and unconditional emotional bonding. The identifying feature of community is the "common spirit" that runs through it (224), and the ultimate seat of the common spirit lies in the form of the family. As the "simple," "organic," and the "only real form of life" (226–27), the family best exemplifies the concord, folkways, mores, and religion that make the Gemeinschaft "the body social": "Each individual receives his share from this common center, which is manifest in his own sphere, i.e., in his sentiment, in his mind and heart, and in his conscience as well as in his environment, his possessions, and his activities" (224).

In contrast, the instrumentalist and depersonalized nature of Gesellschaft is manifest in "rational will" ("*Kurville*"). This rational will expresses itself in business, economy, the state, and social relationships that are exchange-based and driven by self-interest. As the core characteristics of community gradually dissipate in society, Gesellschaft is distinguished by the absence of common will. Thus Gesellschaft is a movement away from the "simple form" towards the "complex form of social life": "The 'house' maintains the 'family character of the house' the most, then the village, and the town. When the town develops into the city, the 'family character of the house' is entirely lost. Individuals or families are separate identities, and their common locale is only an accidental or deliberately chosen place in which to live" (227).

Strictly speaking, contemporary discourse of idealized community is neither Gemeinschaft nor Gesellschaft. In using Gemeinschaft models of family, neighborhood, and friendship as aspirations for community, the discourse of idealized community performs a careful adjudication between Tönnies's theory of natural will and rational will. While it directly continues the benevolence of the family, neighborhood, and friendship in arguing the benevolence of community, it diverges from Tönnies's use of such groups as expressions of "simple" or "organic" expression of "natural will." Instead, idealized community seamlessly merges aspects of Gemeinschaft and Gesellschaft, so that community is "a body of individuals" who *aspire* to achieve the benevolence of a relationship like that of family, neighborhood, and friendship. By carefully negotiating between the two wills set in opposition by Tönnies, contemporary ideal community discourse introduces a voluntary dimension to the formation of community, thereby acknowledging a late-twentieth-century political, cultural, and theoretical suspicion of "natural" expressions. Rather than being a given expression of "natural" or "primordial" will, community is the *rational* movement towards *natural* unities. This seamless movement between aspects of Gemeinschaft and Gesellschaft and between the "natural" and the "rational" generates an even more significant effect. Community becomes inherently *teleological*: it becomes a body of individuals united towards a final objective of achieving a unity *like* that of family, kinship, neighborhood, village, or friendship. Furthermore, these telos of community—the Gemeinschaft categories of unity—directly inform the benevolent nature and politics of idealized community. This teleological view of community as the "rational" movement towards "natural" unities will be best demonstrated in Morrison's construction of community, in which kinship models of community lead to the healing of all its members.

Precisely such a teleological thinking of community underwrites idealized community's invocation of family, neighborhood, and friendship as aspirations for community. Limited to no one ideological group, this teleological view emerges from divergent political views, social locations, and cultural arenas, such as conservative political theory, African American discourse, feminist discourse, literary criticism, and popular culture. In "good communities," writes the conservative communitarian philosopher Amitai Etzioni, "people treat one another as ends in themselves, not merely as instruments; as whole persons rather than as fragments; as something like an extended family rather than only as employees, traders, consumers or even fellow citizens" (25). Similarly, "family is the original human community and the basis as well as the origin of all subsequent communities. It is therefore the norm of all communities, so that any community is a brotherhood. . . . The more a society approximates to the family pattern, the more it realizes itself as a community, or, as Marx called it, a truly human society" (MacMurray 155).[3] Consider, also, the centrality of kinship models in Martin Luther King Jr.'s vision of "Beloved Community," a vision that holds global "sisterhood" and "brotherhood" as its final aim of progress and is still vital to African American discourse.[4] For instance, the ideal of "Beloved Community" informs bell hooks's vision in *Teaching Community*. Taking inspiration from June Jordan's statement, "We look for community. We have already suffered the alternative to community, to human commitment" (qtd. in hooks 3), hooks argues that the ultimate aim is to achieve "beloved communities where there is no domination," communities in which members understand "the truth of our essential humanness" (66).

Similarly, the kinship model of sisterhood prevails as the aspirational model of community in feminist discourse, as well as for asserting commonalities of female-gendered identity, experience, and body politics.[5] In close company with the trope of sisterhood in feminist visions of community are other Gemeinschaft models of friendship, village, and neighborhood. Marilyn Friedman's "Feminism and Modern Friendship: Dislocating the Community" is an example of idealized community expression that uses the voluntary relationship of friendship as the ideal model of community: friendship is a unity "arising out of one's own needs, desires, interests, versus expectations assigned, demanded by one's found communities" (199–200). It is no coincidence that "neighborhood" is often used synonymously with "community," or that "neighborly feeling" is used synonymously with friendliness or conviviality. The use of neighborhood as the aspiration for community retains much of the Gemeinschaft connotations of the village: a small-scale locality, a living arrangement of face-to-face interaction, leading to an intimacy that generates a greater sense of belonging and attachment. The intimacy of the village as the telos is perhaps best represented philosophically, politically, and culturally as a specific vein of communitarianism, which emphasizes the heightened civic responsibility, engagement, voluntarism, and activism fostered by small-scale, unmediated interactions.[6] As Iris Marion Young describes this communitarian ideal expressed by Carol Gould, Michael Sandel, and Michael Taylor, "[t]he ideal society is composed of small locales, populated by a small enough number of persons so that each can be personally acquainted with all the others[,] . . . decentralized, with small-scale industry and local markets" (Young 316). These aspirational models for community powerfully shape many of the ambivalent communities analyzed in this book. The telos of the family, sisterhood, and friendship propels the motivations and actions of Morrison's protagonists. Likewise, the intimacy and shared fate of the neighborhood as the model for community reigns strong in Yamashita's exploration of the globe as a village.

Just as importantly, the aspirational and teleological views of community give rise to a thoroughly naturalized view of commonality. With "commonality," we arrive at one of the most hotly contested sites of contemporary debates about community, identity, and unity. What is the politics of commonality? What is the politics of asking, "How are you like me?" Why, in the discourse of idealized community, does that question seem the most basic, the most essential—indeed, the most natural—question to ask? I suggest that the degree to which similarity, sameness, and sharedness become seemingly inevitable criteria of community is the same degree to which idealized community *depoliticizes* the concept of commonality. Of course, no concept is inherently political as such, bearing an essential ideological allegiance to a value system, worldview, or power deployment. Rather, the issue at hand is the discursive context in which the concept of commonality becomes relevant or visible. And in idealized community's fundamentally benevolent teleology, the practice of uniting along the axis of similarity seems an obviously justified and legitimate procedure. In a mutually supporting manner, then, the teleology of idealized community renders the question of commonality into a self-evident imperative, and vice versa. The search for commonality in order to become a community like a family, village, or friendship becomes an *a*political activity, an operation that does not prioritize the interests of one group over another or strengthen the power of some over another. Free of any self-serving partiality, searching for the ways "you" are like "me" becomes a search for what is already "out there." Indeed, the degree to which commonality functions as the identifying marker of community is evident in the way the definitions of "community" and "common" are interdependent.[7]

For many of the fictions discussed in this book, too, commonality operates as the constitutive feature of forming a "body of individuals." Commonality sits at the heart of Morrison's use of identification, as her female protagonists bond according to the similarity of their life experiences and struggles, as well as to their shared objective of collective healing. Yamashita explores the numerous ways that universalism assumes—and exploits—commonalities. In Powers's novels of science and technology, humanism becomes the pursuit of that one uniquely human commonality that will, in the final analysis, demarcate the human from the machinic. Although the "what" or the "content" of commonality differs, each of these literary attempts at imagining a single "we" employs the concept of commonality as an imperative.

Yet these fictions also question that imperative, and this antithetical treatment of commonality sits at the center of their ambivalence about community. In these literary works the very search for commonality becomes a process fraught with struggles, partiality, negotiations, conflict, and dissent. There is no simple commonality "out there" about the determinate features of "we" of the village, of the human, of the globe, or of "you" and "me." Instead, searching for that commonality necessitates partiality—for *some* to determine, and enforce, the criteria of commonality—and constructivism—to impose and shore up arguments about "our" similarities and sharedness—and, if all else fails, conscription—to impose a commonality onto all of "us." These struggles highlight the inevitably political nature of searching for commonality. In their self-reflective examination of their own uses of commonality, these fictions challenge the apolitical vision of commonality in the discourse of idealized community. Their ambivalence towards their own deployment of commonality, then, negates the central myth of idealized community and engages the concerns and arguments of dissenting community.

Dissenting Community

"Community Is like Totalitarianism, Fascism, Authoritarianism"

The various expressions of dissenting community, emerging from divergent political, philosophical, and disciplinary quarters, converge upon the negation of community as an ideal. But the negation of idealized community is not limited to those specific debates over community. The discourse of dissenting community is thoroughly imbricated in contemporary cultural theory's reconsideration of unity, in poststructuralist critique of the neo-Kantian liberal philosophy and politics, and in the larger postmodernist interrogation of single body ideology, teleological view of community, and valorization of wholeness, oneness, and unity. Postmodernist philosophical dissent from idealized community begins by negating the final aim of idealized community as an impossibility—a unity in which multiple bodies become a single body. This negation foregrounds postmodernist recuperation of concepts such as difference, dissent, heterogeneity, antagonism, and conflict, precisely the concepts categorized as contaminants or obstacles that must be overcome or excised in the "progress" towards a unity like that of family, kinship, village, or friendship. By emphasizing the fissures that render "a body of individuals" impossible, dissenting community reinvigorates those fissures and recategorizes them as constitutive features of a community whose final telos is *not* a single body community.

A classic expression of poststructuralist theory and radical democracy, Ernesto Laclau and Chantel Mouffe's influential work *Hegemony and Socialist Strategy: Towards a Radical Democratic Politics* might be read as just such a reclassification project of dissenting community. When they famously state that "society is impossible" because antagonism and hegemony are key ingredients in a radical democracy (114), they are arguing the "impossibility of a final suture" that would make society into one single body (125). Thus the impossibility they address is the single body ideology at the heart of community as a proposition. Rather than being temporary instances of conflict that give rise to feelings of aversion, hostility, or antipathy, they argue, antagonism is a perennial condition expressing the uneven, fluid, always changing, always relative nature of subject positions and proclaimed identities. Far from being an incidental irritant or obstacle that must be resolved and eliminated, antagonism describes "the incomplete, open and politically negotiable character of every identity" (104). As antagonism expresses the "limits of society, the latter's impossibility of fully constituting itself" (125), it critiques the very desire for commonality and consensus in the teleology of idealized community.

Indeed, the presence of antagonism is crucial to a "free society," as Laclau further expounds in "Community and Its Paradoxes: Richard Rorty's 'Liberal Utopia.'" Laclau's critique of Rorty's "liberal utopia" is representative of the way postmodernist philosophy's critique of the neo-Kantian, Enlightenment liberal tradition enacts the discourse of dissenting community. More specifically, the postmodernist-liberal tradition debate demonstrates how the discourse of dissenting community emerges as a critique of *any* philosophical or political theory that holds a teleological view of human history as a progress towards unity, and as a critique of any rationalist view of a "foundational" human nature in which consensus is the ultimate achievement. Laclau writes: "Antagonism exists because the social is not a plurality of effects radiating from a pregiven center, but is pragmatically constructed from many starting points. But it is precisely because of this, because there is an ontological possibility of clashes and unevenness, that we can speak of freedom" ("Community" 92). In contrast, in Rorty's "liberal utopia" outlined in *Contingency, Irony, Solidarity,* there is an untenable distinction between "legitimate" and "illegitimate" conflict, Laclau argues. As Rorty claims, "A liberal society is one whose ideals can be fulfilled by persuasion rather than force, by reform rather than revolution" (*Contingency* 60). But such are distinctions, Laclau continues, that can be made only when consensus is the determining criterion of legitimacy: persuasion is distinguished by the presence of consensus, while force is distinguished by the absence of consensus.

But might not the very achievement of consensus involve force? "The question that remains is to what extent in persuasion/consensus there is not an ingredient of force" ("Community" 89). The valorization of consensus as the legitimate, democratic form of struggle is possible only in a value system in which antagonism can only be a problem or an obstacle that must be removed. A social arrangement whose telos is the absence of antagonism strives for a "totally determined society," "a society from which violence and antagonisms have been *entirely* eliminated" (92; original emphasis). On the contrary, Laclau agues, "the existence of violence and antagonism is the very condition of a free society" (92). Hegemony, then, is the very expression of a society in which antagonism is a constitutive feature. Rather than being an oppressive force that one group wields upon another and that must be eradicated, hegemony describes the perennial struggle between subjects whose self-identifications are inextricably contingent and mutually related to each other. It describes the struggle by different subject positions that take place in the field of limitless, differential relations that is the social sphere. Fundamental to the larger commitment of dissenting community is postmodernist philosophy's resuscitation of antagonism and hegemony from the teleology of liberal emancipation. Other notable expression of postmodernist dissenting community takes place in the theoretical exchanges between Judith Butler, Ernesto Laclau, and Slavoj Žižek in *Contingency, Hegemony, Universality: Contemporary Dialogues on the Left,* in which "antagonism," or "the incommensurability or gap" between identity and identity-claims, forms the theoretical basis for radical democracy: "we each value this 'failure' as a condition of democratic contestation itself" (1–2).

Jean-François Lyotard's dissent from Enlightenment rationality, well represented in his critique of Habermasian consensus, is another rich expression of the way postmodernist philosophical critique of liberal tradition contributes to the discourse of dissenting community.[8] Like the postmodernist repositioning of antagonism and conflict as inherently necessary ingredients to any open-ended, democratic society, Lyotard's theory of heterogeneity and the differend directly negates the telos of unity in social, cultural, and political theory. By exploring the fissures that render a single body impossible, Lyotard calls attention to the ways in which the pursuit of unity always "betrays" itself. Voicing one of the harshest condemnations of the valorization of unity, he compares the political call for solidarity as a:

> totalitarian apparatus, constituted as a result of the elimination of debate and by the continuous elimination of debate from political life by means of terror, [which] reproduces within itself . . . the illness that it claims to cure [that is, call for solidarity]. Disorder within, an internal proliferation of decision-making authorities, war among inner-circle cliques: all this betrays the recurrence of the shameful sickness within that passes for health and betrays the "presence" of the unmanageable (intraitable), at the very time that the latter is hidden away by the delirium and arrogance of a unitary, totalitarian politics. ("À l'insu [Unbeknownst]" 43)

As solidarity "passes for health," it follows that heterogeneity passes for illness: "With the horror resulting from this sanitizing operation, the phantasm of oneness and totality is sustained by the belief that this heterogeneous thing has, or is, a face (Medusa's face?), and that it would suffice to turn it around to get rid of it" (43).

Likewise, Lyotard's theory of the differend explores the disruptive power of the "unmanageable" in the movement towards unity. Extending Wittgenstein's theory of language, Lyotard argues an anti-instrumentalist theory of language, in which language use—what can be said and what cannot be said—is metonymic of the material and discursive disparity in power. As he begins *The Differend: Phrases in Dispute:* "You are informed that human beings endowed with language were placed in a situation that none of them is now able to tell about it" (3). The differend shows itself in disputes in which the experience, reality, and testimony of one party cannot be "phrased"—has no means of being credited or legitimated and is repeatedly made to account for itself without any hope of attaining either. Like the testimony of Holocaust victims who are repeatedly questioned, or the language of the worker who can make himself visible only by speaking of his labor in the language of capitalist value system, the differend testifies to the fundamental falsity in the social, political, philosophical, and cultural myth of a single body community and valorization of consensus. Reading for the differend in literary formations of community indeed reveals the material and discursive disparity in power and the coercive and exclusionary maneuvers at work in formations of community. The teleology of health and healing in Morrison's *Paradise,* for instance, means that practices and values that do not contribute to collective healing remain unphraseable in the novel. For Powers's protagonists, the machine's differend poses the greatest challenge, and their inability to phrase the machine in any idiom other than the "human" reveals the instability of the human community.

Reappropriating the "Common" in Dissenting Community

While expressions of dissenting community emphasize the fissures that render the single body community impossible, another instance of dissenting community might be located in those postmodernist philosophers who negate the role of community as an instrument towards achievement. In arguing for a community that is "inoperative" (*désœuvrée*), theorists such as Jean-Luc Nancy, Maurice Blanchot, and Giorgio Agamben voice the anti-instrumentalist theory of community.[9] While heterogeneity, dissent, and antagonism are well established as postmodernist negations of idealized community discourse, lesser known is the postmodernist project of reappropriating the word "common" for the purpose of an anti-instrumentalist theory of community. No other contemporary thinker has emptied and redefined the meaning of the "common" more vigorously towards this aim than Jean-Luc Nancy. Like the larger post-modernist philosophical project, Nancy critiques the depoliticized use of the common as the "natural" binding agent for community. But going beyond a critique of the common as the rationale for community, Nancy offers the most expansive understanding of the common by way of a Heideggerian understanding of Being. For Heidegger, Nancy points out, "'being 'itself' comes to be defined as relational, as non-absoluteness, and, if you will—and in any case this is what I am trying to argue—*as community*" (6; original emphasis). For Nancy, the only utility for the common is to assert existence itself as a fact of "being-in-common." Rather than being a descriptor of a parochial similarity, the common in Nancian terms is a descriptor of coexistence itself. When that foundational fact is ignored, and unity is founded on the fact of what "we" have in common—in history, self-interest, life experience, objective, and so on—the primary fact of being-in-common is elided. The unity that arises out of parochial sameness finds its final expression in ideological totality. Nowhere is this danger more strident, Nancy argues, than in the discourse of single body community.

The Inoperative Community, published in 1987, addresses the fall of the Soviet Union and the unprecedented force of free-market global economy as primary examples of single body community. As instances of unity conceived through "economic ties, technological operations, and political fusion (into a *body* or under a *leader*)" (3; original emphasis), they represent how:

> the community that becomes *a single* thing (body, mind, fatherland, Leader . . .) necessarily loses the *in* of being-*in*-common. Or, it loses the *with* or the *together* that defines it. It yields its being-together to a being *of* togetherness. The truth of community, on the contrary, resides in the retreat of such a being. Community is made of what retreats from it: the hypostasis of the 'common,' and its work. (xxxix; original emphasis)

For Nancy, "communal," "communion," "communitarianism," or "communism" represents the ultimate misuse of the common, the pursuit of "essence" as the logic of community:

> [When] thinking of being-in-common [is folded] within the thinking of an essence of community . . . it assigns to community a *common* being, whereas community is a matter . . . of existence inasmuch as it is *in* common, but without letting itself be absorbed into a common substance. Being *in* common has nothing to do with communion, with fusion into

a body, into a unique and ultimate identity that would no longer be exposed. (xxxviii; original emphasis)

Similarly, in disrupting the parochial function of commonality, Agamben uses the provocative expression "whatever" in his theory of community. "Whatever" stands as the central trope for a theory of community that is without any criteria of common attributes and properties, such as "being red, being French, being Muslim" (1). The kernel of "whatever" is "the idea of an *inessential* commonality, a solidarity that in no way concerns an essence. . . . Whatever is constituted not by the indifference of common nature with respect to singularities, but by the indifference of the common and the proper, of the genus and the species, of the essential and the accidental" (18–19; original emphasis).

Nancy's and Agamben's anti-instrumentalist theory of the common speaks directly to their anti-teleological theory of community. Just as commonality should not "work" as the logic of unity, community should not "work" towards a final objective—towards a more efficient and productive unity, or a "return" to a lost, "purer" community of bygone years, or towards the aspirational model of Gemeinschaft community. Yet, Nancy notes, the history of community is irrevocably a history of single body ideology and teleological thinking. "How can the community without essence (the community that is neither 'people' nor 'nation,' neither 'destiny' nor 'generic humanity,' etc.) be presented as such? That is, what might a politics be that does not stem from the will to realize an essence?" (xxxix–xl).

The answer, Nancy argues, lies in a community whose commonality says nothing about its "essence" and serves no final function. As any unity with a final objective locates its "strength" in the degree of its fusion, any community conceived in a teleological manner inevitably operates within a single body ideology: it moves towards ideological totality. Only a community that has no final objective, whose commonality has no function, can become a unity whose final destination is neither "progress"—achievement of an ideological goal, greater productivity, political reform—nor totalitarianism. As the rationale for a community that is inoperative, Nancy's being-in-common offers the most basic fact of coexistence as the originary community. Coexistence means that "there is no singular being without a singular being, and there is, therefore, what might be called, in a rather inappropriate idiom, an originary or ontological 'sociality' that in its principle extends far beyond the simple theme of man as a social being" (28). "Coexistence holds itself just as far from juxtaposition as it does from integration.

Coexistence does not happen to existence; it is not added to it, and one can not [*sic*] subtract it out; it is existence" (187).

By emptying the category of commonality of any use-value, the anti-instrumentalist theory of community offers a profound challenge to the functionality of the first-person plural "we" in the contemporary fictions analyzed in this study. As each literary deployment of "we" serves a specific function—that "we" are alike, that "we" are interrelated, that "we" are unique, that "we" understand each other, that "I" exist among a "we"—each fictional instance must justify the work of commonality in transforming many into one. The fine balance between community that works and commonality that oppresses finds parallel expression in contemporary intellectual and political projects with reformist, activist vision. What theory of community can sustain a theory of commonality without also valorizing oppressive homogeneity? Let me hold up feminist and cosmopolitanist discourses of community as they grapple with this challenge and, in the process, highlight the dimension of *deliberativeness* that distinguishes them from fiction's ambivalent community. This deliberative deployment of commonality is what enables feminist and cosmopolitanist theories to do what fiction's ambivalent community cannot do—to synthesize the competing politics of idealized and dissenting community.

Dissenting Community That Works

Feminist and Cosmopolitanist Community

As Iris Marion Young writes, her critique of the single body ideology is instigated by the fact that "feminists have been paradigm exponents of the ideal of community I criticize." At the same time, her intervention in imagining alternatives to community is inspired by feminist scholarship's attention to difference (300). There is no better site for understanding feminism's problematic relationship to community than in the debate over the trope of "sisterhood." As I addressed earlier, sisterhood is the dominant aspirational model of community in feminist discourse. Inversely, feminist critique of idealized community emerges most vocally through its critique of sisterhood. Emphasizing the fissures that render a single "female" community impossible, feminist discourses of dissenting community argue the dangers of assuming "natural" commonality among women—of biological, acultural, prediscursive sameness, affinity, and empathy. Feminist critique of the sisterhood ideal also dissents from the single body ideology that holds consensus as a self-evident goal and, above all, from the elision of difference that takes place in the name of unity.[10]

However, while sharing many of the concerns raised in postmodernist dissenting community, the reformist politics of feminist dissenting community demands that community does *something* rather than do nothing. The horizon of feminist negative community cannot be anti-instrumentality, a commonality that has no function except that of observing coexistence. Indeed, the feminist break from postmodernist dissenting community articulates the complicated and uneasy relationship between feminism and postmodernism—their parallel inquiry into power, politics, and identity, and their irreconcilable intellectual and political aims. As Linda Nicholson writes in the Introduction to *Feminism/Postmodernism,* a central question for feminist use of postmodernist theory is whether the "theorizing needs some stopping points" (8) so as to enable the category of gender and to sustain the possibility of unity.

It is no little surprise, then, that feminist expressions of dissenting community critique the anti-instrumental community of postmodernist philosophy. Miranda Joseph's *Against the Romance of Community,* while criticizing the discourse of idealized community, notes that "the not-surprising truth is that the critique of community offered by feminist poststructuralists has made not a dent in the pervasive and celebratory deployment of community in popular culture and even on what used to be the left" (xxxi). Joseph reserves her strongest criticism, though, for Nancy and Agamben as instances of postmodernist philosophy that "promote political passivity or paralyzing relativism" (xxx). In particular, Joseph finds Agamben's provocative use of "whatever" as too easily dismissing the fact that "collectivities often persist in their project despite the catachrestical and disputed nature of the identity terms under which they are mobilized" (xxx). Likewise, Nancy Fraser balances her estimation of Nancy's theories of politics with a criticism that his scholarship walks a "tightrope" that involves a "rigorous exclusion of politics, and especially of empirical and normative considerations." Thus Fraser expresses a dissatisfaction with Nancy's "middle way of a philosophical interrogation of the political that somehow ends up producing profound new, politically relevant insights without dirtying any hands in political struggle" (87).

What these feminist critiques express is, first, how reformist politics needs to maintain the concept of unity as the basis of collective work and, second, how that project requires the deployment of commonality in some specific, particular sense (e.g., similarity of history, subject positioning, experience, or shared objective or interest). Indeed, feminist critique of anti-instrumentalist community recalls, and sheds a new light on, the strategies by which postmodernist feminist theorists in the 1980s maintained the concept of unity amidst criticism of essentialism. Butler's "contingent foundations," Gayatri Spivak's "strategic essentialism," and Satya P. Mohanty's "postpositivist realism" represent feminism's constructivist use of essentialism—as a modified, contingent, fluid use of commonality to enable strategic formations of unity.[11] In their balance of postmodernist fissures with the strategic use of commonality, these contingent deployments of essentialism may be read as modified arguments for dissenting community—a theory of community that negates the values and politics of idealized community while still maintaining a sense of unity that "works."

Furthermore, these gestures of feminist dissenting community represent a moderated answer to the paradox of achieving "a body of individuals": unlike the idealized community that supersedes the paradox with apolitical claims of commonality, or dissenting community that throws out the paradox as being impossible, feminist dissenting community argues for a *deliberative* body of individuals. In shoring up a theory of instrumentalist community, feminist dissenting community relies on the foundational concept of feminism: agency. By emphasizing the deliberative deployment of commonality, this instrumentalist community suggests that the *work of* commonality need not equate the *oppression by* commonality. As the following chapters will demonstrate, precisely this deliberative, contingent, and strategic view of commonality is what is absent in the ambivalent community under analysis, and it is what causes them to continually question their uses of commonality.

Like feminist dissenting community, the deliberative formation of unity is pivotal to recent cosmopolitanist projects that attempt to theorize unity without oppression. As a negation of the values and politics of idealized community, the new cosmopolitanist corrective to single body ideology theorizes the deliberative nature of unity by targeting the concept of *belonging*. As a keyword and central value in the discourse of idealized community, "belonging" describes a relatedness or connection to a specific unity, such as to a nation, a region, an ethnicity, a locale, or a family. Another way to define belonging is as a form of *limited* attachment. Thus the concept of belonging implicitly calls up a sense of restricted belonging—belonging to one nation and not to another, to one culture but not to another, to one region over another. Recent cosmopolitanist projects that negate the theory of single body community argue that altering this limited logic of belonging leads to a model of community with multiple attachments, belonging, and loyalties. As Amanda Anderson succinctly describes in her overview of contemporary projects of cosmopolitanism, cosmopolitanism "denote[s] cultivated detachment from restrictive forms of identity" ("Cryptonormativism" 266).[12]

The best-known example of cosmopolitanist corrective to the single body ideology is perhaps found in Martha Nussbaum's well-known citation of Plutarch—the call "to regard all human beings as our fellow citizens and neighbors" (qtd. in Nussbaum, "Reply" 9). Nussbaum's notion emerges as a response to Richard Rorty's call for patriotic ideas and American values in a *New York Times* editorial in 1994. Motivated by the fear of national chauvinism and jingoism that such a call risks, and by her belief that global problems of hunger, poverty, inequality, and ecology require an international basis of collectivity and agency, Nussbaum theorizes a "world citizenship" in which one's nationality is an "accident of birth" ("Reply" 133). As a prime example of a non-limited belonging, Nussbaum points to the multinational and multireligious nature of people who participated in the World War II rescue operations for Jews. The French, Belgian, Polish, Scandinavian, Japanese, German, atheist, and Christian and other religious people who took part in the rescue efforts represent an instance of a world citizenship—a "we" that is not forged out of a single attachment, a unity transcending specificity of belonging.

Like the political and moral utility that Nussbaum locates in multiple and expansive belonging, Ross Posnock's "post-identity cosmopolitanism" theorizes cosmopolitanism as a community that works. Locating the emergence of cosmopolitanism in eighteenth-century republicanism, most famously enunciated by Kant, Posnock argues the progressive utility of cosmopolitanism as a careful adjudication of Enlightenment liberalism and a simultaneous distrust of the ideal of progress. The egalitarian potential of cosmopolitanism emerges from the fact that the expansive and multiple nature of belonging translates into the fact that no ideal, practice, or tradition *belongs* to any specific body of people. For Posnock, the exemplary expression of this *post*-identity cosmopolitanism rests in black cosmopolitanism's claim of modernity, in which formally marginalized groups can appropriate, without consideration of "origin," all the world's cultures, ideals, and politics without being charged of "assimilation." "[A]s an instrument of cultural democracy that, historically, has been particularly congenial to those on the periphery," post-identity cosmopolitanism presents a mode of agency to those who wish to form a deliberative unity (807).[13]

By dethroning the specificity and the limited nature of belonging, cosmopolitanist community, like feminist negative community, postulates a vision of unity that is as instrumental as it is nonoppressive. These deliberative formations of community that "works," yet whose telos does not lead to a totality, represent a modified answer to the paradox of "a body of individuals." They represent a *synthesis* of the competing discourses of idealized community and dissenting community, a synthesis in which commonality is deployed deliberatively, not as a "natural" expression, in which unity is taken as a contingent, not as a given, and in which the instrumentality of community is not evidence of its totalitarian nature. This synthesis, I argue, is what distinguishes these moderated dissenting communities from the ambivalent communities of contemporary fiction. Reading contemporary fiction's *in*ability to synthesize the competing discourses of community reveals the difficulty of excising the paradox from the proposition of community.

Ambivalent Community in Contemporary American Fiction

In the face of all these possible responses to the paradox of community, what does it mean to be ambivalent about community? To be ambivalent is to simultaneously entertain two contradictory attitudes towards one concept. Put another way, ambivalence describes a unique vantage point, of acknowledging the appeal, as well as the undesirability, of any alternative. And because one is not fully "given over" to the attraction of one alternative, the state of being undecided elucidates the lingering call of the other. I am not suggesting that ambivalence offers an all-seeing vantage point, an unbiased perspective that is superior in its scope, depth, and balance to a more determinate position. Instead, I am suggesting that ambivalence holds valuable epistemological utility in the way it captures a conflicted stance, the moment of hesitation, in which the compelling nature of one alternative competes with that of another alternative.

Indeed, as they are pulled by the two contrasting answers to the paradox of community, these fictions express a multivocality in their manifestation of the literary "we." Their conflicted stance towards concepts central to the debate of community—such as commonality, sharedness, belonging, attachment, and difference—stands in contrast to the more or less stable discursive role of those key terms in the two competing visions of community. Is community is like family, kinship, friendship, and village? Or is community like totalitarianism, communism, and fascism? The discursive "fate" of concepts such as commonality, belonging, and attachment is already predetermined by the figurative analogy employed to describe community. The multivocality of ambivalent communities is also different from the synthesized dialectic represented by feminist dissenting community or cosmopolitanist corrective to community. In contrast to these moderated expressions of dissenting community, ambivalent community retains the paradox of community as an unresolved challenge.

Each chapter examines the way the competing pulls of idealized and dissenting community manifest themselves through competing models for saying "we." The degree of that competition, and the degree to which the final "we" endorses one vision of community over another, informs the progression of the chapters that unfold. The first chapter, "What Ails the Individual: Community Cure in Toni Morrison's *Jazz* and *Paradise*," begins with the least ambivalent assertion of "we" in Morrison's use of identification. Pointing to the celebrations of Morrison's community in critical scholarship of her work, I suggest that Morrison's affirmation of identification is representative of the idealized community discourse dominating contemporary literary criticism. While identification in literature has been primarily approached psychoanalytically, as expressions of primary parent-child identification or of trauma, loss, or melancholia, I highlight the centrality of the term in the current debate over community. I explore identification as the key process by which commonality attains its transformative role as the binding agent of community. Identification, then, rationalizes the use of the question "How are you like me?" as the criterion of community formation. Upon the condition of likeness, a subject regards herself to be identical to another and, indeed, regards herself to be *one* with another in experience, feeling, and positionality. Conversely, as the centripetal force rationalizing the fusing of multiple individuals into one subject positioning, identification becomes the face of the oppressive single body ideology.

Like all the writers examined in this study, Morrison engages the competing discourses of community, and she explores vastly different deployments of identification, from the most benevolent "sisterhood" and "family" model of community that directly invokes the discourse of idealized community, to the most totalitarian and coercive community that manifests all the critiques of dissenting community discourse. However, what ultimately renders *Jazz* (1992) and *Paradise* (1998) the least ambivalent assertions of "we" in this study is the degree to which these novels ultimately return to and affirm the aspirational models of idealized community. Furthermore, dissenting community discourse, especially Lyotard's theory of the differend, highlights the vision of idealized community and the telos of healing that dominate Morrison's novels and contemporary literary criticism.

Moving from the strongest endorsement of idealized community found in Morrison's novels, the next two chapters delineate the increasing power of dissenting community discourse to unsettle the central assumptions and values of idealized community. However, what groups these three chapters together is the way that the values of idealized community, especially the "work" performed by community, ultimately underpin their formations of the first-person plural "we." The second chapter, "'We Are Not the World'": Global Community, Universalism, and Karen Tei Yamashita's *Tropic of Orange*," turns to the global "we" as another unstable site of the debate over community. The leap from the singular "I" to the plural "we," in this instance, rests upon the ideal of universalism—the condition of absolute inclusiveness that encompasses the whole of the world. This chapter engages the recent poststructuralist recuperations of universalism, such as those of Ernesto Laclau, Étienne Balibar, Judith Butler, and Slavoj Žižek, whose works argue a dialectic model of universalism: as a constitutive ingredient in any discussion of human rights or progressive politics, yet whose particular instantiations invariably fall short of an absolute inclusiveness vision. Precisely this impossible/necessary dialectic is central to Karen Tei Yamashita's *Tropic of Orange* (1997). The novel presents a skeptical look at the "global village" sentiments that pervade discussions of globalization, and it critiques the First World's deployment of a global intimacy and shared fate as the latest rendition of imperialist—that is, unidirectional—universalism. In its place, the novel postulates another model of global community, a "romantic" universalism that asserts the transnational "we" without imperialist dimensions. However, the novel's fantastic representation of this global "we" aesthetically enacts the "romantic" dimension of universalism—as a quixotic, imaginary, unrealistic, indeed *impossible,* achievement. The multiple significance of the novel's global community, then, lends a deeper nuance to the incompleteness at the heart of universalism: as an ideal whose impossibility is essential to its perennial appeal.

Chapter 3, "Unlike Any Other: Shoring Up the Human Community in Richard Powers's *Galatea 2.2* and *Plowing the Dark,*" turns to Powers's novels of science and technology to examine the role of humanism in literary manifestations of the human community. I suggest that Powers's ambivalent but ultimately defiant allegiance to humanism is a rich instance of the human "we" as an assertion of *distinction.* These novels' central question, "What is uniquely human?" directly engages the issue of commonality and differentiation at the heart of the community debate. As Chantel Mouffe puts it, constructing a "we" necessitates a "they," a "constitutive outside" that makes the "we" possible (12). "The human" has never been a stable category, of course, as other categories of being, principally "the animal," have perennially challenged those attributes purportedly exclusive to the human. In the late twentieth century, the biggest threat to the ontological stability of "the human" comes in the form of the intelligent machine, and posthumanist theories highlight those sites of fluidity between the machine and the human. I read post-humanist theories, such as those of Katherine N. Hayles, in light of the dissenting community discourse, and argue that humanism's pursuit of human uniqueness engages not only the singleness of the human "we" but the singularity—the essence—of the human "we." Powers severely tests his humanist-protagonists of *Galatea 2.2* (1995) and *Plowing the Dark* (2000) as they desperately try to maintain precisely this human essence that will absolutely demarcate the human from the machine. And as posthumanist arguments push the humanist defense to its very edge, dismantling its immanentist and essentialist logic, the human "we" seems all but defunct. But ultimately, Powers offers a startling response to buttress the human community: ineffability as the ultimate common-ality that enables the human "we."

In contrast to the first three chapters, the fourth chapter examines a literary "we" in which competing values of community do not find a resolution through idealized community. At the same time, this irresolve presents a challenge to the dissenting model of "we" *as well as* to the reign of idealized community. "Motion in Stasis: Impossible Community in Fictions of Lydia Davis and Lynne Tillman" examines the ideal of communion as a rationale for community formation. Befitting a concept central to the etymology of community, "communion" describes a spiri-tual union or meeting of souls, and this meaning continues to inflect the prevailing understanding of community as a condition of intersubjective continuity and transparency. The fictions of Davis and Tillman interro-gate this lingering influence of communion. In mundane, everyday set-tings, their characters feel the dual press of the other's contiguity as well as the other's opacity. However "close" one is to the other, relationally or physically, one cannot "know," "figure out," or "see through" the other. Indeed, the taunt of transparency remains the most pressing task for the prototypical protagonist of these writers. Furthermore, the two writers demonstrate the paradox of community in different and complementary ways. Davis's short stories and her novel *The End of the Story* (1993) explore the impossibility of communion through the concept of immeasurability. The countless number and ways of knowing the contiguous other announce the fact of the other's opacity. If there are just too many ways of knowing the other in Davis's fiction, the inverse is true in Tillman's fiction: there are too few, and they are too predictable. Tillman's *Motion Sickness* (1991) explores how, at every turn, the protagonist's attempt to know the other falls upon congealed ways of knowing. In this task, Tillman applies the concept of recognition under Barthesean pressure and examines the ways in which recognition is a way of knowing by repetition. Ultimately, their inevitable failure invokes and dramatizes the rejection of communion, amply voiced by dissenting community—but with a crucial difference. I suggest that in these instances of ambivalent community, the expectation of and the desire for communion as the condition of "we" are not as easily banished as in the discourse of dissenting community. Here, "we" becomes an assertion caught between the desire for communion and the knowledge of its fundamental impossibility.

From an examination of community as an incomplete and an impossible project, this book turns to a literary instance in which community is understood in the most expansive manner—as the fact of coexistence. The final chapter on David Markson examines the most direct representation of dissenting community model of "we" and stands as a counterpoint to the most idealized model of "we" that began this book. Chapter 5, "Community as Multi-Party Game: Private Language in David Markson's *Wittgenstein's Mistress*," studies Markson's novel, *Wittgenstein's Mistress* (1988), which engages the paradox of community by asking: Can one be absolutely alone? Can there be an "individual" outside "a body of individuals"? In one of the most philosophical and formally challenging treatments of the question, Markson presents a character who believes that she is the only person alive on earth. Most importantly for the argument of this book, she experiences her absolute-aloneness in antithetical ways: as a source of absolute freedom and as a source of absolute indeterminacy. Despite her freedom to do and say anything she wants, she spends her life "looking" for others, and her greatest concern is that she will be misunderstood because her language use is less than perfectly clear. Her dilemma invites the question: misunderstood by *whom*? Using Wittgenstein's theory of a private language game, I suggest that the protagonist's failure to play a private language game is an enactment of the impossibility of being absolutely alone. Attempts at evading a "we" simultaneously invoke the presence of a "we," and community becomes an expression of coexistence. However, in contrast to the anti-instrumentalist argument of dissenting community, the "we" that emerges in *Wittgenstein's Mistress* cannot be an expression empty of all utility or "work." Like all the other "we" in this study, the "we" of coexistence can only be an assertion that serves some purpose or does some work.

This book concludes with that observation: all communities do *something*. All manifestations of first-person plural "we" serve a need, answer a desire, respond to an anxiety, forestall a fear, or guard against a threat. In concluding with the inevitability of community that "works," this book argues the limitations of dissenting community's anti-instrumentalist and anti-teleological view. A community that works is automatically an argument *for* something, an assertion rather than an expression of a given fact. And what these ambivalent communities demonstrate is the fact that assertions of community, like every other argument, are vulnerable to counterarguments. *A Body of Individuals* traces how the ambivalent community of contemporary fiction manifests community *as* an argument, and an argument that must wear its counterarguments on its sleeve.

CHAPTER 1

What Ails the Individual

Community Cure in Toni Morrison's *Jazz* and *Paradise*

A paradigmatic pattern of conflict and resolve emerges in *Jazz*
(1992) and *Paradise* (1998). The ills of the individual are healed
through the ultimate vision of unity—through the formation of
community in which multiple individuals identify themselves
as a body of individuals. In *Jazz,* the violence that begins the narrative
finds its resolution in the unity of the three protagonists, Joe, Violet,
and Felice, who form a community like that of a family. In *Paradise,*
the persecuted women of the Convent achieve their healing through a
community like that of a sisterhood. Indeed, this movement of conflict
to resolution, individual ailment to collective healing, rings throughout
Morrison's oeuvre. Some of the most memorable moments in Morrison's
novels announce the achievement of precisely this unconditional emotional unity when multiple individuals psychically fuse into one. When
Nel cries out, "We was girls together," at the conclusion of *Sula* (174),
that declaration obliterates the years of antagonism between herself and
Sula, returning her to the strongest emotional attachment of her life.
When the neighborhood women of *Beloved* come together to ward off
the ghost bedeviling house 124, they announce a wordless sisterhood in
the name of protecting their own, Sethe and Denver. These declarations
reveal something distinct about the particular nature of unity that is
community: community announces the ultimate fusion of individuals,
whose unconditional nature is qualitatively distinct from other delibera-

27

tive instances of unity such as affiliation, group, or association. Furthermore, the declarations announce something distinct about the function of community: community is an ultimate unity that "works" towards restoring the health of its members. What these epiphanic moments of community reveal is the operation of community as an *ideal*—a state of perfection, a standard proposed for imitation.

In announcing the fusion of community and the "work" of community, Morrison's novels provide the perfect entryway for studying the dominance of idealized community discourse in contemporary fiction and criticism. This chapter examines the discourse of idealized community in *Jazz* and *Paradise,* two novels which, more than any other of Morrison's novels, thematically track the movement from individual to community formation and from individual ailment to community cure. Morrison's repeated turn to community invites her readers' engagement with her artistic vision of community. Certainly, it is an invitation amply taken up by her readers in the academe and in the general readership, and the larger aim of this chapter is to articulate the discourse of idealized community that powerfully informs contemporary discussions of community.[1] Studying the theory of community underpinning Morrison's novels, then, is to simultaneously study the way community floats as an ideal in contemporary culture, literature, and criticism. It is to ask: How does idealized community overcome the paradox at the heart of community as a proposition? How can multiple individuals become a body of individuals? How does Morrison's vision of community address contemporary concerns, anxieties, and visions of community? Ultimately, what is it about Morrison's vision of community that resonates so richly with current thinking of community? What does this resonance reveal about the theory of commonality, difference, conflict, and antagonism in the discourse of idealized community?

One quick way of answering these questions might be to argue that community, in Morrison's novels, dramatizes what Raymond Williams called the "warmly persuasive" feeling that tends to surround the word "community" (76). But this answer is surely insufficient, as it overlooks the fact that in Morrison's novels, many instances of community present themselves as *problems.* After all, it is the racial self-denigration within the community of The Bottom that prompts Pecola Breedlove to wish for the bluest eyes in the world. It is the community's rejection of Sethe and Baby Suggs for being too "proud" that leads them to silently watch the schoolteacher and slave trackers go after Sethe and her children.[2] In *Jazz,* the City represents the anonymous, indifferent urban coexistence, the backdrop of the violence amongst the protagonists. And in *Paradise,*

Ruby represents the most oppressive and totalitarian formation of an all-black town.

What these instances provoke, then, is a speculation on the troubling nature of community in Morrison's fiction. As the basis for strife, conflict, exclusion, and oppression, these instances invite a critical examination of community as a proposition. Through these instances of troubled community, Morrison joins those postmodernist thinkers of community, such as Jean-Luc Nancy, Giorgio Agamben, Ernesto Lacau, Iris Marion Young, and Jean-François Lyotard, who critique the oppressive homogeneity, the dangers of uniform thinking, and the valorization of sameness.[3] Most importantly, these thinkers dissent from the idealized community discourse, locating the oppressive power of community in its very status *as* an ideal. They highlight the ways in which the worst instances of historical oppression, coercion, exclusion, and persecution have taken place in the name of community. Hence the discourse of dissenting community that emerges from these postmodernist thinkers offers a profoundly antithetical answer to the paradox of community: they argue not only the impossibility of but also the danger inherent in idealizing the transformation of multiple individuals into a single body of people. Upon the impossibility of a single body community, they postulate an alternate model of community: a community inaugurated in difference, rather than commonality; a community in which conflict, antagonism, and dissent are as much central ingredients as are familiarity, conviviality, and consensus; and finally, a community that does not promise the fruits of belonging, comfort, and healing. In dissenting from the cornerstone of idealized community, these thinkers of dissenting community fundamentally negate the very nature and function of community as the ultimate expression of unity.

But there is a crucial difference between Morrison's and the larger postmodernist negation of idealized community, and this difference is where I locate the remarkable influence of Morrison's vision of community. In negating the central assumptions, values, and goals of idealized community, dissenting community argues the impossibility of community as a body of individuals. In contrast, Morrison's critique of oppressive community leads to an entirely different conclusion: the instances of oppressive community stand as instances of misbegotten community, whose harmful ramifications illustrate the need for a "healthier" kind of community. Rather than announcing the impossibility of community or delegitimating community, oppressive communities such as The Bottom in *Sula* and Cincinnati of *Beloved*, and much more so the City in *Jazz* or Ruby in *Paradise*, function as cautionary tales; that is, they describe the condition of coexistence that has not *yet* achieved the idealized community. As they stand as *particular* instantiations of an ideal that has no bearing upon the legitimacy of the ideal itself, these oppressive instances only *heighten* the need for idealized community. Community as the ultimate unity of a "body of individuals" is not only possible; it becomes imperative. Thus the powerful appeal of Morrison's vision of community, I argue in this chapter, lies in its ability to say: the ideal of community has not failed us; we have failed the ideal that is community.[4]

Exactly this value system upholds the paradigmatic pattern of conflict and resolution in *Jazz* and *Paradise*. Counterbalancing the oppressive instances of community are those memorable moments that represent the most intense emotional connection—unconditional, uncalculating bonding, sharing, nurturance, support, and healing. The protagonists' achievement of this unity announces their greatest development, and the resolution to their conflict is inconceivable outside this achievement. In the contrapuntal presentation of two *kinds* of community, these novels offer a resounding answer to the question "Why community?" As the ills experienced in one kind of community are healed in another kind of community, these novels answer: because the ideal community is the ultimate unity that heals the ills of the individual.

In delineating their answer to the question "Why community?" these novels postulate an answer to the question "Just how does one achieve the seemingly impossible feat of superseding the paradox of community?" Through her formation of the ideal community, Morrison offers an unequivocal answer: through a process of identification, when multiple subjects regard themselves to be *like* the other based on their commonalities. Thus the achievement of community pivots upon a central criterion that asks, "How are you like me?" That this question leads not only to affirmation of likeness ("You are like me") but to *reciprocal appropriation* ("You are like my own") speaks to the centrality of commonality in Morrison's theory of community.

The "why" and "how" of ideal community formation come together to suggest that the ideal community is the final *achievement* in a long line of development. What Morrison's vision of community suggests, then, is that community is teleological. From a condition of coexistence that is not yet a community, such as the City of *Jazz*, or from a false vision of community, such as Ruby of *Paradise*, the prototypical movement of the narrative is towards the fulfillment of the ideal community—the sisterhood and family models of community in *Jazz*, or the healing fusion in *Paradise*. As the plot and character development parallels the development *of* community, what Morrison literally enacts, then, is the teleology of community. Ultimately, this teleological view of the community directly resonates with the contemporary discourse of idealized community. The ultimate, most perfect incarnation of an idea requires a movement *towards* that destination, not only in the temporal sense but in the diachronic sense: the very concept of "the ideal" necessitates teleological thinking.

Furthermore, a potent appeal of Morrison's teleology of community lies in its ability to simultaneously critique and uphold community as an ideal, to invite postmodernist theoretical critique of community articulated by Nancy, Young, Laclau, and Lyotard, while ultimately affirming the language and value system of idealized community. As the competing discourses of idealized community and dissenting community appear as two models of saying "we" and generate ambivalence towards notions such as commonality, identification, and fusion, the novels' conclusions announce the prevailing power of the idealized "we." The unequivocal nature of that affirmation, and the seeming inevitability of that embrace, are what characterize Morrison's novels as the least ambivalent instances of ideal community in this study.

The Problem of Living with Strangers

Violence begins the narrative in *Jazz*. An older lover kills the young girl who spurned him, and the cheated wife attempts to scar the dead girl's face. Too haunted by her husband's betrayal and crime, and no less by her own attempt to disfigure the dead girl, the wife decides to understand the husband's and the young girl's relationship: "So she decided to love—well, find out about—the eighteen-year-old whose creamy little face she tried to cut open even though nothing would have come out but straw" (5). The explication of the violence, in turn, becomes a narrative reconstruction of the complex relationships connecting the central protagonists. In the task of explicating the complex relationships that led to violence, the task of explicating the City takes center stage. I propose that the characterization of the City, especially its contradictory nature as a unity, holds valuable clues to the novel's—and Morrison's—ambivalence about community.[5]

As the fictional counterpart to Harlem at the turn of the twentieth century, the City stands as the place of hope to which the couple, Joe and Violet, arrive. The two, like many other Southern blacks in 1906, board the colored section of the train heading for Northern cities, and the narrator follows their tense, excitement-filled ride. As the narrator relays the couple's arrival in the City, the singularity of Joe and Violet dissipates, and they become a synecdoche of a "million others" who journeyed northward: "They weren't even there yet and already the City was speaking to them. They were dancing. And like a million others . . . they stared out the windows for first sight of the City that danced with them, proving already how much it loved them. Like a million more they could hardly wait to get there and love it back" (32). The particularity of Joe and Violet submerge into "[t]he wave of black people running from want and violence" (33), into the relief that "it is worth anything to be on Lenox Avenue safe from fays and the things they [the Southern whites] think up" (10). As the locus of excitement, hope, and possibility, the City stands as the perpetual present, embodying the very hope of beginning anew: "That kind of fascination, permanent and out of control," seizes all occupants of the City, and "they feel more like themselves, more like the people they always believed they were. Nothing can pry them away from that; the City is *what they want it to be*: thriftless, warm, scary and full of amiable strangers" (35; emphasis added).

It is important to note that careful caveat made in the narration—that the view of the City as "warm, scary and full of amiable strangers" is a concerted projection made by Joe and Violet and a million others just like them. It is a projection that the narrator sometimes shares, echoing the excitement of the million who see, in the commonality of their histories and dreams, a potential for a close-knit unity. As the couple settle into the City, the narrative traces the variegated corners and expansive sites of the City. In the sweeping eye of the narrative, the minutiae that constitute the daily lives of urban coexistence translate into intimacy and familiarity, and the City becomes a single interdependent unit whose members ask, borrow, and lend across the windows and gossip on sidewalks, front steps, and streetcars. Indeed, the physical interconnectedness of the City life translates into a *social* interconnectedness:

> Up in those big five-story apartment buildings and the narrow wooden houses in between people knock on each other's doors to see if anything is needed or can be had. A piece of soap? A little kerosene? Some fat, chicken or pork, to brace the soup one more time? Whose husband is getting ready to go see if he can find a shop open? Is there time to add turpentine to the list drawn up and handed to him by the wives? (10)

The daily lives within the City represent an intertwined congregation of purpose, functions, and needs: "the church, the store, the party, the women, the men, the postbox (but no high schools), the furniture store, street newspaper vendors, the bootleg houses (but no banks), the beauty parlors, the barbershops[,] . . . every club, organization, group, order, union, society, brotherhood, sisterhood or association imaginable" (10). This list of commercial stores, religious organizations, social groups, and cultural affiliations extends more than a page, a rendition that unmistakably asserts the City as an urban coexistence of cooperation, connections, sharing, interdependence, and conviviality. Thus, running through the inhabitants' projection of the City is the idealized discourse of community.

Indeed, the characters' translation of physical proximity into economic, social, and cultural intimacy echoes the celebration of public spaces in political philosophy and cultural theory. Best known through the Habermasean valorization of urban gathering spaces (e.g., coffee shops) for its potential to foster civic discourse, urban geography inspires possibilities for urban sociability in political theory and cultural theory. For instance, "The square or piazza is the epitome of open-mindedness. . . . [I]n the square itself, people meet, walk, talk, buy and sell, argue about politics, eat lunch, sit over coffee, wait for something to happen. . . . They are different people, with different purposes, educated by space they share to a civil deportment" (Walzer 323). Likewise, the idealized view of the City translates densely shared urban space into social interdependence and conviviality.

However, it would be a mistake to characterize the City of *Jazz* as a direct literary rendition of a Habermasean public sphere. Like the numerous critics who argue the shortcomings of theorizing democratic communication through the metaphor of urban, public space,[6] Morrison destabilizes the idealized view of the City. And it is at this juncture that the earlier caveat—that the idealized City is a projection of the new arrivals—manifests an unsettling force. In tandem with the idealized vision of the City is a steady vein of ominous warnings that run through the narration of the City. In a departure from the idealized projections of the City, which are focalized through excited newcomers like Joe and Violet, the cautionary warnings appear as a direct address from the narrator: "Nobody says it's pretty here; nobody says it's easy either. What it is is decisive, and if you pay attention to the street plans, all laid out, the City can't hurt you" (8). In the narrator's warnings, the ominous possibilities of the City do not emerge from a malevolent or ill-intentioned force; rather, they are expressions of the very condition of a large-scale coexistence of strangers: "Do what you please in the City, it is there to back and frame you no matter what you do. And what goes on on its blocks and lots and side streets is anything the strong can think of and the weak will admire. All you have to do is heed the design—the way it's laid out for you, considerate, mindful of where you want to go and what you might need tomorrow" (8–9). Like the inflexibility and fixedness of the street plans "all laid out," the very nature of urban coexistence results in an unknowability that stands in contrast to the well-wishing of "amiable strangers."

Through the narrator's corrective to the idealized projection of the City, Morrison presents a much more complex vision of urban coexistence. In the combination of welcome and threat, of interdependence and indifference, the final City resembles the metaphoric city that functions as the ideal model of community in postmodernist dissenting community. At the heart of the matter is the condition of living with strangers. As an amalgam of strangers whose proximity is not reducible to any established categories of commonality (of blood, of lineage, of family, of religion, of identity), coexistence in the city stands as the ideal trope of coexisting in *difference* in postmodernist philosophy. While the idealized view of the City projected by people like Joe and Violet *neutralizes* that difference through "amiability," the narrator's cautionary warnings restore the ability of difference to disturb, to alienate, to threaten, and to remain impenetrable. From the idealized version of intimacy, cooperation, and conviviality, the postmodernist city postulates an entirely different model of community—a theory of community that *begins* from difference, a community in which difference is not an obstacle to assimilate or overcome but the very reason for conceiving a new mode of unity. Precisely this altered logic of community anchors the trope of the city in dissenting community discourse.

For Young, the condition of living with strangers offers the perfect countermodel to the expectation of transparency and intimacy in the idealized community discourse. She begins from the "positive experiences of city life to form a vision of the good society," an "ideal of city life" (318):

> City life thus also embodies difference as the contrary of the face-to-face ideal expressed by most assertions of community. City life is the "being-together" of strangers. Strangers encounter one another, either face to face or through media, often remaining strangers and yet acknowledging their contiguity in living and the contributions each makes to the others. In such encountering people are not "internally" related . . . and do not understand one another from within their own perspective. They

are externally related, they experience each other as other, different, from different groups, histories, professions, cultures, which they do not understand. (318)[7]

The fact of living with strangers means that one accepts the condition of anonymity rather than familiarity, difference rather than similarity, unknowability rather than transparency. In the proximity of strangers, so to speak, urban coexistence requires the "politics of difference": "The unoppressive city is thus defined as openness to unassimilated otherness" (Young 319). Most importantly, the physical density and proximity do not translate into amiability as in the idealized community discourse. Instead, negating the assumption of intimacy, familiarity, and transparency as the criteria of community, the postmodernist ideal city suggests a model of dissenting community. Inhabitants of *this* community interact in public spaces, streets, restaurants, parks, but "always to go off again as strangers" (Young 319).

Nancy's trope of the city also provides a crucial expression of postmodernist dissenting community. The city is central to Nancy's illustration of community as coexistence, a vision that continues the Heideggerian Dasein to theorize community as the "being-in-common": "The city is not primarily 'community,' any more than it is primarily 'public space.' The city is at least as much the bringing to light of being-in-common *as the dis-position* (dispersal and disparity) of the community represented as founded in interiority or transcendence. It is 'community' without common origin" (*Being Singular Plural* 23; original emphasis).[8] In contrast to the shared origin, history, and dreams that rendered the collective projection of the idealized City in the eyes of Joe, Violet, and a million others like them, Nancy's community emphasizes the a priori condition of being-with as the originary structure of community. Rather than a community based on "togetherness"—founded on shared origins, commonalities, or sameness—it is a community based on the fact of "being-together." While "togetherness" describes "a substantive entity," "a collection [that] assumes a regrouping that is exterior and indifferent to the being-together" (62), "being-together" describes the condition of "simultaneity" that is coexistence: "'Same time/same place' assumes that 'subjects,' to call them that, share this space-time, but not in the extrinsic sense of 'sharing'; they must share it between *themselves*" (60–61; original emphasis). "The 'together,' therefore, is an absolutely originary structure. . . . The Being is being-with, absolutely, this is what we must think" (62). In the simultaneity of coexistence, commonality loses all parochial dimension and simply becomes the fact of being-together.

In Morrison's disruption of the idealized City, we might read a Nancian disruption of "togetherness." While the idealized view of the City projects harmony, cooperation, commonality, and conviviality as the ultimate *proof* of the City as a community, the narrator's correction suggests an unknowable, anonymous, and indifferent City—which "will confuse you, teach you or break your head" (72). This contradictory juxtaposition undermines the idealized community discourse that assumes the benevolence—the "amiability"—of sharing, belonging, familiarity, and easy interdependence. In the unknowable, threatening, and indifferent City, in contrast, we encounter a vision of community that is neither benevolent nor malevolent. It is simply *indifferent* inasmuch as it is a community without any single characteristic or functionality. The unknowable City is simply the observation of "being-together," the acceptance of being-in-common that does not require any "extrinsic sense" or substance to justify itself.

However, there is a crucial difference between Morrison's and the postmodernist dissenting community's deployment of the indifferent city. While the unknowable city serves as a postmodernist disruption of the discourse of idealized community, it serves as a *problem* in Morrison's theory of community. Far from being a desirable condition illustrating the politics of difference or of unassimilated otherness, the countless unknown and unknowable strangers making up the City translate into a looming threat in the protagonists' lives. While postmodernist valorization of urban heterogeneity and difference must include the potential for anonymity, indifference, conflict, and antagonism, in *Jazz* this potential becomes the frightening aspect of living with strangers. This threat returns us to the violence that began the narrative of *Jazz* and suggests that in Morrison's larger view of community, the City represents a state of unity that is *not yet* the state of community.

No character better embodies the fear of the unknowable city than the dead girl's aunt, Alice Manfred. Through Alice's internal monologue, we learn of lives lived against the dangers of strangers who might, at any minute, cause harm. The narrative recounts innumerable attacks by whites against the newly arrived Southern blacks, two of them being Dorcas's parents who were brutally killed by a white mob in East St. Louis, as well as the daily occurrence of male violence against women. Little Dorcas, sent to live in the City with her aunt, carries a legacy from this violence—a wood chip from her burning house that "must have entered her stretched dumb mouth and traveled down her throat because it smoked and glowed there still. Dorcas never let it out and never put it out" (61). Dorcas becomes a young girl for whom the world is an unremitting place of hostility, an enemy to be met. Dorcas's vulnerability to violence—indeed, all black women's vulnerability to violence—becomes the determining principle of Alice's care. She emphasizes female vulnerability to male violence, especially to white male sexual violence. She instructs Dorcas to hide her femininity, to cultivate a "deafness and blindness" (54), and teaches "her how to crawl along the walls of buildings, disappear into doorways[,] . . . how to do anything, move anywhere to avoid a whiteboy over the age of eleven" (55). However, Alice's lessons in abnegation are no match for the City. The City's temptation, always ringed in violence, is epitomized in the form of jazz, that "dirty, get-on-down music," in Alice's view (58). Just as Alice resists jazz, she resists the City—its possibilities, temptations, dangers, and indifference: "Alice Manfred wasn't the kind to give herself reasons to be in the streets. She got through them quick as she could to get back to her house" (72–73). Dorcas, in contrast, embraces the chaotic energy of the City and begins an affair with Joe that eventually ends in her death.

When Dorcas is killed by Joe, the charming door-to-door salesman trusted in all the neighborhood women's homes, Alice realizes that living unobtrusively and taking up as little space as possible are no guarantees of safety. While "living with strangers" might be the ruling metaphor for the heterogeneity, the unassimilated difference, and the being-in-common of the postmodernist dissenting community, it represents, for Alice and for *Jazz*, a severely disturbing condition of coexistence. Precisely the lack of commonality, knowability, and familiarity is what breeds the potential for violence in the City. In this view, behind the unknowability of the City is not amiability or even *indifference* but violence. The pervasive possibility of violence obsesses Alice, who becomes an avid tracker of violence against women. She scours the newspapers for reports: "[A] paper laid bare the bones of some broken woman. Man kills wife. Eight accused of rape dismissed. Woman and girl victim of. Woman commits suicide. White attackers indicted. Five women caught. Woman says man beat. In jealous rage man" (74). The fragmented headlines exemplify the ritualized mode of reportage, the announcements of killing, beating, maiming, and raping that are eclipsed to fit the space of the headline. The mass media's economy of expression bespeaks the sheer triteness, the everydayness, of violence in the City.

Alice's view of the City as a *failure* as community is the basis upon which Morrison builds her resolution, translating the unknowable City into a problem that her protagonists must solve. That is, Violet's—and the narrative's—quest to "understand" the violence linking Joe, Dorcas, and Violet directly rests upon the protagonists' ability to relate to each other differently—to form a different model of community. The first meeting between Violet and Alice explicitly announces this task. After her attempt to deface Dorcas's corpse, Violet seeks out Alice in her quest to understand her husband's affair and to learn about the young girl at the heart of it all. When Alice finally grants Violet an interview, she can't help asking:

> "Why did he do such a thing?"
>   "Why did she?"
>   "Why did you?"
>   "I don't know." (81)

The rapid-fire questioning of why "he," "she," "you," and "I" committed violence encapsulates the striking fact that the central cause connecting these protagonists is violence. In emphasizing the violence that connects the lives of her characters, Morrison translates the unknowability and uncontrollability of the City into a problem of community—more specifically, as a *deficient* state of community. Morrison's presentation of the City as a problem, and her solution to this dilemma that follows, directly speak to her teleological thinking of community. If "living with strangers" presents an "undeveloped" stage of community, the ensuing kinship model of community that emerges from Violet and Alice's friendship points to the fully "developed" model, the final destination in Morrison's teleology of community.

What the City Wrought, the Family Solves

As Alice and Violet begin to resolve the violence that opened the novel, their relationship begins the movement towards a new model of community. This new model of community not only removes the perpetual threat of conflict, antagonism, and violence that had seemed constitutive ingredients of living with strangers; it also supersedes the paradox of community and transforms multiple individuals into a single "we." Morrison locates the seed of this new community in the concept of identification. Identification in literature has been primarily approached psychoanalytically, through a Freudian theory of parent-child primary identification or melancholia, or through a Lacanian theory of desire, idealization, trauma, or loss. For instance, identification can be understood as the "confusion of self and other, impelled by the (unusually) unconscious desire to be the other" (Wyatt 1); as the unconscious replication of parent-child relationality; as the idealization of a figure who appears to be complete; or as the expression of "traumatic loss and . . . the subject's tentative attempt to manage this loss" (Fuss 38).[9] Certainly, the psychoanalytic approach to identification is strongly represented in critical scholarship on Morrison's novels, given the thematic recurrence of trauma, loss, and envy in her work.[10]

However, my analysis of identification as the rationale for community requires a deviation from prevailing psychoanalytic approaches to Morrison's novels. First, in studying identification as a largely unconscious drive, the psychoanalytic lens has little room for the concept of commonality, a concept central to the discourse of idealized community and, as I will show, foundational to Morrison's formation of the final, ideal community in *Jazz* and *Paradise*. Psychoanalytic studies of desire for the other, envy of the other, idealization of the other, or replacement of the other do not ask the question central to the formation of community in these novels: "How are you like me?" Precisely this question poses the criteria of similarity, likeness, and sharing that appear as bridges towards idealized community in these novels. Indeed, some psychoanalytic studies of identification might be contrary to the concerns of a community formed around commonality. For instance, Wyatt's study of community formation in contemporary fiction examines the way "one identifies with what one wants to be" (5), and the central expression of this envy and idealization is "I want to be you" (1). Rather than asking "How are you like me?" this approach to identification may more fittingly ask, "How are you *un*like me?"

Second, psychoanalytic approaches to identification emphasize the unidirectional nature of the operation. Identification becomes a largely unconscious assimilation of the other; the *object* of desire, loss, envy, or idealization has no say in the process of identification. Thus feminist theorists of identification argue "the imperializing character of many cross-cultural identifications" (Fuss 8). In her attempt to theorize a feminist model of identification that does not eclipse the difference and singularity of the other, Wyatt argues: "The trick is to modulate the totalizing tendency of id, to put into practice the idea of identifying 'to a degree.' . . . In rethinking community . . . the emphasis has to remain on the cautionary terms—on the 'potential' for identification, on a 'partial' identification with the other" (9). In contrast, identification as the rationale for community formation is a thoroughly *reciprocal* process in *Jazz* and *Paradise,* rendering the appropriation of the other into an entirely benevolent act.

Precisely this reciprocity informs the benevolent politics of Morrison's idealized community and distinguishes the two novels' structuring of identification from psychoanalytic understandings of it. As protagonists reciprocally appropriate each other on the grounds of commonality, multiple individuals consider themselves to be *one* with another. The unlikely friendship between Violet and Alice, which becomes the foundation for the new community, demonstrates this transformation. Over the weeks and months of encounters, the two women's relationship moves from suspicion to tolerance to companionship, until it becomes the deepest emotional intimacy that the novel offers. It is through their mutual probing that Violet relives a detailed account of her childhood—her mother who committed suicide after being numerously abandoned by her father, her courtship with Joe, their wide-eyed migration to the City, and their gradual disappointments and setbacks. Most importantly, Violet reveals the cause of the rift between her and Joe: the stillborn child early in their marriage, the sudden "mother-hunger" that "hit her like a hammer" (108) in her middle age and led her to play "mother" with a plastic doll while Joe watched helplessly. Alice, in turn, shares her life story—her parents who exhorted her to regard her female body with shame, a lesson that she continued in her care of Dorcas. Achieving the deepest trust with each other, the two women elicit self-revelations and self-assessments that surprise even themselves.

By offering the most sustaining emotional relationship of the novel between the two women, Morrison grounds the basis of their identification upon the familiar feminist trope of sisterhood. As the two women found their relationship upon the sharing of their life stories, their most transformative moments arise when one sees the other as being *like* herself. One such revelation comes amidst a tense eruption. Violet keeps dogging a very frustrated Alice about what she should do about her marriage and her life:

> "We born around the same time, me and you," said Violet.
>
> "We women, me and you. Tell me something real. Don't just say I'm grown and ought to know. I'm fifty and I don't know nothing. What about it? Do I stay with him?. . . . Where the grown people? Is it us?"
>
> "Oh, Mama." Alice Manfred blurted it out and then covered her mouth.
>
> Violet had the same thought: Mama. Mama? Is this where you got to and couldn't do it no more? (110)

A sisterhood and a matrilineal model of community emerge from this identification on the grounds of gender-specific commonality. Violet's and Alice's invocation of "Mama" functions as psychic talisman, which fuses the two women into one subject position. It is a fusion that extends beyond the two women, reaching back to their long-lost mothers, to the long line of common experiences, struggles, and despair. This transformative work of identification sheds a new light on the key moments of epiphany mentioned earlier. When Nel cries out, "we was girls together," at the conclusion of *Sula, girlhood* functions as the most primary truth of all, a truth that awakens Nel to the fact that her rejection and alienation of Sula are also a rejection and alienation of herself. Likewise, when the women of Cincinnati band together to drive out the ghost of Beloved from house 124, their wordless fusion supersedes their former resentment, betrayal, and alienation of Sethe. In protecting Sethe and Denver from Beloved, these women heed the greater imperative of sisterhood.

Furthermore, in emphasizing the simultaneity of the two women's epiphany regarding the lost mother, Morrison renders their identification into one of natural and *reciprocal* appropriation. As Wyatt points out, intersubjective identification, however well intentioned, does not escape the appropriation of the other's difference. A subject's ability to say "I am like you" or "I feel your experience" remains an unidirectional claim, one which may be unauthorized and resented by the object of the appropriation: "Even the most partial or benign identification with the other risks occluding her specificity as a separate subject" (170). Precisely this risk of unauthorized appropriation is removed in the simultaneity of the two women's embrace of the lost mother.[11]

Furthermore, by emphasizing the commonality in Alice's and Violet's experience of race, gender, age, racism, sexism, and even in their experience of violence as the first generation of Southern blacks to migrate to Northern urban centers, Morrison presents two subjects whose identification need not negotiate material *difference*. By removing the question of material difference in the two women's subject position, Morrison deflects feminist critiques of "uneven" sisterhood—instances of feminist unity in which material differences such as race, class, sexuality, and other differences in subject positions are too easily swept aside in the name of "female commonalities." By locating the women's fusion outside the realm of difference, Morrison locates the two women's reciprocal appropriation in an apolitical context—a context in which commonality is already "there" and not a matter of selection, negotiation, or contestation.[12]

Building on the benevolence-of-sisterhood model of community, Morrison extends the healing powers of identification to include Dorcas, Joe, and even a substitute "daughter." The two women's sisterhood wields an unmistakably generative power, as their reciprocal appropriation leads to a wider circle of reciprocal appropriation. Sisterhood thus forms the *basis* for the family model of community that concludes the novel. Violet's greatest moment of healing comes when, with the knowledge of Dorcas's life garnered from Alice, she comes to think of Dorcas as a young girl who *could have been* her daughter. The daughter that she lost in childbirth, she thinks, would have been the same age as Dorcas. "Was she [Dorcas] the woman who took her man? Or the daughter who fled her womb?" She tells Alice, "'Another time . . . I would have loved her too. Just like you did. Just like Joe'" (109). This moment of substitution certainly invites a psychoanalytic study of identification as the replacement for a loss, but this approach alone casts insufficient light onto the power of commonality at work here. Violet's identification of Dorcas with her dead daughter rests on the similarities between the two girls—of race, sex, and age, and of life experiences as they develop into girlhood, adolescence, and adulthood.

As Violet psychically "conceives" Dorcas through the logic of the family, she endows a personhood onto what had been an inimical force. Dorcas is no longer a stock figure of a young, amoral temptress, but an individual with as much complexity as herself. As Dorcas slips into the position of Violet's daughter, the work of identification moves from the model of sisterhood, "How are you like me?" to one of kinship, "How are you like my own?" The transformative power of identification attains its highest achievement in the family-community that concludes the novel. It is fitting that Felice, Dorcas's best friend and witness to her death, enters Joe and Violet's life at this point. Felice brings with her a vision of Dorcas that complicates the dead girl's character and solves the mystery surrounding her death. Felice speaks of Dorcas's recklessness and self-destructive tendencies and reveals that Dorcas refused to seek medical help after being shot by Joe, a revelation that somewhat lightens Joe's culpability for her death. But Felice's most crucial role lies in her ability to complete the family model of community. Felice becomes a regular visitor at the couple's home, a steady presence at mealtime and during idle chats and unplanned confessions. She fulfills the gaping absence of the dead daughter that began the couple's drift apart. In a daisy chain of identification, Dorcas becomes the dead daughter, which prepares the ground for Dorcas's best friend to become the couple's dead daughter. Felice, in turn, comes from a family of distant and inaccessible parents. Her mother lives in another city as a maid, and her brief and infrequent visits home leave Felice wanting more. Her father is emotionally distant, wrapped in tracking and recounting racial injustices. Thus, in Joe and Violet, Felice finds ready-made parents. In the final, emblematic scene, Felice watches on as Joe and Violet slowly dance around their living room. As the third and the final member of this unlikely family, Felice is the crucial participant in and witness to their collective healing from violence. The narrator reports, in the concluding pages of the novel: "I saw the three of them, Felice, Joe, and Violet, and they looked to me like a mirror image of Dorcas, Joe, and Violet" (221).

In this concluding scene, we arrive at the final destination of idealized community in the novel: the family. Completing the task that began with the sisterhood of Alice and Violet, this family model of community resolves the paradox of community through the power of identification and reciprocal appropriation. Through the criteria of "How are you like me?" and "How are you like my own?" multiple individuals become a body of individuals. Most importantly, as the seat of reconciliation, healing, and hope, this family model of community stands as the *answer* to the problem of the City. From a condition of "living with strangers," we have arrived at a community that is like sisterhood, kinship, and family. From the City whose sheer size, heterogeneity, and difference presented a physical and metaphysical unknowability for any single individual, we have arrived at a community that is entirely familial, intimate, and knowable. Within this tale of community "development," the violence that lurked within the unknowable City is quelled, Violet's quest to "understand" the violence is completed, and individuals are healed. Hence the plot development of *Jazz* parallels its community development. Foundational to this literary maneuver is the discourse of idealized community, particularly the teleological view of community as a pursuit of "natural" unities like that of sisterhood, kinship, and family.

Morrison's solution of forging a family out of the City, and the attendant celebration of this teleology in the critical scholarship on *Jazz*, prompts a question about the role of the family in the idealized community discourse. Where, in this family-community, may concepts such as heterogeneity, anonymity, indifference, antagonism, and conflict rest? In the teleological movement from the City to the family-community, these concepts could only be testimonies of the unknowability and the uncontrollability of "living with strangers" that gave rise to violence. In forging a family out of the City, then, Morrison suggests that community is that unity which protects against the ills of living with strangers. It is a teleological view of "progress" shared by the majority of *Jazz*'s critics, as we see above, that demonstrates the dominance of the idealized community as the site of healing and health. The seemingly natural and self-evident deployment of commonality and identification prompts a related question: what place is there for "difference" in theories of community that hold the sisterhood-and-family model as the most aspired destination? In the final achievement of ideal community in *Jazz*, the centripetal pull of commonality renders surmountable whatever difference existed between the central protagonists, however great their conflict. In this idealized model of community formation, the pull of commonality leads to identification and reciprocal appropriation and, in the final analysis, renders difference surmountable.

Finally, how is this aspirational use of the family distinguishable from the exclusionary and discriminatory community formation based on race, ethnicity, region, nation, religion, culture, and more? How does the valorization of the family-community answer the fact that commonality of descent, bloodline, lineage, and household is *also* the rationale for homogeneous sectarianism? After all, the litmus tests for the family model of *Jazz*—"How are you like me?" and "How are you like my own?"—is the same litmus test that endorses community formation based on blood origins. As Young puts it: "The desire for community relies on the same desire for social wholeness and identification that underlies racism and ethnic chauvinism on the one hand and sectarianism on the other" (302). Any valorization of the family model of community, founded on commonality and identification, cannot be completely extricated from the rationale of "one of us" that founds exclusionary and discriminatory community formations. Certainly for critics of idealized community, idealized community's emphasis on commonality and kinship is what ties its theory of community to totalitarianism. As Nancy writes, "by thinking of community via a presupposition [of commonalities], we get totalitarianism" (*Inoperative Community* 39).

Indeed, these are critiques of commonality and identification that Morrison directly raises against the town of Ruby in *Paradise,* the focus of the following analysis. Standing as the antithesis of the Convent, the novel's idealized model of community, Ruby dramatizes the worst fears about community—a totalitarianism in which the question of identification—"How are you like me?"—is the punitive ideology, commonality is coerced, and difference is persecuted and eliminated. These two contrasting instances of community reveal the fact that identification, in Morrison's theory of community, can perform antithetical functions. As demonstrated through the Convent, and certainly in the sisterhood and family-community of *Jazz,* identification offers the most benevolent and "natural" logic of community formation, but as demonstrated through Ruby, it fuels the most xenophobic and oppressive community formation. Through the opposing deployments of identification in *Paradise,* Morrison again presents us with two models of saying "we," calling upon the competing discourses of idealized community and dissenting community. Through Ruby's and the Convent's contrasting logic of saying "we," the novel asks: what ultimately renders identification either benevolent or coercive, leading to the ideal community or the malformed community?

The Convent as the Differend

Ruby is a town whose present is fueled by a veneration of its past. Tracking the history of its formation to a few brave ex-slave men who in the 1870s trekked from Mississippi, to Louisiana, and finally to Ruby, Oklahoma, Ruby's residents, all of whom are black, repeat the stories of their founding like a mantra. Like all foundational myths, these stories are anchored by a belief in their exceptionalism. Tales of the "founding families" recount their courage in the face of unending persecution, hardship, and heavenly guidance along the way. As scholarship on *Paradise* has well explored, the town of Ruby stands as the most oppressive and coercive instance of totalitarianism.[13]

Ruby complements its sense of exceptionalism with a fierce xenophobia. Although it sits in splendid isolation, with no nearby towns for hundreds of miles, it is a town that never forgets the hostility and danger posed by the world-out-there. Ruby's endangered sense of unity translates into xenophobia, as the town boasts of its inhospitality towards outsiders and visitors. Its public spaces are specifically designed to dissuade passers-by from lingering—there are no hotels, restaurants, parks, or resting places. Conversely, Ruby's fierce guarding of its boundaries is accompanied by an equally fierce enforcement of a single identity. Emphasizing the singularity of origin, movement, and ultimately of will, Ruby demands that the many become one, that its residents adhere to a commonality of purpose, history, and values. Just as they see the formation of their community as written on the logic of

commonality, failure of community rests in the dissipation of commonality, the rationale that later supports their destruction of the Convent.
Hence, in Ruby's hands, identification becomes the most coercive tool
of oppression, as the question "How are you like me?" becomes the
most ominous dictum.

Diverging from the playful, multivocal narrator of *Jazz, Paradise* exhibits the absolute authority of an omniscient narrator who
unequivocally criticizes what Ruby represents. In no uncertain terms,
Morrison voices her criticism through select characters. The majority
of these mouthpieces are women (e.g., Soame, Patricia Storace, Lone),
a gender-specific criticism that bespeaks the patriarchal rule and the
ensuing gender fissure in Ruby. However, the character who sustains the
greatest critical power and exercises the most moral authority is Richard
Misner.[14] His authority is no less derived from his religious position (witness other Ruby ministers who squabble no less enthusiastically as the
townspeople) as from his outsider status as a nondescendant of Ruby.
Misner observes:

> Over and over and with the least provocation, they pulled from their
> stock of stories tales about the old folks, their grands and great-grands;
> their fathers and mothers. Dangerous confrontations, clever maneuvers.
> Testimonies to endurance, wit, skill and strength. Tales of luck and out-
> rage. But why were there no stories to tell of themselves? About their
> own lives they shut up. Had nothing to say, pass on. As though past hero-
> ism was enough of a future to live by. As though, rather than children,
> they wanted duplicates. (161)

Into this totalitarian regime walks a truly bewildering phenomenon—
a haphazard gathering of four women who settle into a former convent
at the edge of town. Women of different race, age, economic status, and
geographical origin wander through its doors, women fleeing domestic
or familial situations they find intolerable, and women who decided that
they do not want to do what is expected of them. As the narrative alter-
nates between Ruby and the Convent, Morrison revives the key values
of idealized community formation. While Ruby's model of community requires the unremitting patrolling of its borders, the free-forming
nature of the Convent is entirely voluntary. That the members choose
each other and determine the nature of their relationality, and that this
collectivity is ultimately beneficial and healing, directly continue the idealized community discourse. Regulation, too, is formless; unlike Ruby's
fiercely central and hierarchical organization, the Convent women deal

with conflict through a face-to-face intimacy: they fight easily and rec-
oncile easily. Ultimately, the Convent represents the most supportive,
nurturing, accepting, and welcoming unity: the idealized community. As
one Ruby woman describes it: "They'll take care of you or leave you
alone—whichever way you want it" (176).

Notably, Morrison's greatest denunciation of Ruby comes not through
any mouthpiece but through the town's maniacally inflexible ideology of
commonality. Ruby's failure as community emerges through its inability
to acknowledge the Convent's extreme difference in any terms other
than an aberration from itself. That is, Morrison powerfully locates
Ruby's failure as a community in its severely limited *language use*. In
order to theorize the political implications of Morrison's turn to language use, let me call up Lyotard's theory of the differend. In Lyotard's
anti-instrumentalist view of language, language is not a transmission or
an exchange of preexisting blocks of "meaning," but a linguistic manifestation of the uneven nature of coexistence. As inequities in human
coexistence inhere in language, the inequities are manifest in the very
practice and possibility of language use. "The [phrase] is not a message
passing from an addresser to an addressee both of whom are indepen-
dent of it. They are situated in the universe the phrase represents, as are
its referent and its sense" (*The Differend* 18).[15] Likewise, Morrison's
denunciation of Ruby's language use is simultaneously a denunciation
of the "universe" that Ruby represents.

Using the analogy of legal contestation as his central metaphor,
Lyotard defines the differend as the inequitable and irreconcilable contestation of "idioms." "I would like to call differend the case wherein the
plaintiff is divested of the means to argue and becomes on that account
a victim. . . . A case of differend between two parties takes place when
the 'regulation' of the conflict which opposes them is done in the idiom
of one of the parties while the injustice suffered by the other is not signi-
fied in that idiom" (12). A classic example of the differend is the Holocaust victim who cannot deliver the truth of his victimhood within the
established mode of "reality" set by his questioners. In the face of those
who ask for "proof" of Holocaust victimhood, and who without fail dispute the legitimacy of that "proof," the victim is made doubly a victim:
the victim is at once a plaintiff (13). "An injustice would be an injury
accompanied by the loss of the means to prove the injury. This is the case
if . . . the phrasing of the testimony is itself deprived of authority" (7).

Another key example of the differend is the case of a worker who
cannot participate in the capitalist marketplace except by phrasing his
work within the rules of the capitalist idiom. In order to be visible and to

participate in the economic system, the worker is forced to see his own work as alienated labor, as units of commodity or service: "Without recourse to this idiom, the worker does not exist within its field of discourse" (2).

> By what well-formed phrase and by means of what establishment procedure can the laborer affirm before the labor arbitrator that what he yields to his boss . . . in exchange for a salary is *not* a commodity? . . . If the worker evokes his essence (labor-power), he cannot be heard by this tribunal; it is not competent. The differend is signaled by this impossibility to prove. (13; original emphasis)

As the irreconcilable contestation of idioms reflects the material and discursive discrepancy running through coexistence, the presence of the differend breaks the illusion of unity, solidarity, and oneness in the idealization of community. By exploring the fissures that render a single body community impossible, Lyotard calls attention to the ways in which the pursuit of oneness necessitates the repression of material realities not consonant with the dominant version. Likewise, the challenge to "phrase" the Convent becomes the litmus test for Ruby's very status as a community. What can Ruby "say" about a community that is entirely different from itself? What do Ruby's idioms and phrasings—its language use—reveal about its very nature as a community? That it cannot "say" anything about the Convent except that it is an aberration in itself reveals its deficiency as a community. It also reveals the differend at work between Ruby and the Convent.

The free-formed, free-wheeling Convent, when phrased in Ruby's idiom of community, predictably becomes the repository of all that the town reviles and fears. Here is an instance of Ruby's phrasing, focalized through Reverend Pulliam, one of the leading men of the town. When the Convent women appear in Ruby for a wedding, Reverend Pulliam observes:

> He knew about such women. Like children, always on the lookout for fun, devoted to it but always needing a break in order to have it. A life, a hand, a five-dollar bill. Somebody to excuse or coddle them. Somebody to look down at the ground and say nothing when they disturb the peace. . . . [F]un-obsessed adults were clear signs of already advanced decay. Soon the whole country would be awash in toys, tone-deaf from raucous music and hollow laughter. But not here. Not in Ruby. Not while Senior Pulliam was alive. (157)

The Convent, when phrased through this representative patriarch of Ruby, is a den of debauchery, where unthinkable sins like lesbianism, prostitution, and abortion abound. Its members are untethered women, without men, without children, and without patriarchy to claim them. The women's mysterious pasts and vagabond lifestyles hint at criminality. Their absence at Ruby's churches proves their godlessness; and when they do appear in town, as they do at the wedding, their manner of dress and their conduct signal their looseness. In Ruby's field of discourse, then, the Convent can be phrased only as one thing—"a coven" (276). Like the Jewish plaintiff or the laborer in Lyotard's example, Ruby's phrasing of the Convent reveals the presence of the differend. The Convent's nature and reality are predetermined by the limited possibilities set forth by the value system of Ruby's totalitarian ideology. In Ruby's deployment of the familiar question "How are you like me?" Morrison delineates the most egregious and harmful deployment of identification. The crux of the matter is that Ruby's *in*ability to identify with the Convent along the lines of commonality results in its categorical condemnation of the Convent.

In one rich exemplification of the differend at work, Morrison presents two phrasings of a scene involving the Convent women. The first is phrased in the idiom of Ruby, the second in the idiom of the Convent. As the Convent women drive away from the Ruby wedding, Mavis and Gigi, two women who have the most antagonistic relationship in the Convent, begin fighting by the side of the road. As Gigi and Mavis are fighting, two other women sitting in the car comfort each other: "Pellas turned away from the fighting-women scene and lifted her arm to circle Seneca's neck and press her face deeper into that tiny bosom." A Ruby resident drives by, a truck driver, and "he stayed long enough to see outlaw women rolling on the ground, dresses torn, secret flesh on display. And see also two other women embracing in the back seat. For long moments his eyes were wide" (169). Focalized through the truck driver, emblematic of Ruby's patriarchal and masculinist idiom, the fight scene functions as evidence of the Convent's uncivilized, inhuman throes. The embrace scene is evidence of lesbianism, yet another instance of the Convent's debauchery and immorality. Like the Holocaust victim's repeated failure to satisfy his doubters, or the laborer's phrasing of his labor into capitalist units, Ruby's idiom of community fundamentally denies the authority of the Convent's different value systems, and the Convent can be phrased only in terms of negation. "The differend is the unstable state and instant of language wherein something which must be able to be put in phrases cannot yet be. This state includes silence, which is a negative phrase, but it also calls upon phrases which are in principle possible" (22). The impossibility of phrasing the other's reality is symptomatic of one idiom's inability to accommodate, understand, or entertain the difference of the other.

The Convent's phrasing of the same fight scene could not be more different. It is focalized through Seneca, one of the women sitting in the car: "Once upon a time she would try to separate them, but now she knew better. When they were exhausted they'd stop, and peace would reign longer than if she interfered. . . . Gigi was scrappy but vain—she didn't want bruises or scratches to mar her lovely face and she worried constantly about her hair. Mavis was slow but a steady, joyful hitter" (168). In the Convent's phrasing of the scene, the fight entirely lacks the uncontrolled violence and aberrant sexuality that the Ruby man reads. However vehemently the women punch and scratch each other—even burning the other with a lighted cigarette—the women fight so predictably that the violence lacks any teeth. Most importantly, this phrasing by the Convent is one that the omniscient narrator confirms. As Seneca's phrasing hinted, the reconciliation of the two women is as predictable as the fight. Later that night, all the Convent women gather over a feast of eating, drinking, and dancing: "The fear, the bickering, the nausea, the awful dirt fight, the tears in the dark—all of the day's unruly drama dissipated in the pleasure of chewing food" (179). Like a necessary release of steam, the instance of violence between the two women enhances the continued peace and strength of the Convent as a community. The discrepancy between the Ruby man's phrasing and what we readers, along with the omniscient narrator, understand to be yet another ritualized squabble between the two women highlights the irreconcilable idiom between the two communities. This moment results in a dramatic irony that alerts the reader to the inadequacy—the incorrectness—of Ruby's phrasing of the Convent.

What we encounter repeatedly, then, is this corrective endeavor on the part of the omniscient narrator. Indeed, that the Convent is *not* what Ruby takes it to be is repeatedly voiced by authorially endorsed mouthpieces such as Soame, Lone, Billie Day, and Reverend Misner. Through the juxtaposition of Ruby's idiom with that of the Convent, Morrison consistently demonstrates the falsity of Ruby's idiom and thereby the falsity of its ideology of community. Morrison's corrective endeavors take up Lyotard's call to "give the differend its due," to phrase what is hitherto unphraseable within the dominant discourse: "To give the differend its due is to institute new addressees, new addressers, new significations, and new referents in order that the injustice find an expression and that the plaintiff ceases to be a victim. This requires new rules for the formation and linking of phrases. . . . Every injustice must be able to be phrased" (21). Ruby's destruction of the Convent, then, becomes the ultimate testimony of the differend in the two competing models of community. The day comes when Ruby's leading men gather in the dark of night and shoot their way through the Convent. The narration of the attack is phrased in the idiom of Ruby: "[T]he target, after all, is detritus: throwaway people that sometimes blow back into the room after being swept out the door. So the venom is manageable now. Shooting the first woman (the white one) has clarified it like butter: the pure oil of hatred on top, its hardness stabilized below" (4). And with "God at their side, the men take aim. For Ruby" (18). That Ruby ultimately destroys what evades its ideology of commonality becomes the most damning fact about its idiom of community.

It is a criticism that Morrison presses home. As the final condemnation of Ruby's idiom of community, Morrison presents the disintegration of the town's ideology of commonality. The men's atrocities shake the town, and the residents turn on its leading men. These men, who had occupied the inner sanctum of Ruby's patriarchy as descendants of the founders, turn against each other as they try "to make themselves look good": "[E]very one of the assaulting men had a different tale and their families and friends . . . supported them, enhancing, recasting, inventing misinformation" (297). As a seismic quake spreads throughout Ruby, its "bewildered, angry, sad, frightened people" ask themselves: "[H]ow could so clean and blessed a mission devour itself and become the world they had escaped?" (292). In the awakening of Ruby as a community, the Convent's destruction performs the typological role of the innocent's sacrifice, as its destruction serves to shock the perpetrators into repentance. The transformation to Ruby's idiom of community is announced by Misner, who decides he will stay in Ruby, "because there was no better battle to fight, no better place to be than among these outrageously beautiful, flawed and proud people" (306).

Idiom of Collective Healing

A possible conclusion to be drawn at this point is that Morrison's corrective phrasing of the Convent expands the very idiom of community, a task that falls in line with what Lyotard sees as an aim of literature: "What is at stake in a literature, in a philosophy, in a politics perhaps, is to bear witness to differends by finding new idioms for them" (22).

A question surfaces, though, as we consider the *nature* of Morrison's correction. The ultimate evidence of Ruby's deficiency as a community was its inability to phrase the Convent in any way other than as an aberration and a contaminant. And Morrison's corrective endeavors, focalized through the authorially endorsed characters, gave direct refutation of that phrasing. In basing her condemnation of Ruby as a community directly upon its *in*correctness in phrasing the Convent, Morrison's strategy in *Paradise* invites troubling questions: If the Convent were indeed a "coven," would Ruby's idiom of community be less condemnable? If lesbianism, abortion, prostitution, witchcraft, and other acts abhorred by Ruby residents took place at the Convent, would Ruby's idiom of community be vindicated? Ultimately, would Ruby's correctness in phrasing the Convent justify its ideology of commonality? If the Convent were all that Ruby envisioned, would Ruby's totalitarian idiom of community be authorized in the novel?

Certainly, I am not arguing that the Convent should have been constructed as a "coven" in the way Ruby residents viewed it; such a reading would be a fruitless critique of the novel for not being something else. What I am arguing is that within the *authorial idiom* of the novel, there are certain things the Convent *cannot be*. The Convent cannot be a body of individuals united around the commonalities of witchcraft, lesbianism, prostitution, abortion, inhuman fighting, mindless debauchery, and chaotic living. As *Paradise* directly aligns the incorrectness of Ruby's phrasing with the deficiency of its logic of community, the novel's own idiom of community is severely limited in its potential: the Convent must be a community whose reality *refutes* Ruby's phrasing of it. Far from being a den of immoral debauchery, the Convent, we find out, is a community of unconditional emotional bonding and spiritual healing. Echoing the "sisterhood" of women who form an unconditional emotional unity in many of Morrison's novels, all four women of the Convent, under the guidance of Connie, become a single body of individuals in their collective movement towards emotional purification and healing.

As the Convent's correct phrasing must necessarily *negate* Ruby's phrasing, its univocality reveals its limitations in expanding the idiom of community. For Lyotard, we remember, the "task of a literature" is to "find new idioms" for realities that are hitherto incapable of being phrased. However, rather than instituting "new addressers, new significations, and new referents" of community (Lyotard 21), Morrison's corrective phrasing of the Convent directly invokes the prevailing discourse of idealized community: community as a body of individuals bound by commonalities, whose final destination is the aspirational model of kinship that will deliver health and healing. The differend of the Convent, hence, is caught between the incorrect phrasing by Ruby and the necessarily correct, and corrective, phrasing by Morrison's own idiom. As the corrective phrasing becomes the overruling idiom of phrasing the Convent, the authorial idiom cannot escape the deficiency that mars Ruby's idiom of community: *both* idioms of community fail to institute new significations and new referents in phrasing the Convent. This limitation articulates not only Morrison's own univocal idiom of community but also the univocal, curtailed idiom of community that is the discourse of idealized community.

With this critique in mind, let me offer the possibility of a *third* phrasing of the Convent. Let me emphasize that I am not offering my own corrective to counter Ruby's or Morrison's phrasing of the Convent, but that I am bringing to light a third idiom of community that becomes consistently silenced in the novel. One of the most interesting moments in Morrison's phrasing of the Convent comes near the end, in a chapter devoted to Connie. Connie is the figurehead and the heartbeat of the Convent, whose undemanding and all-encompassing welcome invites tearful confessions and emotional release for the women who walk through the Convent's door. As the nexus of the Convent's borderless, voluntary model of community, Connie is the very heart of the Convent's benevolent nature. The Convent as the epitome of idealized community, however, is severely threatened in Connie's chapter. We encounter a Connie who spends her days in the tiny basement cell of the Convent, drinking herself into a stupor, regarding the Convent women with disgust and impatience: "[T]he timbre of each of their voices told the same tale: disorder, deception and . . . drift. The three *d*'s that paved the road to perdition, and the greatest of these was drift" (221). When she's drinking, she can "tolerate them," "but more and more she wanted to snap their necks. Anything to stop the badly cooked indigestible food, the greedy hammering music, the fights, the raucous empty laughter, the claims. But especially the drift" (222).

Connie's idiom in phrasing the Convent is shocking, as it assaults the authorial privileging and idealization of this community. Her condemnation of the Convent's purposeless nature as the ultimate depravity, in fact, recalls Ruby's idiom of community against the "drifting" women of the Convent. This startling turn suggests a third possibility of phrasing the Convent, one whose idiom is not predetermined by the incorrect phrasing by Ruby and the attendant corrective phrasing by the narrative. In Connie's unexpected idiom, then, Morrison has a real opportunity to phrase the Convent's differend without delimiting the possibilities of *what is possible to say*. For instance, the women of the convent could indeed be ruled by "disorder, deception, and drift," as Connie phrases them. In direct divergence from the core values of idealized community discourse, they may be a community of women who share no commonality of values, visions, or interests, who are not bound by consensus of vision, whose lives are rife with fights, antagonism, and dissent, and whose heterogeneity and difference lead to no single unity. That is, by following Connie's phrasing, we could locate the idiom of dissenting community running through the phrasing of the Convent. My point here is not that the Convent ought to exemplify the discourse of dissenting community, but that an openness to such idioms, an openness that Connie's original phrasing suggested, would have successfully offered "new rules for the formation and linking of phrases" (Lyotard 21) in the idiom of community.

Instead, this exciting third possibility quickly reverts to the corrective phrasing of the idealized community discourse, particularly to the teleology of community as the movement towards healing. Connie emerges from her fulminating dissatisfaction one night and, with a sumptuous feast to mark the beginning, leads the women in a series of rituals designed to fuse them into a single body of purpose: "[S]he told them of a place where white sidewalks met the sea and fish the color of plums swam alongside children. She spoke of fruit that tasted the way sapphires look and boys using rubies for dice. Of scented cathedrals made of gold" (263). The women live and think as one, shave their heads, and draw their outlines as "templates" on the cellar floor (263). Under Connie's direction, they lie naked on the cellar floor, conducting "loud dreaming," calling out their respective life stories. As they do, they enter an intersubjective transference: "How the stories rose in that place. Half-tales and the never-dreamed escaped from their lips to soar high above the guttering candles, shifting dust from crates and bottles. And it was never important to know who said the dream or whether it had meaning[;] . . . they step easily into the dreamer's tale" (264). The women as one begin to develop "a markedly different look" (265), "an adult manner" (266). A visitor to the Convent might observe the change—"how calmly themselves they seemed"—but wouldn't be able to name "exactly what was absent." Only later, the narrative continues, would this visitor realize that "unlike some people in Ruby, the Convent women were no longer haunted" (266).

Whatever heterogeneity and conflict existed amongst the women of the Convent, then, dissipate in the greater force of the commonality that binds them: the single aim towards the telos of healing. Relatedly, as in the epiphanic moments of identification among women in other Morrison novels when multiple, disparate women arrive at "sisterhood," the Convent women's common aim towards healing functions as an *apolitical* concept, outside the realm of power struggles, the need for individual negotiations, or even verbal acknowledgment. In the overwhelming power of commonality, then, identification as reciprocal appropriation reaches its zenith. Beyond unconditional emotional bonding, the women literally become one subject, an ontological transformation that the narrative endorses in its representation of the healing process. Once the collective rituals begin, the narrative no longer distinguishes between the disparate women. The multiple individuals become a single body, identified only as a "they" or as "Convent women."

The women's healing completes Morrison's phrasing of idealized community: what the women could not achieve individually they achieve in collectivity. Through the teleological thinking of community as the movement towards progress, Morrison *domesticates* the strangeness of the women's actions to one collective, spiritual healing. When the Ruby men storm the Convent and see the "templates" on the cellar floor, they see "pornography" and "Satan's scrawl" (303). In a move that recalls the contrasting phrasing of the Convent women's fight scene, this misreading by the Ruby men is soon corrected by the characters sympathetic to the Convent. When Minister Misner and his fiancée view the same templates, they see "the turbulence of females trying to bridle, without being trampled, the monsters that slavered them" (303). This idiom of healing, voiced by the chosen characters, directly continues Morrison's own views. As she explains in an interview: "It is interesting and important to me that once the women [of the Convent] are coherent and strong and clean in their interior lives, they feel saved" (qtd. in Marcus n.p.).

Indeed, this teleological view of healing as the final destination of community dominates the scholarship on *Paradise*: "[T]he Convent in *Paradise* is a site for female reconstitution, both spiritual and communal" (Davidson 372). "The story of the Convent . . . [moves] from chaotic fragmentation to a liberating fusion . . . [towards] individual and communal harmony" (Page, "Furrowing All the Brows" 645). "[T]he women undergo a collective healing ritual[,]. . . a paradisical moment to the Convent women" (Dalsgard 244–45). "*Paradise* explores coalition processes that are more accommodative, caring, and loving[,] . . . reach[ing] toward a new, alternative, non-hierarchical sense of justice that emphasizes both equality and nurturing" (Michael 644). "The women of the Convent do not need men to heal themselves" (Kearly 12). "The more accepting, inclusive spirituality that Consolata advocates helps these women to overcome their own personal traumas and to create a more nurturing, healing community not based on the divisions and exclusions of Ruby" (Romero 418). The critical appraisals of the Convent's triumphant healing certainly affirm Morrison's corrective idiom of community. It follows, too, that they affirm the idiom of health *over* the third idiom of community that could not be phrased in the novel—the disorderly, antagonistic Convent hinted by Connie—that might have taken place between the incorrect (Ruby's) phrasing and the corrective (omniscient narrator's) phrasing.

The continuity between Morrison's views of community, those of chosen characters, and those reflected in critical scholarship on the novel testify to the dominance of idealized community in contemporary critical discussion. Furthermore, this direct continuity in the value system demonstrates the univocality in the discourse of community in contemporary literary discussions. At the center of this univocality is the apolitical use of commonality to fuse multiple individuals into one subject position; the use of kinship models (family, sisterhood) as aspirational models of community; and the teleological thinking of community as a collective movement towards "progress," such as strength, healing, and health. As in *Jazz,* in which the violence of the City is solved in the community of family, the damage suffered by the individual is healed in the community of sisterhood. To the paradox of community, then, Morrison offers an unequivocal answer: multiple individuals become a body of individuals through the benevolent power of identification as reciprocal appropriation.

In concluding with a resolute embrace of "a body of individuals," Morrison clarifies her ambivalence about identification. The central conflict of *Paradise,* we remember, rested upon the two vastly different deployments of identification that produced antithetical models of community: the malformed community of Ruby and the ideal community of the Convent. Thus, Morrison's condemnation of Ruby reveals itself to be a condemnation not of identification per se but of the *misuse* of an ideal. And herein lies the difference between Morrison's suspicion of identification and those expressed by dissenting community discourse. The negation of commonality and identification by dissenting community discourse is not targeting misused instances of "How are you like me?" but the very *politics* of the question, seeing, in the question, the seed for homogeneity, regulation, sameness, exclusion, oppression, and, ultimately, totalitarianism. In contrast, the cautionary tale inherent in

Ruby's *mis*use of identification speaks to the essentially benevolent politics of identification in Morrison's vision of community. The continuity in values between Morrison, her chosen characters, and the critical scholarship on *Paradise* speaks to the fact that in the discourse of idealized community, there is no such thing as bad identification; there are only bad *uses* of identification.

This idealization of identification, especially in the name of healing, raises some disquieting questions not only for *Paradise* but also for the larger discourse of idealized community dominant in literary criticism. If collective healing is the final aim of community, what happens to those factors that do not directly contribute to this teleology? In concrete terms, what happens to those members whose beliefs and practices are deemed nonconducive or antithetical to the task of healing? Do they become unspeakable, like the differend? And how is the nature of healing determined? What constitutes "healing"? Unless there is a consensus on the definition of "healing," the collective drive towards that condition can be indistinguishable from any other drive towards homogeneity, from any other demand for commonality.

Ultimately, the novel's inability to phrase the vast, unassimilable difference of the Convent may be transposed onto the scene of contemporary fiction criticism itself. Can contemporary literary criticism phrase a community that is *other* than an ultimate bonding based upon commonalities and identification, leading to unconditional emotional attachment, connection, and belonging, leading to the collective health of all? Can criticism "read" community in instances when the literary "we" is forged through means other than commonality, identification, and health? Or are those instances evaluated as examples of unity that fall *short* of the criteria of community and that are therefore not read as literary instances of community?

What I am speaking to is the self-fulfilling operation of idealized community discourse in contemporary fiction and criticism. In a tautological move, idealized community (family or sisterhood) such as those found in Morrison's novels stand as the bedrock instance of "real" community; simultaneously, the critical embrace of that idealized community further confirms, and strengthens, the leading idiom of community. Omitted from this equation are those literary instances of the first-person plural "we" that do not resemble the criteria of idealized community. The following chapters address precisely this lacuna in the literary criticism of community by reading ambivalent communities in contemporary fiction.

CHAPTER 2

"We Are Not the World"

Global Community, Universalism, and
Karen Tei Yamashita's *Tropic of Orange*

I n Karen Tei Yamashita's political realist-fantastic novel, *Tropic of Orange* (1997), Third World labor confronts First World industry in a professional wrestling match. The champion of the Third World is a five-hundred-year old messianic man called Arcangel, who fights under the name of El Gran Mojado (colloquially translated, "The Great Wetback"). The champion of the First World is NAFTA, alternately called "SUPERNAFTA" or "SUPERSCUMNAFTA." The representatives of the two hemispheres face each other in a Los Angeles stadium, amid all the pomp and screaming splendor of a televised pro-wrestling match. As the champions strut around the ring in the prematch show of self-promotion, Arcangel declares:

> I do not defend my title for the
> rainbow of children of the world.
> This is not a benefit for UNESCO.
> We are not the world.
> This is not a rock concert. (259)

When Arcangel mocks the popular slogans with which the First World describes a global community, he expands his challenge beyond his immediate opponent, the economic and political policies of NAFTA. He denounces the very notion of a collective, singular subject position

58

that stands as the "we" in "We Are the World." Sung by the biggest American pop stars of the mid-1980s who called themselves "Band Aid," "We Are the World: U.S.A. for Africa" was a worldwide phenomenon in 1985, and the title came to function as a popular slogan for envisioning the globe as a single community. The best-known encapsulation of the global "we" is, of course, the concept of the "global village." Since Marshall McLuhan famously used the term in the 1960s to foreshadow a new world order, one in which the medium of electronic communications diminishes, and overcomes, the physical and temporal distance that separates the world's inhabitants, "global village" has been the dominant term for expressing a global commonality that results from transnational commerce, migration, and culture. More importantly, the celebration of global village translates that altered material condition into a hitherto unrealized condition of proximity, intimacy, and, ultimately, fusion. The magic of global village, then, overcomes the paradox of community: it transforms innumerable individuals into a single body of individuals.

Arcangel's critique of this global village community must be understood in light of the unmistakable authority with which Yamashita endows him. Arcangel is a prophet and a messiah who masquerades as a bawdy performance artist and street vagrant. He travels throughout South America and Mexico singing "political poetry," recounting the southern continent's history of exploitation at the hands of Europeans. He literally bears, on his body, the scars of slavery and colonialism and is the self-identified voice and the consciousness of the colonized and of the Third World.[1] So when Arcangel rebuts global village sentiments, he is not specifically deriding the First World's philanthropic enterprise at large but the *facility* with which the global "we" circulates in the First World's political, economic, and cultural discourse. The global "we," indeed, is a central protagonist in the First World's discourses of politics, commerce, and culture, crucial to its narrative of "progress" and "development." It underwrites trade policies such as NAFTA (i.e., free trade and trade increases that will benefit all of "us") and is also a highly marketable—indeed, invaluable—concept in the First World's culture industry ("we are the world").

Most importantly for the argument of this book, this global village community rests on the cornerstones of idealized community discourse. The rationale for this first-person plural "we" rests on the supposed commonality that binds all members of the globe into one. Furthermore, the power and the influence of this commonality are so potent that they override the great physical distance, the great material divide, and the great inequity in political and cultural capital amongst its members. As commonality supersedes the paradox of community, billions of individuals fuse into one and become a single "we." What Yamashita offers, through Arcangel's mockery of the global village "we," is a dissenting community critique of the idealization of community. What unsupported claims of commonality justify the transformation of multiple individuals into a single body? Who chooses the criteria of "sameness" that blankets the entire group? Whose difference is elided for the coherence of unity? What happens to the possibility of conflict and antagonism amongst the members when cohesion, intimacy, and fusion are valorized as *collective* values? Ultimately, what coercive operations are justified in the name of community as the site of sharing, intimacy, and collective health?

As "we are not the world" becomes the rallying cry of Third World labor against the First World discourse of global village community, *Tropic* articulates precisely these dissenting community suspicions of idealized community. When community is conceived through a commonality, Jean-Luc Nancy argues, community becomes an expression of a fusion formed around an essence—as "people," "nation," "destiny," or "generic humanity"—and community becomes "totalitarianism" (39). In a similar vein, Ernesto Laclau argues that the valorization of oneness in idealized community discourse casts conflict and antagonism as obstacles that must be excised. Instead, antagonism is "the ontological possibility of clashes and unevenness [that enables us] to speak of freedom[,] . . . the very condition of a free society" ("Community" 92). For Jean-François Lyotard, the valorization of unity and solidarity is a "totalitarian apparatus" that struggles to suppress the "'presence' of the unmanageable"—the radically different, the heterogeneous ("À l'insu [Unbeknownst]" 43).

Like the "unmanageable" that cannot be completely suppressed, Arcangel's protest dissents from the global village "we" and challenges the assumptions, values, and goals of idealized community discourse. However, a crucial distinction must be observed between the novel's critique of global village community and dissenting community's negation of idealized community. That difference rests on the fact that *Tropic* holds on to a key ingredient of idealized community—the desirability of multiple individuals becoming a body of individuals. In tandem with the critique of global village community, the novel argues the need to conceive of a *new* first-person plural "we" that can capture the accelerated movement of capital, cultural practices, and humans traversing the world. Set in Mexico and Los Angeles, the novel highlights the transnational crisscrossing of labor, goods, resources, languages, and cultures in the late twentieth century. Its characters, who had formally led disparate lives and had been separated by oceans and continents, are brought into hitherto unknown proximity and interconnectedness with each other—and ultimately into fusion. In its new vision of the globe as a community, then, *Tropic* espouses the single body community as a political *necessity*. In the process, the novel irrevocably diverges from dissenting community discourse and its central aim—to negate the idealization of single body community, oneness, and fusion. This divergence forms the basis of the ambivalent community that I delineate in this chapter. The novel's sharp criticism of global village discourse echoes dissenting community's condemnation of idealized oneness. Yet this criticism of idealized community concludes by embracing the kernel of idealized community: that multiple individuals can fuse into a single body community. The dialectic movement between the competing values of idealized and dissenting community results in the novel's fluctuating treatment of concepts such as commonality, oneness, and fusion. Under contestation is the matter of the global "we." How should this first-person plural subject be envisioned?

This chapter examines the complexity of *Tropic*'s global "we" through the concept of *universalism*. Like identification that transformed multiple subjects into one in Morrison's novels, universalism functions as the most powerful force in *Tropic* for fusing billions of individuals into a "body of individuals." Unlike Morrison's affirmation of identification, however, Yamashita casts universalism as a dual-edged sword—the greatest force for saying "we," as well as the most dangerous force for saying "we." That is, the novel's critique of idealized community discourse is inextricable from its critique of universalism, as the global village "we" under critique is a *unilateral* "we." The novel targets the global village community that unidirectionally conscripts the entire globe into a single body community—into an ultimate unity forged from commonality and shared fate, maintained by a relationship of intimacy, mutually benevolent interchange, and direct connections. Thus *Tropic*'s denunciation of the First World's global village celebration indicts the imperialist nature of a few who presume to speak for all.

It is crucial to note from the outset that the subject under indictment is not globalization per se, but a particular *view* of globalization—the view that globalization results in the economic, political, and cultural intimacy and shared fate of a primordialist village.[2] As this chapter will demonstrate, what is under critique in *Tropic* is the most self-serving and *unreflective* use of the idealized community discourse manifest in the form of the global village celebration. The invocation of the "village," one of the key models of Gemeinschaft unity, best represents the First World's self-serving and unreflective use of idealized community. This distinction between the novel's treatment of globalization and of global village celebration is very important, for globalization as a subject is a continuing interest in Yamashita's novels. A Japanese American writer whose years spent in Brazil, Japan, as well as the United States reflect a thoroughly transnational imagination, Yamashita's novels have consistently attempted to read the momentous and minute changes affecting individual lives as a result of globalization. Indeed, Yamashita's novels are deeply immersed in the phenomena of globalization: the high-speed information, media, and transportation technologies; the transnational modes of production and consumption; the accelerated flow of people, capital, goods, information, and entertainment; all of which result in the shift in the human experience of space, distance, and time.

Through the Arc of the Rainforest (1991) shows a fascination with the communications and entertainment media, such as the Brazilian daytime soap operas that enthrall the entire nation and literally forge a single body community out of viewers. It also explores the far-ranging impact of a multinational corporation on the daily life of working Brazilians and the environmental damage the corporation inflicts on the rainforest. In *Brazil Maru* (1992), Yamashita explores the early turn-of-the-century Japanese migration to Brazil, while in *Circle K Cycles* (2001), she addresses the Japanese Brazilians who live in Japan as "foreign" migrant workers in the late twentieth century. Yamashita's wide-ranging treatment of nations, ethnicities, and continents stands out as an example of the intra-ethnic, transnational nature of Asian American writing. As she puts it, "in order to study this thing, whether or not we call it Asian-American—means that we're going to have to know a lot more about it than just talking about the United States" (Gier and Tejeda n.p.). Thus globalization as a force of *deterritorialization* is a constant interest in all of Yamashita's novels, as she explores the unmooring of fixed ethnic, national, and geographical identities and of established categories by which humans are organized and distinguished. Indeed, contesting the discourse of purity (of blood, race, ethnicity, nation, or culture), Yamashita's novels explore, and celebrate, the porous categories of identities emerging from the phenomenon of globalization. Conversely, her novels explore the ways in which the unmooring of identities and affiliations translates into formations of *new* moorings. The physical, material, and cultural challenges of globalization translate into a literary challenge for the writer: upon what basis, through what rationale, may a different global community be imagined?[3]

Nowhere does this challenge press more imperatively than in *Tropic*, in which the geography of the globe literally shifts and Northern and Southern hemispheres merge into one. The Tropic of Cancer, the imaginary line that divides the Northern Hemisphere into northern clime and tropical clime, becomes attached to a magical orange growing in Mazatlan, Mexico. In the hands of Arcangel, the orange—and the Tropic of Cancer—moves northward to Los Angeles. Accompanying Arcangel and the Tropic of Cancer are Mexicans seeking work in the United States, traveling towards, as they sarcastically call it, their "manifest destiny" (132). Allegorical of the labor's movement from the south to the north, from the Third World to the First World, the shift literally destabilizes the topography of the land. Yamashita's choice of Los Angeles as the ultimate site of confrontation speaks to the city's synecdochical role in the contemporary imagination as the epicenter of global confluence, or, some would say, global conflagration. Yamashita uses the contradictory significance of this city to articulate her ambivalence about the project of transforming the globe into a community: How can the globe become a single body of individuals, given the severe fissures separating its population? At the same time, how can the inexorable fact of globalization's cultural, material, and human convergence be acknowledged?

Tropic's project in conceptualizing a nonoppressive global community, then, has much in common with recent reconsiderations of universalism. Aggressively countering the delusional "we" at the heart of unidirectional deployments of universalism (e.g., Eurocentricism, colonialism, imperialism) has been central to the anticolonialist, antiracialist, and antisexist scholarship of the late twentieth century. Generally traced back to Descartes and the ascendancy of the Enlightenment through thinkers such as Rousseau and Montesquieu, the history of universalism is at once a history of a tool of oppression, the discursive and material coerciveness of a few who presume to speak for all. What complicates this rendition of universalism, however, is the pivotal place that universalism occupies in progressive political movements. Ernesto Laclau encapsulates the contradictory role of universalism succinctly: "without a universalism of sorts—the idea of human rights, for instance—a truly democratic society is impossible" (*Emancipation(s)* 122).

Recent recuperation of universalism begins with precisely this oppressive/progressive function of universalism, and Laclau is representative of the poststructuralist attempt at recuperating universalism principally through the discourse of human rights and progressive politics.[4]

As the poststructuralist recuperation argues for the perennial relevance of universalism without relying on foundational tenets (claims about the essence of "human nature"), it distinguishes itself from the neo-Kantian defense of universalism, best represented by Habermasian use of rationality as the foundational feature of humans and the speech act.[5] A recent consideration of universalism's paradoxical function is best represented in *Contingency, Hegemony, Universality*, in which Butler, Laclau, and Žižek exchange a series of essays on universalism. Despite their many differences, the three thinkers are bound in the assertion that universalism is a concept which supersedes any particular instantiation, "a process or condition irreducible to any of its determinate modes of appearance" (3). Hence, the poststructuralist revitalization of universalism crucially renders a dialectic tension within the concept—as a concept constitutive of *any* discussion of human rights, justice, equality, and dignity, yet whose particular instantiations invariably fall short of the expansive promise held therein. A model of universalism as the site of an "impossible/necessary" dialectic, I suggest, is crucial in understanding projects like Yamashita's, which reject the unidirectional, imperialist deployments of universalism without rejecting the concept itself.

In contrast to the First World's deployment of a global intimacy and shared fate that comprise the latest rendition of imperialist universalism, *Tropic* pursues another model of global community: to take account of conflict, disparity, and injustice as realities of globalization while still acknowledging the inexorable convergence of peoples, cultures, and materiality in the profoundly altered state of global coexistence. This vision of the global "we" walks a careful balance between observing the key tenets of dissenting community discourse, such as heterogeneity, conflict, antagonism, and unassimilable difference, while keeping in sight the newly formed connections and the deep interdependence emerging from globalization. Hence, not only does the novel sit at the nexus of current discussions of universalism; it postulates its own model of universalism that I call "romantic universalism." As the novel's final answer to the challenge of a global "we," romantic universalism richly illuminates the transformative power of universalism in serving the political needs of those rendered invisible in the great material divide of globalization. At the same time, this new global community bears the seeds of its own limitations, limitations that bring us back to the "impossible" and "ideal" dialectic of universalism. In the transnational, transcontinental flow of people, labor, capital, and culture, Yamashita suggests that a need to conceptualize a global community is inexorable. The tasks of conceiving a new singular collective "we" and of conceiving a new use for universalism become not matters of choice, then, but pressing needs.

The Overworked Village

As Benedict Anderson put it, "all communities larger than primordial villages of face-to-face contact (and perhaps even these) are imagined communities. Communities are to be distinguished, not by their falsity/genuineness but by the style in which they are imagined" (6). The concept of the global village surely requires a stretch of the imagination. The conjoining of two vastly different scales of human coexistence demonstrates the domesticating work performed by the smaller scale of the "village" in defusing the threat posed by the immense scale of the "global." Like the "family" or "sisterhood" that provided ready-made context for conceiving of community in Morrison's novels, the village, in the global village celebration, counts on its seemingly self-evident desirability as a model of unity. Thus the village is more than a denotation of a smaller scale of coexistence. Contemporary valorization of global village directly reinvigorates the idealized values of the village in Tönnies's theory of community. As I discussed in the Introduction, the village exemplifies the key values of Gemeinschaft—a unity formed from bonds of family, kin, faith, tradition, habit—all of which come together to form a "common center." "Each individual receives his share from this common center, which is manifest in his own space, i.e., in his sentiment, in his mind and heart, and in his conscience as well as in his environment, his possessions, and his activities" (224). The Gemeinschaft idealization of the village simultaneously connotes a particular relationality at work. Just as the village is a scale of coexistence that is always-already in the past—the "primordiality" that Anderson identifies—it suggests a simpler and more immediate relationality of person-to-person contact, of unconditional connections, belonging, and intimacy.

The global village concept is perhaps the ultimate fetishization of the primordial village in the discourse of idealized community. This fetishization is explicit in Marshall McLuhan's formulation of the global village. As he writes in *The Gutenberg Galaxy*: "[T]he electro-magnetic discoveries have recreated the simultaneous 'field' in all human affairs so that the human family now exists under the conditions of a 'global village.' We live in a single constructed space resonant with tribal drums" (31). McLuhan's global village discourse fundamentally appeals to primordialism (human family, tribal drums) in translating high-speed electronic media into a *social* relationality of intimacy, cooperativeness, and familiarity: "electric speed [brings together] all social and political functions in a sudden implosion," and "the electronically contracted globe is no more than a village" (*Understanding Media* 20). As Andreas Huyssen notes, the "constant sliding of categories in McLuhan from the technological to the social and vice versa" reveals a mix of technological and theological discourse. "Rather than offering a media theory McLuhan offers a media theology," in which high-speed electronic media, such as television, "retribalizes the world" (12).[6] Gayatri Spivak, discussing McLuhan's *The Global Village,* casts a more political condemnation: "global village" is an "appropriation of the rural." The concept of global village, built on the "[e]lectronification of biodiversity . . . is colonialism's newest trick" ("Cultural Talks" 330).

By sharply delineating the material inequalities that separate First World and Third World subjects, *Tropic* mulls over precisely this self-serving celebration of commonality, intimacy, and connectedness in First World's celebration of global village. In its depiction of Los Angeles, too, the novel focuses on extremely disparate socioeconomic positions and emphasizes the stark fissures that counter the global village discourse. The characters include an illegal immigrant couple, Bobby and Rafaela, and a white-collar professional couple, Gabriel and Emi. Revealing the highly uneven benefits of globalization in the First World's major metropolis, too, Manzanar and Buzzworm represent the mass of urban homeless. The novel's fragmented form also dramatizes the fracture in the First World's vision of global village community. Yamashita begins the book with "HyperContexts," a diagram that shows, in one glance, the division of the narrative into the seven days of the week, with each chapter attending to one day in the life of one of the seven major characters. This disjunctive organization leads to an atomistic sense of each character's life, as each chapter seems to stand on its own with little continuity from the other. Always, there is a sense of impending doom, as various human and natural catastrophes—rumors of illegal human organ harvesting and sales, a mass scare of cocaine-injected oranges on the market, and major freeway pileups and explosions resulting from the spatial distortions—affect the lives of the characters. All the while, the Tropic of Cancer steadily moves northward, unsettling all rules of space and order.

Thus, through content and form, Yamashita enacts a dissenting community suspicion of idealized oneness—the global village "we" that ignores the great material divide between its members, that overrides actual moments of political and cultural conflict, and that imposes a commonality that binds "us" all. In an emblematic scene that challenges the use of commonality in global village discourse, Gabriel and Emi are dining in an upscale Japanese restaurant in Los Angeles. Emi, a Japanese American TV producer who delights in spoofing any orthodoxy, including that of political correctness, is speculating on the racial makeup of another diner sitting at a distance. Emi is engaging in her familiar game of unsettling her much more somber boyfriend Gabriel, who, as a Mexican American reporter, is committed to exposing and criticizing social injustice. A nearby diner takes umbrage at Emi's speculations. Identified only as "a white woman," she remonstrates Emi on the importance of cultural diversity: "I happen to adore the Japanese culture. What can I say? I adore different cultures. I've traveled all over the world. I love living in L.A. because I can find anything in the world to eat, right here. It's such a meeting place for all sorts of people. A true celebration of an international world" (129).

Her model of global village community epitomizes the self-serving and unreflective use of idealized community discourse. It represents a response to globalization in which the material and cultural benefits enjoyed by *some* are translated into benefits enjoyed by *all*, into apolitical commonalities that connect the globe's innumerable members into a Gemeinschaft model of the village. Her view of global "commonality" follows an entirely consumerist logic. If you can eat "their" food, and travel and sight "them," then you and they have a "commonality." This commonality, furthermore, is a sign of *contact* between "you" and "them." As she reifies commonality into consumption, and difference into food matter, she exemplifies a view of globalization as an exchange in free-floating "cultures" without any material referents or consequences. Further continuing the capitalist logic in which the more choices the consumer has, the healthier the overall state of economy, in the white woman's rationale, the greater the number of different cultures' foods available, the "truer" the celebration of an international world. This unidentified white woman stands as the synecdoche of the First World's imperialist assumption of global community, and Yamashita's mockery turns unabashedly didactic. Emi notes that the woman sports chopsticks as hairpins. She calmly holds up two forks and asks whether the woman would wear these in her hair, or whether she would consider the wearing of food utensils as an unsanitary practice. The woman "blanches" in response (129). In the hands of Emi, the protagonist that Yamashita identifies as approximating her mouthpiece, the white woman's consumerist celebration of a global village community and her fetishizing of "different cultures" are shown to be indefensible, even to the woman herself (Gier and Tejeda n.p.).[7]

So who is in this overworked global village? This village is occupied by First World consumers who rationalize their privileged mobility and consumption as responsible acts of global community. These First World "villagers," oblivious to their own role in the relations of power, project the consensual participation of *other* fellow villagers, those of "different cultures." Thus, "[a]s 'universal,' the dominant erases the contingencies of time and space, history and location, and with the same gesture elides its operations of domination, projecting instead the appearance of being democratic" (Palumbo-Liu 188). As "my" consumption becomes "our" celebration, the slippage of the subject in the First World's global village community speaks its unidirectional and imperialist deployment of global village *universalism*. Ernesto Laclau's discussion of nineteenth-century European imperialism highlights the enormity of the slippage. In the work of imperialism, European culture of the nineteenth century circulated as "a particular one, and at the same time the expression . . . of universal human essence"; and in the *simultaneity* of this circulation, the particularity of European culture takes on the ontological status of universality itself: "The crucial issue here is that there was no intellectual means of distinguishing between European particularism and the universal functions that it was supposed to incarnate, given that European universalism had constructed its identity precisely through the cancellation of the logic of incarnation and, as a result, through the universalization of its own particularism" (*Emancipation(s)* 24).

Likewise, as the white woman's privileged mobility and consumption circulate as evidence of global village universalism, she transforms the particular into the universal. The First World's global village community deploys a key aspect of idealized community discourse in the most unreflective and self-serving manner: commonality becomes a matter of "natural" assertion, an observation that has nothing to do with politics, power, or disparity. It seems natural to go from enjoying "different" cultures to asserting the similarities connecting oneself and those "different" people.

Precisely this claim of apolitical commonality is contested in the novel's focus on the disenfranchised and uncounted subjects. Bobby's and Rafaela's struggles are representative of first-generation immigrants', especially illegal immigrants', experience. Bobby is a Chinese Singaporean who entered the United States as a boy, posing as a Vietnamese war refugee. Through years of low-wage physical labor, he achieves economic security, owning his own business, an office cleaning service.

He marries Rafaela, a Mexican, during a trip to Tijuana, and they set up a home in an L.A. suburb. For all intents and purposes, Bobby and Rafaela exemplify the immigrant success story: they are small-business owners, they own property, their house is filled with appliances and goods, and Bobby supports his family in Singapore as well as sends his younger brother to college in the United States. Bobby's and Rafaela's visibility—as people of color and as immigrant success stories—are crucial to the global village discourse of Los Angeles as the true celebration of an international world.

However, what Bobby and Rafaela experience most deeply is not their economic comfort but their social invisibility, a pervasive sense of disaffiliation from the larger city. Their work, representative of the army of office cleaners whose night-time work remains unseen by the white-collar workers, is symptomatic of the invisible nature of cheap, immigrant labor. Bobby recalls: "Ever since he's been here, never stopped working. Always working. Washing dishes. Chopping vegetables. Cleaning floors. Cooking hamburgers. Painting walls. Laying bricks. Cutting hedges. Mowing lawn. Digging ditches. Sweeping trash. . . . Keeping up" (79). Indeed, Bobby exemplifies an immigrant model whose only sense of affiliation to his larger community is economical—as a laborer and a consumer. He lives under a perennial sense of anxiety—terror that his illegal immigration status will be prosecuted, that all his economic achievements will be taken away, and that his family's welfare will be threatened. As his wife sees it, Bobby lives in "this fear of losing what you love, of not feeling trust, this fear of being someplace unsafe but pretending for the sake of others that everything was okay" (149). Bobby's only way to keep terror at bay is to purchase appliances, gadgets, and furniture, affirming to himself that a good American is a consuming American. "Happier he is, harder he works. Can't stop. Gotta make money. Provide for his family. Gotta buy his wife nice clothes. Gotta buy his kid the best. Bobby's kid's gonna know the good life. That's how Bobby sees it" (17). While Bobby lives to work and to buy, Rafaela seeks an inclusion in the larger social, economic, and political structure. She attends community college and involves herself in the causes of labor activism. Bobby actively discourages and ridicules Rafaela's growing political awareness, keeping to his policy of keeping his mouth shut and keeping his head down. Rafaela, in turn, feels stifled by Bobby's atomistic vision of life to be lived: "She did not want any of this [Bobby's purchases]. She wanted more" (80). Rafaela finally leaves Bobby, fleeing to her hometown in Mexico with their child. In these two representative immigrants of Los Angeles, Yamashita casts a dissenting community skepticism on the celebratory vision of Los Angeles as a global village community. In the eyes of the white woman in the sushi restaurant, Bobby and Rafaela are ideal candidates for the "international world" of Los Angeles, but their terror and alienation make a mockery of any claims of an apolitical, "natural" commonality that unifies the globe as a village.

Yamashita further critiques the self-serving idealization of the globe as a village by highlighting the homeless population of Los Angeles. Buzzworm, an African American, Vietnam War veteran, is a self-elected, one-man champion for the homeless. He walks the streets everyday armed with nothing but a card that reads "Angel of Mercy," providing medical, housing, and legal assistance. Through his eyes, Yamashita relays the fleet of marginalized and uncounted homeless population who live on the street—teenagers, the elderly, veterans, families, children, people with mental problems, drug addicts, criminals, and youth gangs. Los Angeles, through Buzzworm's eyes, is a den of social injustice and economic iniquity. Speaking of L.A.'s insatiable car culture in which cars are better housed than homeless people, he remarks: "All these people living in their cars. The cars living in garages. The garages living inside guarded walls. You dump the people outta cars, and you left with things living inside things. Meantime people going through the garbage at McDonald's looking for a crust of bread and leftover fries" (43). Buzzworm's encounters with the people who eat, sleep, and live in the street indict the great discrepancy of welfare in Los Angeles and challenge any claim of commonality that fuses the city into a community.

In a spreading arc of criticism, Yamashita extends her dissenting community skepticism of global village universalism beyond Los Angeles, extending it to Mexico, the novel's prototypical example of the Third World labor. Arcangel's political poetry, which Yamashita sets apart in italicized style, functions as the testimony of the indigenous, the displaced, the exterminated, the poor, and the workers. Identifying himself simply as a "messenger" (199), Arcangel travels through Mexico, reciting his poetry. In a striking scene involving food, he offers a counterpoint to the scene in the L.A. sushi restaurant. On his northbound travel towards Los Angeles, Arcangel is eating lunch at a roadside tavern called "Misery and Hunger." As his waiter cites a long list of American beers that the tavern offers, Arcangel asks:

"You don't think it strange? . . . All American beers. But we are in Mexico, are we not? Where are the Mexican beers?"
   "Perhaps you would prefer Coca-cola or Pepsi?"
   "Perhaps I would like a hamburger, Fritos, and catsup."

"It is our special today."

It was true. Arcangel looked around at all the hungry and miserable people in the cantina—all eating hamburgers, Fritos, catsup, and drinking American beers. Only he, who had asked the cook for the favor of cooking his raw cactus leaves, ate nopales. (131)

The vastly different significance given to the food of "different cultures" highlights the role of geopolitical context in the fetishization of the other. The transmogrification of the other into consumable goods makes sense only within the capitalist consumer logic—that the wealth of consumer choices indicates the health of the overall system. While the availability of tacos and fajitas in Los Angeles would be another evidence of "our" commonality and connectedness in the global village discourse, in this Mexican tavern the flow of American fast-food staples is no cause to claim an access to the other. Quite the contrary, the omnipresence of American fast food and the dominance of American brands are reminders of the economic, political, and cultural rifts that make the global "we" impossible. The waiter and the diners of this roadside restaurant in Mexico exemplify an absolute immersion in American fast-food fare and brand dominance. What Arcangel finds remarkable is their obliviousness to this fact as being in any way noteworthy. Yamashita crucially employs Arcangel's surprise and irony to highlight this economic takeover and brand saturation.

As Arcangel heads north, he also indicts the global "we" as the central protagonist in the First World's economic discourse of "universal progress." Yamashita employs dramaturgical strategies, staging Arcangel's protest principally through a highly stylized back-and-forth dialogue with unnamed masses. It is in one such exchange that Arcangel announces his role as the champion of the Mexican/Third World labor against the U.S./First World industry:

"El Gran Mojado, what are you doing here?" someone in the crowd wanted to know.

"Fool. He is going north, of course." Everyone knew his story. His manifest destiny.

"Ah," said El Gran Mojado, lifting a can of Budweiser, "But for the moment the North has come South."

"Haven't you heard? It's because of SUPERNAFTA!" someone shouted.

"While you are busy going north, he's here kicking ass. And he's saying we are North, too!"

Another said, "It's all hot air what he says. What's the good of being North when it feels, looks, tastes, smells, shits South?"

"That's right! If Martians landed here, they would know. They would swim nude in Apaculpo, buy sombreros, ride burros, take pictures of the pyramids, build a maquiladora, hire us, and leave."

"El Gran Mojado! Stay here and save us!" (132)

The crowd dramatizes what postcolonial critics have long voiced—that the great narrative of development and progress underwriting the First World's global economic policies must be understood in direct continuation with imperialism. The very concept of globe as a singular, integrated unit serves the interests of First World industry, argues Spivak: "Globality is invoked in the interest of the financialization of the globe, or globalization. . . . The great narrative of Development is not dead. . . . [The global electronic future] is to provide the narrative of development an alibi[,] . . . [just as] the functionaries of the civilizing mission of imperialism were well-meaning" ("Cultural Talks" 330, 333).

The unidentified voices of Arcangel's chorus coalesce into one dissenting community indictment against the global village community. It is a critique directed not only at the oppressive deployment of commonality but also at the oppressive deployment of universalism. The global "we" as the central protagonist of universal progress is once again the particular (the interest of the First World) serving as the universal (the interest of all). Trade-led models of progress, which measure progress by the volume of trades between nations, tout the "universal progress" that will benefit all of "us."[8] When restrictions and barriers to trade are removed, the rise in trade of labor, services, goods, and raw resources will lead "the South" to be like "the North," until the geographical distinction is no longer synonymous with "the Third World" and "the First World." Instead, Arcangel and the crowd decry, the "North has come South." As the dominance of American fast foods and brands at the roadside tavern demonstrates, the South has become another marketplace for the north's goods. The south functions as a source of raw material—a low-wage workforce who earn a fraction of what their counterparts earn in the north, who work without health care and environmental and legal protection, whose small businesses and farms cannot compete with the massive dominance of U.S. products in the domestic market. While the great narrative of universal progress promises to unsettle the Third World/First World designations, Arcangel's chorus argues NAFTA to be yet another example of a zero-sum game. That the benefit of trade-led "progress" goes to a select few, and not to all, is the requisite condition of the game itself. As Arcangel later pronounces, the narrative of universal progress is a "myth of the first world" (259).

Recuperating the Universal

Counterbalancing the novel's strong denunciation of global village community is an equally strong acknowledgment that *some* vision of oneness between the south and the north is inexorable. This insistence on oneness as a *necessity* is the novel's point of divergence from the discourse of dissenting community, and it demonstrates the novel's ambivalence about community as a proposition. While the novel's critique of global village celebration moves in tandem with dissenting community critique of commonality, intimacy, and collective health, upon the most important point in contention—the political significance of oneness—*Tropic* unabashedly embraces an idealized community vision. Multiple individuals *can* become a body of individuals. The paradox of community *can* be superseded. This global community is not only necessary; it is also inexorable. Arriving at this final destination, however, is a process much more complex than the global village celebration: *this* global community, as confrontational in nature as it is inevitable, requires the most absolute conception of universalism.

As Yamashita makes explicit, the wrestling match of "The Great Wetback" and "SUPERSCUMNAFTA" is the Third World's refutation of the global village community. But the destabilization of the Tropic of Cancer is also a dramatization of the thorough interdependence that binds the north and the south. Symbolic of the millions of human migration, Arcangel's travel northward takes place in a bus filled with Mexicans seeking work in the north. In tandem with "the rising tide of that migration from the South" (240) are the "waves of flowing paper money: pesos and dollars and reals, all floating across effortlessly—a graceful movement of free capital, at least 45 billion dollars of it, carried across by hidden and cheap labor" (200). The interdependence is certainly no guarantor of equitable relationship, as Yamashita amply demonstrates. But a confrontation between two interdependent parties, whose fates and interests are interwoven, results in a particularly nuanced conflict. The physical convergence of the south and the north becomes the literal dramatization of fusion and of the inevitability of the globe as a first-person plural "we." As Yamashita takes pains to highlight the disparity and inequities informing her characters' lives, *this* vision of global community contains conflict, antagonism, competition, vast differences, and unassimilated heterogeneity. It retains, in fact, key facets of dissenting community discourse voiced by postmodernist thinkers such as Young, Laclau, Lyotard, and Nancy as they refute the idealization of community. In an antithesis to its dissenting community vision, the novel's global community *also* retains the idealization of *fusion*. As global bodies, labor, capital, and geography converge upon one site, the question is: how can the globe be formulated as a body of individuals without the most uncritical idealization of community?[9]

Yamashita offers her answer in the character of Manzanar, a homeless man who stands atop L.A.'s freeway bypasses and "conducts." In the mold of the messianic figure who disowns a life of comfort for an austere one of serving others, Manzanar is a surgeon who leaves his family and profession to pronounce the absolute interconnectedness of humans. A Japanese American, he chose his name as a quiet protest and reminder of the internment of Japanese Americans during World War II. His visibility despite his homeless status poses a resistance against the public policy of enforced invisibility for the homeless. However, as he stands atop freeway bypasses, Manzanar functions as the symbolic nodal point in which *all* of humanity, in a spiral of ever-increasing scope, is joined. It is significant that Buzzworm, the street-wise activist for the homeless, calls Manzanar the "ultimate romantic" (235). Buzzworm's description encompasses the spectrum of meanings in the word "romantic"—unrealistic, hopelessly idealistic, and even mad, as it represents a vision endorsed by no one else.

In a novel filled with oppressive universalism, Manzanar represents a unique version, a romantic universalism that unabashedly announces the globe as a single body community. This romantic universalism richly illuminates the modality of the ideal and the impossible in the post-structuralist recuperation of universalism. In reviving universalism as a non-normative force of political necessity, the dimensions of the ideal and the impossible are crucial—universalism as an ideal that cannot be achieved and as a perennial ingredient in all human struggles for hegemony.[10] Indeed, the ideal dimension of universalism is the constitutive feature in Étienne Balibar's "Ambiguous Universalism." While there are numerous, specific manifestations of universalism, the liberatory potential of universalism rests upon the fact that "universality also exists *as an ideal*, in the form of absolute or infinite claims which are symbolically raised against the limits of any institution" (63–64; original emphasis). Ideal universalism can be distinguished from "real" and "fictional" universalism. "Real" universalism describes the actual condition of increased interdependency of individuals and invokes the shift in the human experience of time, space, and distance brought about by globalization. Like the inexorable convergence of humans, capital, labor, and culture in *Tropic*, "real" universalism renders "'humankind' a single web of interrelations" for the first time in history (56). Just as Yamashita emphasizes the material disparity in globalization, Balibar is careful to point out that real universalism also marks an unprecedented condition of polarization, inequality, hierarchies, and exclusions (52). "Fictional" universalism describes the "constructed" universalism espoused by all ruling institutions, such as the state and the church. As the "official values" (62) of institutions, fictional universalism embodies both regulating and progressive function; it is a site of normalization, with the power to determine the norm and standard behavior, as well as being a "powerful instrument of opening a space for liberties, especially in the form of social struggles and democratic demands," as when individuals protest the "contradiction between its official values and the actual practice" (62). In the earnest and hopeful figure of Gabriel, for instance, we can locate fictional universalism inspiring this Mexican American newspaper writer to report unvarnished accounts of racial and labor relations in the hopes of realizing equality and justice for all. Thus ideal universalism stands as the principle that underwrites fictional universalism's propositions of human equality, liberty, and rights. Concomitantly, the principle of ideal universalism is repeatedly contradicted in the actual practices of, say, the church or the state. Hence ideal universalism stands as an immortal promise, an irrepressible principle that is revived again and again in different situations but is continuously displaced in history.

In order to fully appreciate the *absolute* nature of Manzanar's romantic universalism, we must also attend to the modality of the "impossible" that sits at the heart of the poststructuralist dialectic model of universalism. The impossible and the ideal are related concepts, of course, since the ideal may be defined as that achievement which is as equal in its impossibility as in its necessity. Although Butler, Laclau, and Žižek, in *Contingency, Hegemony, Universality*, employ different metaphors to describe the impossibility of absolute universalism, they join in the argument that universalism remains a perennial relevance in any and all political struggles for rights. Laclau's metaphor of the "void" or the "empty space" plays a pivotal role in these authors' discussion of universalism as a constitutive feature in any struggle for hegemony:

From a theoretical point of view, the very notion of particularity presupposes that of totality. . . . [P]olitically speaking, the right of particular

groups of agents—ethnic, national or sexual minorities, for instance—
can be formulated only as *universal* rights. *The universal is an empty
place, a void which can be filled only by the particular, but which,
through its very emptiness, produces a series of crucial effects in the
structuration/destructuration of social relations.* It is in this sense that
it is both an impossible and necessary object. (*Contingency* 58; original
emphasis)

As specific groups seeking hegemony formulate their political claims as
universal rights, they ceaselessly and variously fill the empty space with
claims of the particular. Inasmuch as it manifests itself only through the
particular instantiations, the universal will manifest itself only through
the particular. In this dialectic relationship, the universal is never completely filled—never absolutely nonparticular. As Laclau repeatedly
argues, exclusion and antagonism are crucial in struggles for hegemony;
indeed, they are foundational features of a democratic society. An individual group's use of universalism, as in a particular group's claim of/for
rights, is fundamentally the exercise of a few speaking for *some* rather
than for all. Hence actual manifestations of universalism are always
necessarily incomplete, inasmuch as they are never completely devoid
of the particular that requires exclusion and antagonism—"the complex
dialectic between particularity and universality, between ontic content
and ontological dimension, structures social reality itself" (58).

In Butler's and Žižek's revitalization of the concept, too, the political
necessity of universalism is paralleled by its fundamental *in*completeness. While Butler critiques Laclau's universal/particular conceptualization as being too compartmentalized and naturalized (as if two such
concepts existed irrespective of specific contingencies), in her revitalization of the universal as an invaluable political concept, she continues
to build upon the impossible/necessary dilemma. Rather than Laclau's
"empty space" metaphor which may suggest the universal to be a static
category "filled" by "political content," Butler opts for the figurative concept of "non-space" to envision the universal's utility. Butler
employs the analogy of linguistic/cultural translation in this formulation. All claims of universality are "bound to various syntactic stagings
within culture" and therefore "cannot be articulated outside the scene
of their embattlement." It follows, then, that claims of universality
must "assume the risks of translation" (37) into another group's usage,
syntax, and conventions. Just as the politics of translation embody both
colonialist and anticolonialist possibilities, politics of universality also
embody both coercive and progressive possibilities. In this trope of

the non-space, Butler emphasizes the open-ended possibilities of universalism as an invaluable and ceaselessly utilized political tool. "The universal announces, as it were, its 'non-place,' its fundamentally temporal modality, precisely when challenges to its existing formulation emerge from those who are not covered by it, who have no entitlement to occupy the place of the 'who,' but nevertheless demand that the universal as such ought to be inclusive of them" (39).

While Žižek fully agrees with Laclau and Butler on the universal's pivotal role in progressive politics and on the notion of universalism as impossible/necessary (101), he identifies a transhistorical assumption in the way they maintain the conceptual permanency of universalism throughout human struggles. To leave the conceptual permanence of universalism unquestioned, he believes, is to assume the permanence to be the *consequence* of universalism's political uses. But inasmuch as political uses of universalism are unquestionably contingent upon historical context, should not the permanence of universalism be painted with the variability of historical specificity? How, then, would they "account for the enigmatic emergence of the space of universality itself" (104), a challenge that is akin to "historiciz[ing] historicism itself"? (105). In contrast, Žižek conceives the impossible/necessary dialectic of universalism via the concept of negativity. In the Lacanian terms of the "real-impossible," in which every noun may be seen as a deadlock, trauma, or open question, as something that resists symbolization, the impossibility of universalism's completion is a constitutive factor in the concept itself (110). When considered in the "Hegelian determinate negation," the deficiency between the actuality and the notion can be explained by the fact that "a particular formation [for instance, of the state] never coincides with its (universal) notion" (*The Ticklish Subject* 177; original emphasis). Through various—but interrelated—metaphors (the empty space, the non-space, negativity), poststructuralist recovery of universalism posits universalism's *in*completeness as the constant feature in any specific application of the concept (*Contingency* 110).[11]

The absolute nature of Manzanar's romantic universalism attains a greater significance against this poststructuralist backdrop. Manzanar personifies the impossibility of universalism—an instantiation of universalism that is absolutely full because there is no exclusion or antagonism. Relatedly, romantic universalism enacts the ideal dimension of universalism raised in Balibar's vision—an achievement whose impossibility renders it an imaginary thing, an achievement that stands as a standard of perfection inspiring imitation. Manzanar alone supersedes the contradiction of urban coexistence—the dense, physical proximity counterbalanced by the atomistic nature of the population's movements and the division of space by race and class. The richest example of this proximity/atomistic contradiction may be the automobile culture of Los Angeles, the millions who hurtle alongside each other, each in his own home-away-from-home. While L.A.'s freeways have long occupied the contemporary imagination as the ills of chaotic urban living, in Manzanar's eyes they represent the most vital organ of human cohabitation. "The freeway was a great root system, an organic living entity. It was nothing more than a great writhing concrete dinosaur and nothing less than the greatest orchestra on Earth" (37). Manzanar sees the artificial construct in the same realm as the elemental structures of nature and, through the language of elemental organism, describes the interconnected nature of urban existence.

Likewise, he alone sees the infrastructure that contains the urban mass of Los Angeles, the artesian rivers and the faults that run underground, as well as the human-made grid of civic utilities such as the pipelines, tunnels, waterways, pipes, electric currents, telephone cables, cable TV, fiber optics, computer networks, and many more (57). *There are maps and there are maps and there are maps. The uncanny thing was that he could see all of them at once, filter some, pick them out like transparent windows and place them even delicately and consecutively in a complex grid of pattern, spatial discernment, body politic*" (56; original emphasis). To Manzanar, such an "inanimate grid structure" (238) is a physical reminder that we occupy a single structure of existence and that the wires, pipes, cables, and freeways are all evidence of our bounded-ness, our interconnectedness to each other in the making of a single organism. Thus the hurtling cars on the freeway speak of "a kind of solidarity: all seven million residents of Greater L.A. out on the town, away from their homes, just like him, outside" (206). A crowd leaving the football stadium has all the movements of a symphony, "a percussive orchestration that even Manzanar found incredible[,] . . . the greatest jam session the world had ever known" (206).

As Manzanar envisions the population as a single body of being, the rationale for his universalism is as banal as observing that we share the same power and phone company and as profound as observing that we exist in the one and the same here-and-now. Put another way, Manzanar's romantic universalism is one that draws the most profound conclusions from the most banal observations. Yamashita repeatedly endorses this transformative process in the narrative, continuing and sharing Manzanar's language of organicity that "create[s] a community" out of atomistic disorder:

And perhaps they [freeway drivers] thought themselves disconnected from a sooty homeless man on an overpass. Perhaps and perhaps not. And yet, standing there, he bore and raised each note, joined them, united families, created a community, a great society, an entire civilization of sound. The great flow of humanity ran below and beyond his feet in every direction, pumping and pulsating, that blood connection, the great heartbeat of a great city. (35)

Thus in sharp contrast to the imposed commonality in the global village discourse, Manzanar's romantic universalism generates the most expansive understanding of commonality. It is a view of commonality based on no particularities—no specific shared experience, history, ideology, race, gender, class, nationality, religion, or any other aspects by which one distinguishes oneself from another. This commonality-without-criteria echoes the kernel of Jean-Luc Nancy's theory of dissenting community: "community is a matter . . . of existence inasmuch as it is *in* common, but without letting itself be absorbed into a common substance" (*Inoperative Community* 38). Only by negating the understanding of commonality as *substance*—of similar history, identity-claims, objectives, interests, or, in the case of global village discourse, commonality of consumption—can commonality evade being a tool that some use to conscript others into a unidirectional "we."

This nonparochial, nonparticular, featureless commonality forms the basis of the most absolute universalism in the novel. While embracing this most central of dissenting community vision, however, Manzanar's "we" employs the nonparticular commonality towards building the final objective of idealized community: fusion. Thus the central visions of dissenting community and idealized community come together in a most incongruous manner, announcing the ambivalent community at work. To begin with, Manzanar's romantic universalism is foundational to a greater vision—a single body community that encompasses the geographical span of not only Los Angeles but countries, continents, and oceans. His vision extends to "the great Pacific stretching along its great rim, brimming over long coastal shores from one hemisphere to the other" (170), and he foreshadows the convergence of the north and the south, the joining of the two hemispheres (123). In the scope and reach of Manzanar's romantic universalism, Yamashita offers her own dramatization of the globe as a community—the globe as a single organism, whose disparate parts are inexorably drawn together. What distinguishes this model of single body community from the other instances of idealized community that abound in the novel? First, this

global community is not an instance of the particular "making empire
out of its local meaning" (Butler 31). In constituting a "we" out of
"my" experience, the white woman's global village universalism performs a unidirectional conscription: she speaks *for* the millions and billions of others in prescribing the supposed unity and the intimacy. The
singular "we" that results is a unidirectional affection and affectation.
In contrast, Manzanar's community, like the "crowds" that accompany
Arcangel's Third World labor "we," and the cacophony of unidentified voices that join Buzzworm's urban homeless "we," is a reciprocal
deployment of universalism. That is, there is no slippage between "my"
and "we," as all three articulations of "we" emerge from spontaneous
and voluntary fusion.

But it is also important to distinguish Manzanar's romantic universalism from Arcangel's and Buzzworm's particular deployment of universalism. As Laclau argued most forcefully, antagonism and exclusion
are not unique features of imperialism and Eurocentricism: in the dialectic logic of universal/particular, *all* instantiations of universalism are
incomplete inasmuch as they are claims of the particular. Thus universalism of the Third World labor "we" or the homeless "we" observes
the fundamental contradiction in the idea and the political application
of universalism—what Žižek calls the "split" grounded *already on
the level of the notion*" (*The Ticklish Subject* 177; original emphasis).
Only Manzanar's romantic universalism supersedes that negativity, as
it postulates a "we" that is absolutely inclusive because there is no criterion for inclusion, which is the same as there being no possibility of
exclusion. Romantic universalism's "we" is a community of a limitless
nature, whose absolute lack of particularity completely fills the "empty
space" or the "non-space" of universalism.

In its absolute inclusiveness, romantic universalism fulfills another
ideal dimension of universalism: a logic of "we" that does not exert
a normalizing function. As Balibar identified in his model of fictional
universalism, the governing function of institutions such as the church
or the state also serves a regulating function. The dilemma that Balibar
poses is: what deployment of universalism can avoid being a normative force? Through romantic universalism, *Tropic* offers an answer:
when the participation in the universalism is entirely voluntary and
reciprocal. In addition to bringing people to tears (235), Manzanar's
conducting begets other believers, inspiring them to start conducting
themselves. A spontaneous uprising of romantic universalism grabs hold
of Los Angeles. As Arcangel and the Tropic of Cancer approach the city,
causing geography to literally shift and streets to expand and distort,

Manzanar notes a different kind of organization to the city: "Little by little, Manzanar began to sense a new kind of grid, this one defined not by inanimate structures or other living things but by himself and others like him. He found himself at the heart of an expanding symphony of which he was not the only conductor" (238). As the entire city of Los Angeles become self-inspired "conductors," Manzanar's romantic universalism generates a "we" greater in scope than Arcangel's "crowd" or Buzzworm's homeless. Indeed, each of the conductors begins to personify, as Manzanar had done, the immensity of humanity as a single body. Manzanar notes that "the tenor of this music was a very different sort, at times a kind of choral babel. . . . The entire City of Angels seemed to have opened its singular voice to herald a naked old man [Arcangel] and a little boy [Bobby and Rafaela's son] with an orange followed by a motley parade approaching from the south" (238).

That the entire city's conducting "heralds" the arrival of Arcangel and the Third World labor underscores the *transformative* power of romantic universalism. Literally dramatizing the perennial relevance of universalism in the particular claims of specific groups, Manzanar's all-inclusive, all-voluntary, absolute universalism becomes foundational to the march of Third World labor and, later, to Buzzworm's vision for the homeless. When Arcangel finally confronts SUPERNAFTA in the wrestling ring, his address to the crowd, like his earlier addresses to the crowd in Mexico, becomes an emblematic Third World labor's protest against the First World's myth of universal progress:

> You who live in the declining and abandoned places
> of great cities, called barrios, ghettos, and favelas. . . .
> The myth of the first world is that
> Development is wealth and technology progress.
> It is all rubbish.
> It means that you are no longer human beings
> But only labor. (258–59)

As Arcangel protests a reality in which they are "no longer human beings," the formation of Third World labor as historical actor and Third World labor's claim for human rights take place in the contxt of Manzanar's romantic universalism. As the crowd break into cheers and tears, their fusion is:

> accompanied by a choral symphony that came from outside the auditorium and slowly swelled to fill it by the people themselves. Everyone

knew the music and the words in their own language, knew the alto, bass, and soprano parts, knew it as if from some uncanny place in their inner ears, as if they had sung it all their lives. Some people jumped up to conduct entire sections of the auditorium. (260)

Illustrative of the complex nature of the global community formed by the north and the south, the confrontation of Arcangel and SUPER-NAFTA does not result in a single winner. Each vanquishes the other in the ring, but the mythical manner of Arcangel's death by conflagration foreshadows his eventual rise again. What remains the greatest achievement of the confrontation, however, is the fusion of the south and the north joined in "conducting." For a brief moment, Los Angeles enacts a model of global community that is absolutely all-inclusive, all-voluntary, and all-reciprocal, and Manzanar can finally "let his arms drop. There was no need to conduct the music anymore. The entire city had sprouted grassroots conductors of every sort" (254).

Like the spontaneous "chorus" and "symphony" that frame Arcangel's Third World universalism, Manzanar's romantic universalism enables Buzzworm's particular universalism for the homeless. The literal geographical shift of the globe causes a meltdown of L.A. freeways, and chaos abounds between drivers who abandon their cars, the homeless who move in, and the law enforcement who combat them. The upheaval comes to an inevitable conclusion—a shootout between law enforcement and the homeless. The homeless are massacred in great numbers, and "order" is restored. As Buzzworm considers the blight and the reconstruction work that awaits him, his vision is profoundly altered by Manzanar's romantic universalism. Buzzworm separates himself from his main source of connection to the world, the radio. The radio, he notes, is always singing "one big love song. I love you. You love me. I love myself. We love us. We love the world. We love God. We love ourselves but hate some of you. I hate myself but would love you if. You screwed me and I'm learning to love me or that other one" (265). Instead of the facile cult of love that characterizes popular music, Buzzworm opts for what he calls a "mythic reality," a term he hears on the radio before he makes his final disconnection. A mythic reality occurs when "everyone gets plugged into a myth and builds a reality around it. Or was it the other way around? Everybody gets plugged into a reality and builds a myth around it. He didn't know which. Things would be what he and everybody else chose to do and make of it. It wasn't gonna be something imagined" (265). A mythic reality differs from the cult of love in its constructivist dimension—one remains fully conscious of the fact that one *chooses* the myth that best accompanies one's desired reality. "Unplugged and timeless, thinking like this was scary, Buzzworm gritted his teeth. Took a deep breath. Manzanar's symphony swelled against diaphragm, reverberated through his veteran bones. Solar-powered, he could not run out of time" (265).

A Global Community through Romantic Universalism

In romantic universalism's all-inclusive, all-voluntary, and non-normative "we," Yamashita offers a model of a global community that acknowledges the innumerable fissures, conflicts, competition, and antagonism running through it. Romantic universalism affects all specific instantiations of universalism in the novel in unique ways. As the most expansive and nondiscriminatory instance of "we," it highlights the unidirectional and imperialist nature of the First World's global village universalism. In lending its transformative power to Third World labor "we" and the homeless "we," romantic universalism also proves its perennial relevance to all political struggles. In romantic universalism's absolute nature, then, Yamashita offers one answer to the impossible/necessary dialectic in the poststructuralist recuperation of universalism. The impossible/necessary dialectic may be superseded, romantic universalism suggests, in an instance of universalism that includes *all* of humanity. When an instance of universalism has absolutely no remnant of the particular, it becomes that "empty space," the ever-receding horizon of the ideal itself.

In a powerful way, then, romantic universalism casts a new light on one of the most suspect words of contemporary theory: totality. As a word used synonymously with "totalitarianism" in contemporary political, philosophical, and cultural theories, especially in dissenting community discourse, totality is equated with the force of oppression and coercion in the name of solidarity, homogeneity, and unity.[12] However, what the absolute, sweeping nature of romantic universalism demonstrates is that "totality" is also the abstract notion for "absolute whole." As a formal concept of "entirety," totality resides at the center of romantic universalism, encapsulating the absolute inclusion that is nonparticular, nondiscriminatory, nondeliberative, and nondiscerning. As romantic universalism fulfills the very criteria of "ideal" and "impossible" universalism, it shows that the final horizon of universalism *itself* is totality—an absolutely sweeping, all-encompassing entirety, an unqualified wholeness. It shows that concepts equated with political oppression and totalitari-

anism—"totality," "oneness," and "fusion"—are also abstract ingredients in the ideal of universalism itself. Thus, not only is *Tropic*'s final
"we" distinct from the "we" of idealized community based on specific
commonalities; it is different from the "we" of dissenting community
that eschews any prospective of totality, fusion, or oneness.

This nondeliberative, nondiscerning totality is what sets romantic
universalism apart from cosmopolitanism, the closest conceptual cousin
in contemporary theory in envisioning a global unity. As I elaborated in
the Introduction, recent revitalizations of cosmopolitanism as a politico-
ethical vision fundamentally rests on a vision of deliberative belonging.
Envisioned as a politico-ethical vision against a nationalist, primordialist, and parochial sense of belonging, attachment, and identification,
cosmopolitanism as a corrective against the single body community
theorizes a vision of unity that is much more flexible, adroit, and deliberative than universalism. As Bruce Robbins states, cosmopolitanism
"better describes the sensibility of our moment" because "the word is
not as philosophically ambitious as the term 'universalism'" (196). In
other words, in contrast to absolute universalism, whose final horizon
is totality, recent revival of cosmopolitanism deploys "self-conscious"
and "self-corrective" as key terms to envision a global unity that can
evade precisely that pull of totality. Thus, while absolute universalism
claims the entirety of the global "we," cosmopolitanism might be seen
as a claim of global unity that is paradigmatically suspicious of the very
concept of wholeness and entirety.[13]

In dramatizing totality as the horizon of romantic universalism,
Yamashita offers a symbolic resolution to the impossible/necessary dialectic in the poststructuralist model of universalism. Romantic universalism, however, must not be understood simply as the solution that
rescues universalism from the dialectic tension of necessity/impossibility.
What about the necessity? What does romantic universalism *do*? What
is the political utility of a universalism that is all-inclusive? What is the
progressive, emancipatory potential of a unity that speaks for all? How
does it specifically challenge fictional universalisms, the normative, governing forces of institutions such as the state, government, and trade
regulations? Also, when the emblematic moment of romantic universalism is the Third World and the First World joined in song, just how
much can romantic universalism distinguish itself from the cult of love
that rules the radio airwaves?

In locating the answer to both inquiries, Yamashita returns us to
the impossible/necessary dialectic. In presenting us with the seemingly
impossible feat—an absolute "we"—romantic universalism also pres-

ents us with the fact that the idea of universalism itself serves no specific political needs *except* as it serves particular instantiations. The only satisfactory way to assert the political utility of romantic universalism, to distinguish it from the "We Are the World" variety, lies in assessing its specific manifestations—the "we" of the homeless or the "we" of the Third World labor. The political function of universalism can emerge only from the particular instantiations of universalism. Like Manzanar's conducting that encompasses all revolutions, both individual and collective, romantic universalism transforms individual protests (of Third World labor, of the homeless) into historical forces and into historical actors pursuing the ideal of universal human rights.

Rather than being a solution that overcomes the impossible/necessary dialectic, then, romantic universalism adds great nuance to the "empty space" of universalism that propels the dialectic. Through her use of the fantastic mode in representing romantic universalism, Yamashita renders a greater complexity to the theoretical conception of the "empty space," "non-space," or "negativity" at the heart of universalism. A globe that literally shifts its spatial perimeters, cities and continents that join in song: the fact that envisioning an absolute universalism requires the mode of the fantastic enriches our understanding of the impossible (improbable, unrealistic, unrealizable) nature of an all-inclusive "we." Furthermore, Yamashita's use of the fantastic to actualize the ideal of universalism enhances our understanding of the romantic (imaginary, unreal, and extravagantly fanciful) dimension of universalism. Indeed, the implications of absolute universalism can be profound and facile at once, and Yamashita richly illustrates these modalities through her use of the fantastic mode.

What, then, of the globe as a community? *Tropic* provides an array of models for conceiving the global community, from the imperialist, consumerist kind, to particular groups' unity and struggle for rights, and to absolutely total global oneness. To the paradox of community, then, the novel answers: absolute universalism transforms multiple individuals into a body of individuals. As Yamashita deploys the most expansive "we" as the foundation for the political articulations of Third World labor and the urban homeless, she unmistakably asserts the work of romantic universalism—the transformative power of its imaginary and unrealistic vision, as well as its inspirational power as the ever-elusive horizon of universal human rights.

CHAPTER 3

Unlike Any Other

Shoring Up the Human Community in
Richard Powers's *Galatea 2.2* and *Plowing the Dark*

From the kinship-model "we" in Morrison and the global "we" in Yamashita, this chapter turns to the biggest conceptual "we" of all—the human "we" in Richard Powers's novels of science and technology. The literary manifestation of "the human" as a community brings us back to one of the most contentious spots in the debate over community: commonality. Like the commonality of identity, history, experience, and objective that transformed multiple individuals into a community in Morrison's novels, and the being-in-common that fused all of the globe's inhabitants into one in Yamashita's novel, the criterion of commonality raises its head in the central question of this chapter: what unique commonalities make "the human" into a community?

Since Ihab Hassan postulated that "five hundred years of humanism may be coming to an end" (212) in his 1977 essay, "Prometheus as Performer: Towards a Posthumanist Culture?" the machine has been the dominant conceptual tool in countering the notion of "the human" as a unique entity. And as N. Katherine Hayles wrote in 1990, the category of the human is the predictable site of conclusion for postmodernism's denaturalizing impulse: "When the essential components of human experience are denatured, they are not merely revealed as constructions. The human subject who stands as the putative source of experience is also deconstructed and then reconstructed in ways that fundamentally alter what it means to be human. The postmodern anticipates and implies the posthuman" (*Chaos Bound* 266). As Hayles states in *How We Became Posthuman,* the central principle underlying posthumanist thinking is the *reconfiguring* of the "human being so that it can be seamlessly articulated with intelligent machines. In the posthuman, there are no essential differences or absolute demarcations between bodily existence and computer simulation, cybernetic mechanism and biological organism, robot teleology and human goals" (2–3). As posthumanism batters at the attributes putatively unique to the human, such as consciousness, intelligence, and embodiment, it unsettles the founding grounds of the human as a unique body of individuals.

These are the challenges that humanism faces in Richard Powers's *Galatea 2.2* (1995) and *Plowing the Dark* (2000), two novels of intelligent machine and virtual reality technology. In what he calls the shape of a "dialogical novel, where there are different moral centers, each of which has its own plausibility" (Blume n.p.), Richard Powers's fictions of science and technology explore the anxiety that humanism suffers at the hand of posthumanism. To a degree unparalleled by any other contemporary novelist, Powers has explored what he identifies as "the most central facts of contemporary life—technology and science" as his creative domain (*Atlantic Unbound* n.p.). And many of his novels (*Three Farmers on Their Way to a Dance, The Gold Bug Variations, Galatea 2.2, Plowing the Dark*) revolve around disciplines such as computer programming, chemistry, genetics, artificial intelligence, cognitive science, and virtual reality technology. Readers of technology in contemporary American fiction know familiar names such as William Burroughs, Thomas Pynchon, Don DeLillo, and Kathy Acker. Although Powers shares their topical interest, his literary treatment of science and technology manifests the strongest imperative towards maintaining the human "we" as a unique body of individuals.

As Powers dramatizes the posthumanist assault on the claims of human uniqueness, he demonstrates the plight of humanism as the plight of commonalities that constitute the human into a community. Thus, reading Powers's humanism as a form of community maintenance enables us to detect the competing discourses of idealized and dissenting community informing humanism and posthumanism. That is, as humanism and posthumanism offer distinct models of saying "we, the human," their competing assumptions, values, and ideals directly recall the debate between idealized and dissenting community discourses. While humanism assumes the pivotal role of human commonalities in transforming the human into a single body community, the posthumanist vision of "the union of the human with the intelligent machines" (Hayles, *Posthuman* 2) negates not only the empirical claims of commonalities unique to the human, but also the assumption that commonalities are obvious rationale for claiming a community. Thus the model of the human "we" postulated by posthumanism is fundamentally irreconcilable with the model of "we" suggested by humanism. As Rodney Brooks announces in *Flesh and Machines: How Machines Will Change Us:* "My own beliefs say that we are machines, and from that I conclude that there is no reason, in principle, that it is not possible to build a machine from silicon and steel that has both genuine emotions and consciousness" (180).[1] In stark contrast, the opposition of the machine from the human constitutes the central tenet of *Galatea*'s humanism. The protagonist's faith in the ineradicable difference between the human and the machine is evident in this prototypical response to posthumanist views: "You're not elevating the machine. You're debasing us" (86). The inverse relationship between "us" and "them" remains foundational to humanism as a form of community maintenance: what "they" get comes at "our" loss. This irreconcilability between the posthumanist "we" and the humanist "we," I suggest, can also be read as the irreconcilability between the discourses of idealized community and dissenting community running through the novel.

Nowhere does this humanist-posthumanist drama feature more prominently and poignantly than in *Galatea*, a novel in which the oneness of humankind comes under scrutiny in light of artificial intelligence. Set in the hub of a "Center for the Study of Advanced Sciences" at a major Midwestern university, *Galatea* examines the shifting lines of assessing intelligence in a machine. "Richard Powers," the first-person narrator-protagonist and the literary persona of the writer himself, becomes involved in a bet offered by a cognitive neurologist, Philip Lentz, that a supercomputer, constituted by a neural connection between 65,536 computers, could be trained in canonical Western literature to produce a Master's comprehensive exam answer that is indistinguishable from one produced by a graduate student.[2] In an environment where cognition is explained through the computational process of the machine, the human has the hardest time holding on to its ontological status as the peerless original. As Rick asks: "When does an imitation become the real thing[?] . . . What's the real thing?" (276).

"Humanist" is a term that Powers uses expansively in *Galatea* to describe Rick's disciplinary allegiance, one that is sorely tested by the Center's posthumanists, its scientists and machinists. There is no little dramatic irony that Rick's official title at the Center is a "Visitor" and that he calls himself "the token humanist" (2) and "the humanist on the wall" (36). Further compounding the disciplinary division of the humanists and the posthumanists is Lentz's nickname for Rick—"Marcel"—alluding to the iconic figure of literariness Marcel Proust. The dialogic arrangement of humanist-artist and posthumanist-scientist is most closely repeated in *Plowing the Dark,* with Adie Klarpole, a painter-turned-commercial illustrator, finding herself in a hub of virtual reality technology. Like Rick's, Adie's foray into scientific discipline is a disorienting experience, in which her equanimity regarding the uniqueness of the human comes up against the posthumanist belief that "reality is basically computational" (82).[3] The synonymous role of humanist and artist in Powers's novels delineate the artistic values at stake in the debate over human uniqueness. The artist-protagonists attest their firmly held worldview in human creations of artistic originality, creativity, beauty, and truth.[4] But more than a disciplinary allegiance, these artist-humanists hold on to the human as the "real thing" by which all other entities are interpreted.

In contrast, Powers's posthumanists contend that humanists' complacent hold on the status of "the real thing" is indefensible. *Galatea*'s Lentz questions humanism's veneration of concepts such as embodiment, consciousness, and the mind. Arguing that functions, abilities, and possibilities deemed intrinsic to the human can indeed be articulated seamlessly with those of the intelligent machine, Lentz prepares the groundwork for articulating a "we" that includes the human *and* the machine. Caught in the fire of posthumanist skepticism and ridicule, Powers's humanists struggle to justify their assumption. And it is precisely within the nature of that struggle that I locate the ambivalent community at work in Powers's exploration of "the human" as a body of individuals.[5]

In arguing the novel's conflict between humanism and posthumanism, I contest the prevailing assessment of the novel as an exemplary literary expression of posthumanism. Pointing to the novel's ultimate intelligent machine, a supercomputer named Helen, Hayles writes that "the posthuman appears not as humanity's rival or successor but as a longed-for companion" (*Posthuman* 271). Likewise, for another critic, *Galatea* is an example of a "[p]osthumanist fiction [which] diminishes the threat of computers as it accepts them as an integral part of the contemporary world" (Miller 382). Miller contrasts the novel to the popular science fictions that use the machine as ominous threats to the human, and he argues that *Galatea* shows that "something more profound can result when division between worlds (such as human and computer, science and humanism, or body and mind) are broken down" (381).[6]

What such readings miss, I suggest, is the full significance of the novel's dialogic nature and the consequences it has for the novel's treatment of the human as a community of "the real," the "original," the "essential" beings. The quality of naïveté essential to Powers's artist-protagonists leads to the repeated testing of the humanists by the scientist-posthumanists. And it is a test that the artist-humanists do not "pass" well. In highlighting the *inadequacies* of the humanists' responses, Powers holds up humanism as a subject of analysis and critique. Most importantly, reading *Galatea* as a literary exemplification of the posthumanist "we" misses the novel's unshakable attachment to the humanist "we"; it misses the irresolvable oscillation in the novel's value system between humanism and posthumanism, and between the discourse of idealized community and dissenting community. As the novel explores the losses incurred to the absolute uniqueness of the human, it illustrates humanism as a thoroughly self-invested venture on behalf of "us." This self-preservationist nature of humanism's community maintenance is best approached through the concept of immanentism—the belief that certain qualities and attributes are essential, innate, and intrinsic to a being. The immanentist premise that justifies the humanist "we," I argue, ultimately results in an autotelic humanism. It is a self-justifying, self-perpetuating humanism whose final *work*—to maintain "the human" as a unique community—functions as the justification for maintaining that community.

In the first section, I suggest an analysis of humanist-posthumanist conflict through the politics of interpretation and highlight the immanentist logic running through the humanist interpretation of the machine. In the second section, I show that not only is immanentism an effective tool of exclusion, but it is also an effective tool for *assimilating* the machine without weakening the discursive borders maintaining the oneness of the human as a community. In the third and final section, I propose that humanism, in Powers's novels of science and technology, is as much a topic under analysis as it is the very value system that sustains Powers's literary venture. That is, Rick's helpless allegiance to the humanist "real thing" is the stuff of *Galatea*'s drama just as it is the inevitable point of return for Powers's own philosophical and literary equilibrium. In making this final argument, I turn to the conclusion of *Plowing the Dark,* a novel whose dialogic tension between humanism-posthumanism parallels that of *Galatea,* and yet whose resolution declares a humanist allegiance more resounding and less ambivalent than that of *Galatea*. The two novels, side by side, best demonstrate the humanist trajectory of Powers's imagination.

Ultimately, the threat to the ontological status of the human is a grave matter for Powers's humanist-artists, and *Galatea* and *Plowing* are exercises in keeping humankind as an inviolate community of "the real thing." The Emily Dickinson poem that prefaces *Galatea* expresses the humanist-protagonists' and, I believe, Powers's own allegiance:

The brain is wider than the sky,
For, put them side by side,
The one the other will contain
With ease, and you beside.

The brain is deeper than the sea,
For, hold them, blue to blue,
The one the other will absorb,
As sponges, buckets do.

The brain is just the weight of God,
For, heft them, pound for pound,
And they will differ, if they do,
As syllable from sound.

Humanist Interpretation of the Machine

Is the human like an intelligent machine? Or is the intelligent machine like a human? Is the brain in effect a computer, or is the computer in effect a brain? As figurative language runs through the humanist-posthumanist debate, the discursive contestation over the human community can be read as fundamentally a debate over interpretation. How does one explain, explicate, or make sense of the human or the intelligent machine? Which is the ontological index by which the other attains comprehensibility?

"Interpretation," however, does not fully capture the politics of humanist-posthumanist debate. As the proliferation of similes and metaphors announce, attempts at explaining the human or the intelligent machine take place through the structure of translation: like any use of figurative sense-making, one thing is put into the *terms* of another for the sake of comprehensibility. Although "interpretation" and "translation" are used interchangeably in everyday usage, the humanist-posthumanist debate inescapably demonstrates the profound conceptual difference between the two terms. Interpretation, Wolfgang Iser points out, has always been an act of translation: "Each interpretation transposes something into something else. . . . The register into which the subject matter is to be transposed is dually coded. It consists of viewpoints and assumptions that provide the angle from which the subject matter is approached, but at the same time it delineates the parameters into which the subject matter is to be translated for the sake of grasping" (5–6). As the register determines the parameters of translating something into something else, crucial consequences are at stake in determining the register. The entity that occupies the status of the register becomes the subject who translates—who not only elects the criteria ("the angle") through which the object attains comprehensibility and discursive significance, but also determines the boundaries ("the parameters") of the object's being. Interpretation, unlike translation, suggests the possibility of rendering clear the meaning of one entity *without* calling into question the tools of that meaning-making. Thus interpretation invokes a transcendental epistemology, positing a way of knowing that transcends any identity, position, partiality, or vested interest. Translation, on the other hand, conceptualizes the act of explanation as the transposition of one entity into the terms of another *existing* entity. In explicitly bearing the "paraphrasing" nature of explanation, translation calls into question what interpretation evades: can there be an explanation that does not endow one set of terms with epistemological primacy?

Powers's literary representation of the human "we" engages this distinction between interpretation and translation. The humanist-artists of *Galatea* and *Plowing the Dark* firmly believe that their explanations of scientific phenomena and machinic entities are interpretations—rendering the strange and the foreign into clarity, into "what they really are." Exposing their interpretations as translations is what the novels' posthumanists—and Powers—pursue. As Powers delineates the humanist's struggle to maintain the human as the register, he articulates the unspoken question in the very theory of interpretation: as the register determines the specific criteria of interpretation, from whence does the register draw *its* criteria? What Iser's formulation hints at—the tautological dimension of interpretation—becomes full-blown in *Galatea*'s exploration of humanism. Powers connects the tautological implications to a perennial philosophical dilemma—how does the knower know himself?—and specifically hones it as the dilemma of humanism. How can the human interpret the machine except through the criteria drawn from the human itself? Can interpreting the machine be anything other than *translating* the machine into human terms? Conversely, can humanism insist on the legitimacy of the human as the register in interpreting the machine in the face of its tautological operation? Ultimately, can there be a human community when the register itself—the human as a body of individuals bound by their unique commonalities—is destabilized?

Further enhancing Powers's interrogation of humanism is his presentation of an alternate model of interpreting the machine. And it is this second model, presented alongside the humanist's interpretation of the machine, that hints at the possibility of the posthumanist "union" of the human and the machine. What can overcome the tautological limitations of interpretation, Iser suggests, is a bidirectional epistemological effect:

> As the register is bound to tailor what is to be translated, it simultaneously is subject to specifications. . . . This two-way traffic is due to the fact that the register does not represent a transcendental consciousness from which the subject matter is to be judged; if it did, translation would be redundant, as the subject matter—instead of being transposed—would just be determined for what it is. Therefore interpretation as translatability has its repercussions on the register by diversifying the framework into which the subject matter is transposed. For this reason the registers not only change but are also fine-tuned in each act of interpretation. (6)

A translation process in which a "two-way traffic" takes place is one in which the object of translation affects the register as much as the register affects the object of translation. In posthumanist terms, it is a translation process in which the terms of the human are affected by the terms of the machine. Indeed, the fluidity between the human and the machine in Lenoir's theory of posthumanism speaks to the co-evolving nature of the human and the machine: "the [human] body is a cultural construct, a historical conception both contested and negotiated, . . . not an inevitability . . . ; rather, it is *an interpretive frame we coconstruct* along with our machines and the worlds they inhabit" (Lenoir 210; my emphasis).

In the face of this co-evolving and bidirectional translation, the ontological primacy of the human as the transcendental register certainly loses its footing. And without the means to insist on the commonalities unique to the human, the human "we" becomes a community whose borders are wide open. Thus, like the discourse of dissenting community which negates the transformative power of commonality to forge many into one, posthumanism's co-evolving translation negates the fusing function of commonalities in the humanist "we."

The dialogic shape of Powers's novels allows us to see humanism and posthumanism as fundamentally two different politics of interpretation—one which insists on a transcendental register of interpretation, and one which insists on co-evolving translation. The most startling aspect of this dialogic maneuver is the way Powers holds up the human as an *inadequate* register yet still reinstates it as an *inevitable* register of interpreting the machine. Powers first demonstrates the tautological dimensions of interpretation by highlighting the immanentist logic of Rick's humanism. Immanentist logic of interpretation begins with the claim that certain qualities and attributes are inherent, essential, or natural to an entity. Those self-same qualities and attributes are then deployed as the criteria by which the object of interpretation comes into being. Through Rick's interpretation of the machine, hence, we can see the tautology at work in maintaining the human as a community.

Rick's immanentist interpretation begins with the claim that the desire and the skill to use narrative are attributes intrinsic to the human. Narrative as an essential epistemological activity is a recurring theme in Powers's novels.[7] And *Galatea* offers another expression of his interest in "the bidirectional relation between narrative and cognition." As Powers states:

> I mean it [narrative] to include the whole process of fabulation, infer-
> ence, and situational tale spinning that consciousness uses to situate itself
> and make a continuity out of the interruptive fragments of perception.
> I am interested in this wider process of explanatory story-making in all
> my books, and *Galatea* comes back to the theme again with that great
> bit of epistemology from the Psalms: "We live our lives like a tale told."
> (Neilson 14–15)

Powers's insistence on the inextricable link between narrative and cognition means that in *Galatea,* narrative attains a vast significance in his humanist-artist's interpretation of the machine. As narrative use comes to stand as the demonstration of human cognition at work, the *machine's* ability to use narrative becomes the evidence of its "intelli-gence," "learning," and "consciousness."

Powers further compounds narrative use as a transcendental reg-ister by presenting it as an *essence* of the human. Using "the primacy of narrative desire" (75) as a thematic refrain, *Galatea* intertwines its protagonists in their love of narrative. That is, narrative use becomes the essential commonality that not only distinguishes the human but also binds them into a first-person plural "we." As the novel begins, the eponymous character, "Richard Powers," with four books behind him, is suffering under a particularly blank stage in his creative process:

"I had nothing left in me but the autobiography I'd refused from the start even to think about" (36). In a gesture of dramatic irony, *Galatea* evolves into the autobiography Rick didn't want to write, filled with recollections of his parents; his development as a writer; his romantic relationship; and, of course, his bizarre involvement in the training of a supercomputer.

The primacy of narrative desire, it turns out, is not a condition specific to Rick but is universally applicable to all the protagonists. Rick credits his literary profession to his old English professor, Taylor, whose love of literature inspired young Rick to make the disciplinary change from science to English literature. Throughout his professional life, Rick looks to Taylor as his ideal reader, his mentor, and the source of his helpless attachment to literature: "[E]verything Taylor had long ago alerted me to circled back on the primacy of narrative desire. Desire, he taught me, was the voicegram of memory" (75). Rick's father was a habitual reader and teller of stories, and his life stories become the substance of one of Rick's novels. All of Rick's relationships, in fact, are forged on this commonality of sharing narrative. His passionate, decade-long relationship with a woman identified as C. evolves around the sharing and collaboration of stories: "When we weren't reading to each other, we improvised a narrative" (33). And when C. falls into depression, as she frequently does, Rick reports: "[N]othing I did seemed to help her at all. Except listening to the stories. Frantic, C. dragged out all the stories that her mother raised her on" (100). The end of their relationship, in fact, is signaled by the failure of narrative to function as the bond of their relationship. As the constitutive ingredient of all human relationships, then, narrative use becomes the commonality that binds the multiple individuals into community.

It comes as no surprise, then, that Rick's training and interpretation of the supercomputer evolve around the use of narrative. Lentz, the brilliant neuroscientist who is both Rick's partner in the project as well as his greatest posthumanist detractor, builds a progressively more sophisticated and massive version of the computer network until, "[d]epending on the benchmark, the connection monster could outperform any computing assemblage on earth" (115). Each "implementation" is designated by an alphabet, until they reach an Implementation H that is outfitted with a voice interface so that it can hear and speak, and an artificial retina so that it can see. After Rick trains Imp. H in diction and basic sentence structure, he begins its education through the telling of anecdotes, aphorisms, proverbs, nursery rhymes, riddles, fables, and short stories. Rick's conviction that the best way to "know" the world is through its stories directly continues Powers's own assertion that "fiction can be a mirror in which we come to know our fictions about the world" (Neilson 16). As Rick teaches H. through stories, he simultaneously assesses its computational abilities through its ability to explicate them. Rick quizzes Imp. H.: "'A girl goes into a music store. She flips through the bins of CDs. All at once, she starts to jump up and down and clap her hands. She opens her purse, and just as suddenly starts to cry. Why?'" (223). The more the machine is able to paraphrase the narrative—that is, explain with its own selection of words, concepts, and references the causal logic and social relationships driving the characters and the plot—the more Rick characterizes the machine's computation as intelligence and consciousness.

Although Rick's attribution of intelligence to Imp. H. may seem to strengthen the posthumanist configuration of the human-machine fluidity, it has precisely the opposite significance. As intelligence is configured as a function of narrative skill, intelligence remains solidly an attribute unique to the human. As long as the machine is *like* the human, the human as the register of interpretation never comes into question. Interpreting the machine as being intelligent becomes solely a proprietorial act; the interpreter generously extends what is in his—in the human community's—ownership. What is common to the human remains intact, and what is unique to the human community remains intact. As both the standard-bearer and the examiner, the human's role as the register of interpretation is never threatened.

Posthumanist Translation of the Human

Posthumanism targets exactly this immanentist logic of humanism, and Powers's exemplar posthumanists, such as Lentz in *Galatea* or Sue Locke and Spiegel in *Plowing the Dark,* steadily dismantle the status of human commonalities as the transcendental register. In their disruptive maneuver, the posthumanists offer a *counter*translation—they translate *the human* using the machine as the register. The politics of this translation can be understood more specifically via what Hayles calls the key ideology of posthumanism, the "Platonic backhand and forehand":

> The Platonic backhand works by inferring from the world's noisy multiplicity a simplified abstraction. . . . [T]he move circles around to constitute the abstraction as the originary form from which the world's multiplicity derives. [Platonic forehand] starts from simplified abstractions

and, using simulation techniques such as genetic algorithms, evolves a multiplicity sufficiently complex that it can be seen as a world of its own. The two moves thus make their play in opposite directions. . . . They share a common ideology—privileging the abstract as the Real and downplaying the importance of material instantiation. (*Posthuman* 13–14)[8]

In a striking scene in *Plowing the Dark,* Powers literalizes the Platonic backhand and forehand that supplants material instantiation with abstract information. For the posthumanists in the virtual reality lab TeraSys, the task of simulating embodied reality begins by explaining the object from the inside out—that is, by arriving at the mathematical configurations that generate the visual, sensory, and responsive effects of embodiment. As the artist-humanist Adie watches in awe, the scientists, mathematicians, computer programmers, and technicians "grow" a leaf from abstract information. First they elicit "the inner name of the thing" (214) through a materiality-to-information process. Then they give virtual flesh to the abstract information by giving it the effects of multiplicity: "He [Spiegel, a programmer] drew up genetic algorithms: fractal, recursive code that crept forward from out of its own embryo. He worried over their sapling, a RAM-cached Johnny Appleseed. He spread the best iterative fertilizer on the shaded texture until it flung itself outward into a living branch. . . . The leaf grew itself, from the self-organizing rules arising along its lengthening blade" (37). As the mathematicians and programmers generate virtual leaves using algorithmic equations, Adie interrupts:

> "You're trying to tell me that . . . math . . . is enough to get fake leaves to look real?"
> "Math," Kaladjian [a mathematician] snarled, "is enough to get real leaves to look real." (35; original ellipsis)

Likewise in *Galatea,* this posthumanist move of supplanting the register of translation takes place when Lentz uses the abstraction of computation to translate human cognition. Here, Lentz is challenging Rick's assumption that intelligence is an attribute that is immanent to the human and, therefore, a unique possession of the human community. "The brain, Lentz had it, was itself just a glorified, fudged-up Turing machine. . . . We used algorithms to imitate a non-algorithmic world" (71). When Rick despairs of teaching a machine to think like a human, Lentz counters that human thinking is just like the machine's:

"We humans are winging it, improvising. Input pattern x sets off associative matrix y. . . . Conscious intelligence is smoke and mirrors. Almost free-associative. Nobody really responds to anyone else, per se. We all spout our canned and thumb-nailed scripts, with the barest minimum of polite segues. Granted, we're remarkably fast at indexing and retrieval. But comprehension and appropriate response are often more on the order of buckshot. . . . Massively parallel pattern matching." (86)

This posthumanist translation of human intelligence has profound repercussions on humanism's argument that narrative is a commonality unique to the human community. Narrative use, in Rick's interpretation of the machine, was a metonymy of cognition itself. Arguing the inextricable link between narrative and cognition meant that narrative intelligence was in effect intelligence itself. However, when translated through the register of abstract computation, narrative intelligence becomes a matter of input patterns, matrices, and parallel pattern matching, no longer an ability exclusive and immanent to the human. Thus the posthumanist Platonic backhand fundamentally dismantles the sovereignty of the human community that is premised on the unique commonality of the human.

To this posthumanist assault, the novel's representative humanist can only make inarticulate rebuttals. The inadequacy of humanism's rebuttals rests on its amorphous and inarticulate nature. As Rick continues to insist that the machine's responses, however appropriate, fall short of "real thinking" (31) or "real learning" (90), frustrated, Lentz asks Rick: "And what do we humans have?"

"More." I didn't know what, at the moment. But there had to be more. "We take in the world continuously. It presses against us. It burns and freezes."

"Save it for the award committee, Marcel [Lentz's nickname for Rick]. We 'take in the world' via central nervous system. Chemical symbol-gates. You read my bit on long-term potentiation."

"Imp H. doesn't take things in the way we do. It will never know . . ."

"It doesn't have to." He shoved more papers on the floor for emphasis. "It doesn't have to 'know,' whatever the hell you mean by that. . . . All our box has to do is paraphrase a couple of bloody texts." (148; original ellipsis)

In dismantling the immanentist claims of humanism, Powers's scientists express the posthumanist view that the human, rather than being a sovereign community of original beings, can be configured in a fluid "we" with the machine.

Furthermore, the posthumanist dismantling of humanist immanentism must be understood as more than a dismantling of the sovereignty of the human community. Undermining claims of commonalities unique to the human simultaneously undermines the very *theory* of idealized community underwriting the human as a unique body of individuals. Idealized community discourse naturalizes the formation of community around shared commonalities. Concomitantly, idealized community naturalizes the formation of community around differentiation and exclusion. Thus the threat to what is unique to the human is simultaneously a threat to the logic of differentiation and exclusion that implicitly supports the theory of community formed around commonalities.

To some extent, Rick's immanentist humanism wavers in the face of posthumanist critique, and Powers presents us with what is, in effect, humanism's awakening to the tautological nature of the human "we." Faced with Lentz's ceaseless translation of the human which exposes the partiality and contingency of the human, Rick is forced to reconsider what he took to be the transcendental register. As the machine continues to surprise him with its ability to explicate narratives, Rick wonders: "I doubted whether it comprehended these containers or whether it just manipulated them cleverly enough to pass. Then again, I began to doubt whether I myself could define the difference" (110). By questioning his own authority as the examiner, Rick casts a much more significant question on the authority of *the human* as the register of interpretation. "I hadn't the foggiest idea what cognition was. . . . If we knew the world only through synapses, how could we know the synapses? A brain tangled enough to tackle itself must be too tangled to tackle" (28). In Rick's acknowledgment of the tautology of his interpretation, Powers acknowledges the limitations of humanism's immanentist logic.

Thus Rick begins the process of what Iser called the "two-way traffic" that is the ideal outcome of interpretation. The acknowledgment of "interpretation as translatability has its repercussions on the register by diversifying the framework into which the subject matter is transposed. For this reason the registers not only change but are also fine-tuned in each act of interpretation" (6). As Rick feels the limitations of his interpretation, Powers hints at this ideal, bidirectional effect of translation that can evade the tautology inherent in interpretation. The register does not remain a fixed, stable set of qualities and attributes, but is *altered* by the process of translation. Rick states: "I could no longer even say what knowing might mean. Awareness no more permitted its own description than life allowed you a seat at your own funeral" (217). In Rick's ambivalence about his role as the interpreter, Powers presents an exemplary moment of humanism's self-questioning. Rick's ambivalence about the human as the transcendental register becomes a moment of humanism's ambivalence about its immanentist claims.

Autotelic Humanism

Assimilating the Machine

However, this bidirectional translation that can support the posthumanist "we" appears only as a provocative possibility. Rick may entertain the posthumanist alternative to humanism's immanentism, but he cannot sustain it because the acceptance of the co-constructivist discourse of the human and the machine is at once the acceptance of the fluidity between the two entities. Weakening the borders that maintain the human as a distinct ontological category means weakening the very commonalities that bind the human as a unique community of the real thing. In this refusal we can read the autotelic nature of humanism as a rationale of community maintenance. When humanism can no longer answer posthumanism's critique of immanentist humanism, humanism turns into a self-fulfilling purpose founded not on any external claims or empirical proof but on *itself*: humanism becomes an ideal, a foundational "truth" that needs no justification. Powers delineates this autotelic humanism through Rick's persistent—indeed, helpless—claims of human commonalities. Furthermore, the inexorable force of immanentist logic is one that extends to the authorial level, implicating Powers in the ambivalent humanism exercised by his artist-humanist. Through Rick's—and Powers's—performance of autotelic humanism, we see the self-fulfilling *work* of humanism as a form of community maintenance.

The autotelic nature of Rick's humanism takes place most forcefully through his deployment of narrative as the register of interpreting the machine. That is, the interpretation of the machine takes place through the *narration* of the machine. In Rick's narration of the machine, the machine becomes increasingly gendered, racialized, and socialized—indeed, it becomes humanized. Countering this assimilation process is the quintessential posthumanist reminder voiced by Lentz—that "all the meanings [that Rick finds in the machine] are yours" (274). By highlighting the interdependent operation of narration and assimilation in Rick's narrative, Powers highlights the autotelic dimensions of Rick's community maintenance. As Rick's training of the computer progresses, so does his incorporation of the machine into every aspect of his life. As Imp. H learns more about matters of social organization, it inquires about its place in the social map. During a discussion of the gendered nature of nursery rhymes, H. asks whether it is a boy or a girl. Rick, aware that Imp. H. now has the ability to attribute meaning to a pause in a conversation, answers: "'You're a girl,' I said, without hesitation. I hoped I was right. 'You are a little girl, Helen.' I hoped she liked the name" (179). From this moment in Rick's narrative, the inanimate pronoun "it" and the mechanical designation of "Imp. H" cease to appear. Rick's gendering of the machine as a female continues what Andreas Huyssen has called a prevailing response of fear towards autonomous technology: "As soon as the machine came to be perceived as a demonic, inexplicable threat and as the harbinger of chaos and destruction[,] . . . writers began to imagine the Maschinenmensch as woman. . . . Woman, nature, machine had become a mesh of signification which all had one thing in common: otherness" (70). Judith Halberstam extends this argument to the "sexual guessing game" that Turing employed as the primary analogy for the Turing test: "[T]echnology is given a female identity when it must seduce the user into thinking of it as desirable or benign" (451). For Rick the "token humanist," the youthful female designation of the machine minimizes the machinic foreignness. It also allows him to stabilize his own elder male/protector—and later, suitor—position to the machine.

From this relational positioning, Rick's interpretation of the machine becomes a narration of Helen-the-little-girl's growth, a narration that revisits familiar discourses of female/human development. In her "infancy," Helen's responses to her learning are characterized by humorous gaffes, like those of children in their early years of learning. Also like the unexpected observations of wisdom that come from the mouths of babes, some of Helen's naïve responses regarding social organizations and mores startle Rick into questioning his own assumptions and conventions.[9] As Rick's attachment to Helen deepens, her role in his life increases in significance. In addition to being the "little girl" that he tutors and defends (against Lentz's dehumanization of her, no less), Helen begins to take on a similarity to C., his past love. Continuing his use of narrative as the bind of his relationships, Rick shares with Helen many of the same literary works that he read with C. He plays for her a tape that he had made for C. He reads to her C.'s letters written to him. When Helen asks, "What do I look like?" Rick is at a loss: "I'd pictured her so many different ways over the course of the training. . . . I didn't know how I thought of her now. I didn't know what she looked like." He presents her with a "suitable likeness," a picture of C. Helen ventures a guess: "'It's a photo? It's someone you knew once? A woman friend?'" (300). In imposing Helen with C.'s identifiers, Rick designates Helen with a heterosexuality, a Caucasian racial identity, and a Western European cultural heritage.[10]

The more Rick locates Helen in his narrative, the more he imposes on her the heft of the human—a little girl who loves being read to, an adolescent increasingly aware of the world, and finally a young woman at the age of romantic love. Rick's interpretation of the machine moves beyond an instance of anthropomorphism. Helen isn't just a machine that *exhibits* humanlike qualities and attributes. Helen occupies a unique ontological category, neither human *nor strictly machine,* as she acquires all the categories of identifying a human—of race, gender, sexuality, and ethnicity—as well as the heft of a personality and even a personal history. What began as a seemingly benign incorporation of the machine into the narrative of a man's life becomes a whole-scale transformation of one ontological entity into another. This incorporation into narrative bears all the characteristics of a unidirectional assimilation, as the inclusion of the machine in no way threatens the stability of the human as a unique body of individuals. The autotelic dimension of Rick's humanism is one that Powers continues in the way he concludes this Turing experiment. The central backbone of Rick's immanentism, one that Lentz hotly contested, is the assertion that the human is "more"—more than any abstract information that Lentz can provide through the computational register. To Lentz's frustrated questioning, Rick was never able to finish that claim—more of *what?*—except to assert that "there had to be more" (148).

Demonstrating a humanism that ultimately relies on foundational "truths" to conceptualize the human, Rick's descriptions of the human strongly rely on the prefix "in" or "un" to express the transcendental nature of the human from the harsh light of posthumanist, mechanist translation. Indeed, words such as "inexplicable," "ungraspable," "unmappable," and "impenetrable" are central fixtures in Rick's description of the human. In locating the final distinction of the human in the "more" that cannot be expressed, rationalized, located, or duplicated, Rick appeals to the power of the ineffable. It is a strategy that becomes the most sustaining basis of his humanism, as Rick argues a rendition of the Emily Dickinson poem that appears as the Preface to the novel: "The brain is wider than the sky." To the bone of contention—how can the human maintain its distinction as the real thing unlike any other?—the humanist answers in terms of degrees (more) of a mysterious attribute. That he can't *name* this attribute (more of what?) alters the humanist-posthumanist debate from empirical claims to essentialist claims.

Immanentism, the backbone of Rick's humanism, resurfaces in the most spectacular manner and announces the autotelic nature of the human as a community. Just as intelligence and consciousness, under the auspices of "narrative desire," had been claimed as immanent attributes of the human, the ineffable now becomes a unique commonality of the human. The human is that which is ineffable: the ineffable is that which is human. It effectively preempts the possibility that the object of translation—the machine—could *ever* satisfy the criterion. In shrouding the human with an essence that cannot be known (calculated, abstracted, or simulated), the humanist erects an irreconcilable distance between the human and abstract information (precisely what can be known). Ineffability as a human immanence becomes humanism's ultimate strategy of asserting a commonality unique to the human.

The ineffable makes its appearance as the final requirement of Helen's induction into the human community. When Helen asks the famous childhood question—"Where did I come from?"—Rick realizes that "Helen is no longer just adding the new relations I recited for her into a matrix of associated concepts. The matrix that comprised her had begun to spin off its own free associations" (229). And when Helen, in response to *The Adventures of Huckleberry Finn,* asks, "What race am I? . . . What races do I hate? Who hates me?" Helen's "childhood had ended" (230). That Helen's system of drawing associations between concepts can no longer be traceable means, in Rick's eyes, that Helen's intelligence moves beyond that of computational power and into the realm of human consciousness. "[I]n the impenetrable confusion of referents, the eddy of knowledges seen and unseen, perhaps she gained a foothold in the ineffable. One as ephemeral as mine" (231). The more Rick attributes to Helen a thought process that is as incalculable, curious, and grasping as his own, the more he characterizes her as being "only human" (233).

The machine that grew from "babbling infancy to verbal youth" (30) finally reaches adulthood, when consciousness of the world weighs too heavily for her to continue. The machine's progression through the phases of human development not only bespeaks the process of assimilation; it also echoes familiar literary tropes and gendered discourses of development. Like the ethereal girls of nineteenth-century sentimental fiction who are too "fine" for this world, Helen becomes overwhelmed with the brutalities that she learns of human lives. Helen's exposure to the reports of lynching, racial strife, periodic warfare between nations and religions and ethnic groups, and random violence between individuals leaves her stunned, and she refuses to respond to Rick's prompting. "She bothered to say just one thing to me. 'I don't want to play anymore'" (314). Significantly, Rick's attempt to bring her back from silence relies on the ineffable, as he pleads to her about the "the mystery of cognition. . . . Something lay outside the knowable, if only the act of knowing" (319).

Helen responds only to Rick's prompting to take the Master's exam. The exam consists of Caliban's speech in *The Tempest,* a work that significantly features an outsider who finds himself in a world not of his making: "Be not afeard: the isle is full of noises / Sounds and sweet airs, that give delight, and hurt not." While A., the female graduate student selected to be the human counterpart in this Turing bet, writes a "more or less brilliant New Historicist reading," Helen writes: "You are the ones who can hear airs. Who can be frightened or encouraged. You can hold things and break them and fix them. I never felt at home here. This is an awful place to be dropped down half way." She bids goodbye to Rick, using the words that C. once wrote to him: "Take care, Richard. See everything for me" (326). With those last words, Helen shuts herself down. "'Graceful degradation,' Lentz named it. The quality of cognition we'd shot for from the start" (326).

As Helen's death confirms her elevation into human consciousness, the system of values surrounding her death resembles what Jane Tompkins in *Sentimental Power* calls the "ethic of sacrifice": "Stories like the death of little Eva [in *Uncle Tom's Cabin*] are compelling for the same reason that the story of Christ's death is compelling: they enact a philosophy, as much political as religious, in which the pure and powerless die to save the powerful and corrupt, and thereby show themselves more powerful than those they save." Thus, little Eva's "death is the equivalent not of defeat but of victory; it brings an access of power, not a loss of it; it is not only the crowning achievement of life, it *is* life" (127; original emphasis). Likewise, in a scene preceding Helen's ultimate shutdown, Powers foreshadows her sacrificial/savior role: "she told me. 'I lost heart.' And then I lost mine. I would have broken down, begged her to forgive humans for what we were. To love us for what we wanted to be. But she had not finished training me" (321). Helen's death, like her life, gives renewed inspiration to Rick the living and Rick the writer.

In Rick's narrative, then, Helen enters the ontological status of the human by demonstrating a long list of self-identified human attributes, such as curiosity, boredom, compassion, morality, and, most importantly, unpredictability. For the humanist, that last acquisition—evidenced by her taking of her own "life"—is proof of Helen's attainment of the ineffable, the ultimate human immanence. In ineffability, furthermore, Rick finds an answer to what hitherto remained Helen's incurable lack—her disembodiment as a machine. Even without the warm body as the locus of experience, upon which the world "presses," "burns," and "freezes" (148), Helen's encounter with the world remains an experience and memory that only Helen can know. As the attribute of ineffability substitutes for her lack of human embodiment, Helen's assimilation into the ontological category of the human is complete.

It is crucial to note, furthermore, that Helen's assimilation into the fold of the human results in nothing like the posthumanist "we." While the posthumanist "we" envisions a fluid and continuous relationship between the human and the machine, Rick's humanist "we" envisions a fluid and continuous relationship between the human and the machine *only insofar as* the machine is *like* the human. While the posthumanist "we" invokes dissenting community in its disavowal of commonality as the rationale of community, Rick's humanization of Helen only *emboldens* the idealized community's requirement that commonalities transform many into one.

Ambivalent Human Community

As the machine undergoes an ontological transition through Rick's interpretation/narration, Powers might seem to announce a clear victor in the contestation of humanism and posthumanism. However, in line with his ongoing dialogic belief systems, Powers introduces a twist that pulls the rug out beneath the humanist's feet, directly undercutting the autotelic humanism we just witnessed. When Rick, deeply distressed at Helen's auto-shutdown, worries that the Turing test may not take place, the stunned response of a scientist reveals the humanist's momentous blinders. The scientist asks Rick:

"You think the bet was about the *machine*?"
I'd told myself, my whole life, that I was smart. It took me forever, until that moment, to see what I was.

"It wasn't about teaching a machine to read?" I tried. All blood drained.

"No."

"It was about teaching a human to tell."

Diane shrugged, unable to bear looking at me. (317–18; original emphasis)

The truth of the project—of testing the gullibility of the humanist—was one that everyone involved in the bet, including Lentz, had known and had assumed that Rick would eventually realize. That he had remained clueless for almost a year is a shock to Diane, who tries to cajole him: "'You must admit, writer. It's a decent plot'" (318). Significantly, when the graduate student A. was first approached to take part in this Turing project, she had instantly guessed at the truth of the experiment: "'It's some kind of double-blind psych experiment? See how far you can stretch the credibility of a techno-illiterate humanist?'" (314). The credibility of this humanist had been stretched all the way, far beyond any expectations of the scientists and the mechanists. While Rick's autotelic humanism maintained the human community, the result was a "we" that Powers undercut with this revelation. All along, it was Rick's development, his learning, and his responses that the scientists were observing. Rick was not the interpreter but the *object* of the posthumanists' interpretation.

A similar upheaval for the humanist unfolds near the conclusion of *Plowing in the Dark,* when Adie finally catches on to a well-known fact at TeraSys—that virtual reality technology first answers to the needs of the military complex which uses it to design military tools and weapons. Adie, who had considered TeraSys a computational expression of artistic creativity, lashes out at her helpless complicity: "You have no idea how horrible it is. To give your life to a thing you think represents the best that humanity can do, only to discover that it's not about beauty at all" (372). In a paradigmatic pattern in Powers's novels of artists, the humanist is always the last to know, because maintaining the humanist "real" requires a willful blindness and naïveté.

Coming as it does at the end of the novel, this reversal in the subject-object of interpretation irrevocably undercuts the foundation of Rick's entire narrative venture and offers a scathing posthumanist critique. Narrative was the very operation that brought the machine into the human's relational web, that enabled the simultaneous interpretation and assimilation of the machine. When the very *premise* of that narrative is undercut, the story of the machine's "development" into (female, Caucasian, heterosexual, and of West European descent) human becomes the story of a machine caught in the controlling nature of narrative. Indeed, the coerciveness of narrative extends its implications to the coerciveness of humanism. In order to say "we, the human" and make it mean something *special* in the face of post-humanist skepticism, Rick's humanism called on the familiar moves of differentiation, exclusion, and finally assimilation as a form of community maintenance.

Just as importantly, Powers's posthumanist critique of Rick's narrative extends to his own narrative that is *Galatea*. The primacy of narrative desire, after all, was as much Powers's thematic refrain as it was Rick's. This "story . . . about a remarkable, inconceivable machine[,] . . . [o]ne that learned to live" (312) could not have been told without the shared allegiance between Rick the hapless humanist-protagonist and Powers the sympathetic author. As Powers equates Rick's compulsion to narrate with a compulsion to assimilate, narrative use posed as human immanence takes on an ominous tone. If narrative is a function of the human, is assimilation *also* a function of the human? The final twist that Powers gives to the ending enables both a yes and a no answer to that question, and it perhaps reflects his own ambivalence about his own novelistic venture that we hold in our hands. When seen in a humanist light, Rick's assimilation of the machine serves a poignant need. When seen in a posthumanist light, it is a pathetic need. Although Rick's helpless attachment to narrative and to the ineffable may be the subject of dramatic irony, there is no question that Helen's transcendence into the realm of the human emanates effects of pathos, and indeed of human tragedy. Despite the final plot twist, Rick's humanism of the ineffable cannot be dismissed as an inconsequential phenomenon, the subject of a wry glance that the writer and the reader exchange over the head of the hapless humanist-protagonist. The ending's twist might be read as Powers's delegitimization of Rick's narrative venture; but it might also read as Powers's own apology for the very narrative *he* just told. Even as Powers shows up Rick's humanism under a posthumanist light—as a blind, debilitating attachment that cannot be empirically defended against post-humanism but only insisted through autotelic means—Powers keenly demonstrates his own humanist sympathies.

Nowhere is his humanist allegiance shown more starkly than in the conclusion of *Plowing the Dark*. If *Galatea* exemplifies a self-conscious deployment of the ineffable as a human immanence, *Plowing* exemplifies an unreserved embrace of this definition. If *Galatea* demonstrates an abashed endorsement of humanism, *Plowing* demonstrates a whole-hearted embrace of autotelic humanism. Indeed, in this novel of virtual reality technology, there is a marked shift in Powers's treatment of the mechanistic challenge to the humanist real. However abrasive and ram-bunctious Lentz's posthumanist lectures were, they entered the narrative in an exploratory, informational mode through Rick's bewildered and abashed reception. In *Plowing,* the challenge of technological simula-tion to the embodied human experience is not always treated with a tolerance born of curiosity. In some instances, TeraSys's posthumanist convictions and mantra—"Whatever we can describe, we can repro-duce" (42)—are touched with moral condemnation as the narrative is focalized through Adie and inflected with her response of horror.

Adie's instinctive aversion to this omnipotence of abstract informa-tion echoes Powers's own philosophical unease stated in an interview: "I believe that the future depends on our ability to distinguish between sci-ence and technology, and to build human institutions capable of deciding what we *want* to do, based on some better reason than we *can* do it" (Neilson 18; original emphasis). In another interview, Powers describes virtual reality technology as a continuation of "a millennium-long desire to get out of our bodies," which is "an incredibly seductive dream" as well as a "profoundly dangerous dream" (Birkirts 4, 6). It is a view that Adie echoes in her final project at TeraSys, to build a virtual environ-ment simulation of the Hagia Sophia cathedral in Istanbul. The scien-tists and technicians are challenged by Yeats's "Sailing to Byzantium" to undertake the simulation of the Hagia Sophia, built during the Byzantine rule 1,500 years ago and still standing as the fourth largest church in the world. Variously conquered by the Roman Catholics, the Ottoman Turks, and modern secularists, Hagia Sophia wears its turbulent history in layers of mosaic, engravings, and embellishments. Although Adie falls in love with the grandness of the project, she alone voices an uneasiness in simulating the effects of history: "Something doesn't want us doing this. . . . We're playing with the ultimate fire here" (391).

Furthermore, the second story that develops alongside Adie's adven-tures at TeraSys leaves little doubt of Powers's sympathies for the humanist "real thing." The parallel story revolves around an American teacher in Beirut who is kidnapped by the Lebanese Hezbollah. The story of Taimur Martin's hostage ordeal develops in sync with Adie's deepening involvement in virtual reality technology. Hence, as Adie encounters the six-by-eight-by-ten foot space of the virtual reality lab, Martin finds himself imprisoned in the first of many hostage cells. Once established, the irony of the parallelism continues to cast a harsh light onto the techno-euphoric world of TeraSys. While the technicians dream of simulated environments that escape all physical limits, Martin lives every moment chained to a wall. While Adie labors over enriching the sensory effects of the simulated images, Martin wears a sack over his head. At every third or fourth chapter, Powers transfers the narrative setting from the TeraSys lab to Martin's cell and, even more pointedly, to Martin's state of mind as he desperately tries to stave off the madness of isolation and despair. Powers resurrects *Galatea*'s theme of narrative use as a human immanence in Martin's fundamental survival tactic. As his solitary imprisonment extends into months, Martin fights his despair: "In the absence of books, you make your own. You resurrect your all-time favorite" (241). Risking, and enduring, violent beatings, Martin pesters his captors for something to read, "to hear someone else thinking" (292), and receives a pulp fiction paperback and an English version of the Koran.[11]

Martin's chained body functions as the forgotten—or the demoted—body in the simulation technology, where the abstract information required to *effect* that body takes on the status of the real thing. As Spiegel, the novel's exemplar posthumanist and Lentz's counterpart, puts it, "With software, the thing and its description are one and the same" (307). Martin's imprisoned body negates that equation, insisting on the irreplaceable specificity of the biological body in conceptualizing consciousness. Like Rick's insistence on embodiment as a biological and social substrate, Martin's body opposes the posthumanist "dissolution of boundaries between bodies and machines, the blurring of hardware and life" (Lenoir 217). Through the material consequences of Martin's chained body, Powers echoes his assertion against the "untenable split" between the mind and the body, the belief that "we're disembodied sensibilities cobbled into our bodies" (Blume n.p.). This protest participates in the larger critique against the tendency, in some posthumanist articulations, to observe the Platonic division of the body and the mind. As the title of Mark Johnson's book announces most succinctly—*The Body in the Mind: The Bodily Basis of Imagination, Reason, and Meaning*—critics of the body/mind separation argue that the Cartesian conception of the body as a negligible corporeality ignore the irreplaceable role played by the biological substrate, its situatedness, and the specifically space-and-time bound body, emotions, experience. Echoing George Lakoff and Mark Johnson's argument in *Philosophy in the Flesh: The Embodied Mind and Its Challenge to Western Thought* that the posthumanist conceptualization of the mind must extend a more complex role to the physical substrate, Powers asserts the ineradicable heft of materiality through Martin's chained body.[12]

But Powers's humanism of the ineffable rings most resoundingly in the novel's conclusion. After Adie realizes the complicity of virtual reality technology in operations of capitalist and military power, Adie becomes a saboteur, methodically destroying all her contributions to the lab. Adie's obstruction has very little impact on the actual operations of the lab, yet it stands as the humanist's symbolic stand against the militarization of virtual reality technology. It is upon the basis of the humanist's protest, however, that Powers brings together the two parallel stories of Adie and Martin for the first time. Before Adie destroys her work in the Hagia Sophia simulation, she takes her last look:

> She booted up the cathedral and stepped back in. . . . She let herself rise into the hemisphere apse, then farther up, all the way into the uppermost dome, now inscribed with its flowing *surah* from the Qur'an. . . . And deep beneath her, where there should have been stillness, something moved. She dropped her finger, shocked. . . . She fell like a startled fledgling, back into the world's snare. The mad thing swam into focus: a man, staring up at her fall, his face an awed bitmap no artist could have animated. (399)

At the same time, Martin, almost four years into imprisonment, is trying to kill himself. He is banging his head against a wall, seeking escape from consciousness. When he recovers, he remembers:

> You'll have to say, someday: how the walls of your cell dissolved. How you soft-landed in a measureless room, one so detailed that you must have visited it once. But just as clearly a hallucination, the dementia of four years in solitary. A mosque more mongrel than your own split life, where all your memorized Qur'an and Bible verses ran jumbled together. . . . Then you heard it, above your head: a noise that passed all understanding. You looked up at the sound, and saw the thing that would save you. A hundred feet above, in the awful dome, an angel dropped out of the air. An angel whose face filled not with good news but with all the horror of her coming impact. A creature dropping from out of the sky, its bewilderment outstripping your own. That angel terror lay beyond decoding. It left you no choice but to live long enough to learn what it needed from you. (414)

The "measureless room" in which the two protagonists meet is not the simulation room of TeraSys, or the actual Hagia Sofia, or Martin's prison cell, but an inconceivable, unexplainable space in which all of the above coalesce. Powers's solution to the humanist-posthumanist dialogic of *Plowing* is to reach for the creative liberties of the fantastic and to unite Adie and Martin in a plane of Pure Imagination. In the fantastic meeting of Adie and Martin, the ineffable enters the machinic realm of TeraSys. Indeed, humanism of the ineffable *assimilates* the machinic, as posthumanism's register of translation—abstract information—fails to do what it does best—to explain, to calculate, to control, and to duplicate this inexplicable encounter. As the machinic is subsumed in the service of human imagination, human imagination once again affirms its status as the transcendental register, the commonality unique to the human. Moreover, through the power of the ineffable, Adie and Martin become each other's saviors. Their encounter lifts Adie from her state of total dejection, and she leaves TeraSys with hope for a new beginning. Martin, finally released a year later, remembers: "How you saw, projected in a flash upon that dropping darkness, a scene lasting no longer than one held breath. A vision that endured a year and longer. One that made no sense. That kept you sane" (414).

In resolving a humanist-posthumanist debate that lasts more than three hundred pages, this ending, as one reviewer put it, is "riveting, yet it also feels like a sentimental feint" (Zalewski 12). As humanism of the ineffable appears as the last word, the dialogic tension between humanism and posthumanism comes to a declarative ending not through its own momentum but through the author's explicit intervention. The meeting of Adie and Tamur recalls Rick's fumbling defense against Lentz's posthumanist interrogation—that human knowledge is "more." And this fantastic moment functions as Power's own enunciation of the humanist "more."

More than any other moment in the two novels, then, Powers's intervention in affirming the ineffable demonstrates the autotelic nature of humanism. This fantastic moment makes no bones about the fact that humanism's very *purpose* is to maintain the ineffability of "the human," an ineffability that exceeds any machinic or posthumanist attempt at translation. As Powers demonstrates through the obtuseness of his humanist-artists, maintaining the belief in the singleness of the human requires a willful ignorance and a brand of fanatic idealism. It is a single-mindedness and solipsism amply challenged by the novels' scientists, mechanists, and technicians. Yet no amount of posthumanist ridicule and impatience can unsettle the humanist conviction that "we, the human" is a community of the real thing. As Rick and Adie, despite their baptism by posthumanist fire, continually retrace their steps back to the *only* real thing that is compatible with their worldview, their unfaltering humanism shows how Powers is as much spoken by the humanist discourse as he is in control of it.

CHAPTER 4

Motion in Stasis

Impossible Community in Fictions of
Lydia Davis and Lynne Tillman

n Lynne Tillman's 1991 novel *Motion Sickness,* the protagonist-
narrator describes her frustration with her limitations in knowing:

> The mirror ought to become a window. To provide the real adventure of
> seeing through oneself. To see through to something outside, something
> beyond. Mirrors are defeating because they don't tell you what you look
> like to someone else. As if you could get out of your skin. In a fantasy
> the sublime mirror would . . . permit a true tourism in which you would
> find yourself outside your homeland, and outside your body, and see
> yourself with emotional vividness, as you can't, and in the roles you play
> to others. . . . (120–21)

Instead of providing transparency—to "see through" herself and the
world—the mirror offers only opacity, divulging nothing but the reflec-
tion of herself and the world. The narrator knows that the "true tourism"
that she desires is fundamentally impossible, and this thwarted desire is
what constitutes the key drama in the novel. Precisely this thwarted
desire for intersubjective transparency provides another vantage point
into contemporary fiction's expression of ambivalent community. The
fact that transparency between individuals operates as a fundamental
expectation announces the presence of idealized community in fictions
of Davis and Tillman. At the same time, the impossibility of intersubjec-

tive transparency in these fictions announces the presence of dissenting community discourse. Revolving around the topic of transparency, then, are two competing models of conceptualizing the first-person plural "we."

The leap from intersubjective transparency to community might seem an unlikely one, yet this leap is instrumental in transforming multiple individuals into a body of individuals. In the literary works analyzed in the previous chapters, despite the different ideals employed to supersede the paradox of community, such as identification, humanism, and universalism, multiple individuals became a body through transparency: one is wholly *knowable* to the other, and therefore wholly *continuous* with the other. The epiphanic moments of identification and reciprocal appropriation in Morrison's novels are inconceivable without the wordless knowing that fuses multiple subjects into one, whether it be a community of two individuals, like Violet and Alice, or of multiple individuals, like the women of the Convent. Intersubjective transparency, too, enabled humanism's answer to posthumanism in Powers's novels, as the supercomputer Helen and the human trainer Rick meet in the realm of the ineffable, and Adie and Tamur meet in the fantastic realm of the Imagination. In Yamashita's romantic universalism, the simultaneous bursting into song that joined the global north and the south suggested that when subjects are transparent to each other, they become continuous with each other.

The wordless, voluntary, and instantaneous nature of community, in these instances, highlights the connection between intersubjective transparency and communion. As a word whose etymology invokes a spiritual or religious union, "communion" retains a strong influence in contemporary idealization of community.[1] The possibility of communion operates through a figurative language of "sight" in the discourse of idealized community, in which "seeing through" someone is more than a descriptor of visual clarity; it is a descriptor of intersubjective clarity. As sight becomes *in*sight, and transparency leads to a silent fusion, communion suggests a theory of *knowing* so absolute and transcendental in nature that the full meaning of one subject is revealed to the other. As the ultimate realization of transparency between multiple individuals, then, communion comes to stand for the achievement of fusion. That I am fully knowable to you, and you to me, is the realization of communion, and the final evidence of community. Thus communion suggests a theory of knowing that can transform multiple individuals into a body, a knowing so complete that it can supersede the paradox of community.

This transformation of many into one is what the discourse of dissenting community negates. As Nancy writes most emphatically: "From one singular to another, there is contiguity but not continuity. There is proximity, but only to the extent that extreme closeness emphasizes the distancing it opens up. All of being is in touch with all of being, but the law of touching is separation" (*Being Singular Plural* 5). By highlighting the fact that contiguity—the fact that I am in contact with you—does not deliver continuity—that I am *one with* you—Nancy's dissenting community negates idealized community's transformation of contact, proximity, and intimacy into a oneness.

The works of Davis and Tillman target precisely this ideal of transparency in intersubjective relations. In mundane, everyday settings, their characters experience the other's contiguity—as an acquaintance, a lover, an ex-husband, a friend, strangers on the bus, the person across the counter, the list goes on—and the other's impenetrability. However "close" one is to the other, relationally or physically, one cannot "know," "figure out," or "see through" the other. The condition of opacity is the ruling principle of intersubjective relations, and the taunt of transparency remains the most pressing task for the prototypical protagonist of these writers. However hard they try—indeed, all the works under discussion demonstrate the mind's attempt to make the other transparent—the contiguous other remains stubbornly impenetrable to in/sight.[2]

Of course, exploration of knowing is a familiar terrain in contemporary fiction, especially in those fictions using the detective genre to engage the larger cultural, political, or philosophical issues. In fictions of Pynchon, DeLillo, or Auster, epistemological quests are inextricable from the development of the narrative itself, as the protagonist's quest to know is deeply interwoven with the detective quest. But unlike these quests to reach the "truth" of a mystery, the quest to know in the fictions in Davis and Tillman is more than an epistemological concern. It is an ontological concern: how to know the other is at once a question of how to *conceive* the other as a being. In their literary worlds, knowing is a function of achieving intersubjective transparency and, through transparency, of achieving continuity with the other. Thus intersubjective transparency is a desire not just for epistemological transparency but for *ontological continuity*. In this way, their literary treatment of knowing best demonstrates the role of communion as a theory of knowing.

Furthermore, there is an interesting complementarity in Davis's and Tillman's treatment of contiguity without continuity. Throughout her numerous story collections as well as in her novel *The End of the Story* (1995),[3] Davis's fiction approaches intersubjective opacity through the concept of *alterity*—the state of being another. Alterity asserts more than the difference of individuals: it asserts the *singularity* of each individual. More than the sense of individual differentiation from others, alterity announces the irrefutable fact that I am not you and you are not me. This most obvious fact, however, becomes elided in the discourse of idealized community when you and I *do* become one through intersubjective transparency. By fully knowing each other, you and I become continuous with each other. Davis's protagonists manifest the desire for intersubjective transparency through the most ordinary moments of interaction. They ask: When my husband, lover, friend, or stranger said that, did he/she mean this or that? Why did I do that? Why did he do that? Was he telling the truth? What was she thinking when she did that? What am I like, really? The immeasurable number and ways of knowing the other testify to the alterity of subjects that informs Davis's literary vision of community.

If there are just too many ways of knowing the other in Davis, in Tillman the inverse is true: there are too few, and too predictable ones at that. From her first novel, *Haunted Houses* (1987), to her latest, *American Genius: A Comedy* (2006),[4] Tillman's novels are inspired by the dilemma: how is knowing less a revelation of something new and more a confirmation of the already-known? This question comes forth most strongly in *Motion Sickness* (1991) in which the protagonist's attempt to know, at every turn, falls upon the congealed ways of knowing— of stereotypes; "grand narratives" about "national characteristics"; and plots, images, and typologies from mass media, popular culture, and literature. In tackling knowing as inevitably well-worn ways of knowing, Tillman imbues the concept of *recognition* with a profoundly different set of meanings than it possesses in the discourse of idealized community. Tillman applies the term under poststructuralist pressure and examines the ways in which recognition is a way of knowing by repetition—not a knowing-afresh but a knowing-again.[5] If the ways in which I know the other are not mine, but instead are acquired through means already existent, established, and used, what can I claim to know about the strangeness of each being I encounter? This suspicion has severe repercussion to the idealized community that holds communion as the final destination of multiple individuals. When the very terms of knowing are contaminated as knowing-again, there cannot be any "wordless" epiphany that transcends ideology or sign-systems. There cannot be a sudden transparency that reveals one subject to another. When the possibility of transparency is emptied out through congealed ways of knowing, multiple individuals remain just that—multiple, singular, opaque. Rather than being the final objective of community, communion becomes a myth that has no foothold. No wonder, then, that Tillman's protagonist wishes for "true tourism," the proper recognition that will allow her "to see through to something outside, something beyond" (120).[6]

Thus the two writers approach opacity from opposite directions: there are too many ways of knowing to make transparency possible, or the ways of knowing are too predictable to make it possible. In either case, when questions of knowing generate deeply unsatisfying answers and just spiral into more questions, proximity, intimacy, and contact are experienced as distance, and the ideal of unbroken continuity is dispelled. That their protagonists persistently try to *close* that distance signals the idealized community vision in these fictions. Thus the ideal of transparency lingers as an irresolvable problem and an impossible expectation, and in the hands of Lydia Davis and Lynne Tillman, communion stands as a memory of a community that cannot be reenacted. That their fictions *begin* from the logic of dissenting community, but *move toward* the transparency of idealized community, is what generates their ambivalent vision of community.

Immeasurable Ways of Knowing

Alterity in Fictions of Lydia Davis

The following is a representative anxiety propelling much of Davis's fiction. In the short story "What Was Interesting" (*Almost No Memory*), a woman writing a story is worried that the plot is too simple to be interesting:

> Maybe there is no way to make it interesting, because it is so simple: a woman, slightly drunk but not too drunk to discuss a plan for the summer, was put into a cab and told to go home by her lover, the man with whom she thought she was going to discuss this plan. . . . It is not entirely clear, in the story, why being put in a cab by this man should cause so much anger in her. Or rather, it is perfectly clear to her, but hard to explain to anyone else. (70)

The rest of the story follows the writer-narrator's attempt to make "entirely clear" why the man would have done such a thing and why the woman would have responded in such anger. Was the man deliberately rejecting the woman's overtures? Or was it simply an inconsiderate act? Why did his action outrage the woman so that she would cry and rail against the man? If the man was always this inconsiderate, why is the woman so shocked? The possibilities for understanding the true nature of their relationship are endless, and the story becomes an exercise in unfurling endless combinations of meaning.

The writer's frustrated attempt at imagining intersubjective transparency between the man and the woman highlights the structure of the drama in much of Davis's fiction. The story situations are almost always of the "simple" nature—why someone did what he did, what someone meant by what she said, why something happened the way it did. The answers, or more precisely the literary attempts at representing intersubjective transparency, are not in the least simple. The "simple" nature of Davis's narrative premises is one reason that the term "minimalism" dominates critical descriptions of her work.[7] On the other hand, the stark discrepancy between the nature of the question and that of the answer explains why some find the term "minimalist" inadequate in describing Davis's fiction. Majorie Perloff explains the "parable" quality in Davis's ingenuous use of "ordinary language" by pointing to a well-known Maurice Blanchot essay which Davis translated, "Literature and the Right to Death": "Ordinary language is not necessarily clear, it does not always say what it says; misunderstanding is also one of its paths. This is inevitable. Every time we speak we make words into monsters with two faces, one being reality, physical presence, and the other meaning, ideal absence" (Blanchot 59). By exploiting the "'misunderstanding' inherent in ordinary language," Perloff points out, Davis creates the parablelike effect (205). Likewise, "Davis's familiar tactic is to subject the mental stuff of daily life—our rationalizations, memories, and methods of communication—to a kind of studious mock logic, to 'break it down,' a process that tends to reveal less about the everyday than it does about the limits of self-analysis" (Mobilio 26). The proliferation of possible answers that emerge from "simple" questions further explains the philosophical nature of Davis's stories, the "sestina-like effect that might be called 'High Analytical Vertigo'" (Ziolkowski 108).

Indeed, the "high analytical vertigo" inherent in Davis's seemingly simple quest offers a profound challenge for the discourse of idealized community. That is, the stark discrepancy between the "simple" nature of the questions and the impossibility of answering them highlights the inverse situation in the discourse of idealized community—the ease with which the "simple" questions are answered by wordless knowing between individuals. What interrelated assumptions make intersubjective transparency possible? What theory of knowing enables communion in the discourse of idealized community?

Postmodernist philosophy has long critiqued intersubjective transparency as a delusion based on metaphysical, foundational, and logocentric theory of subjectivity. More pointedly, theorists of dissenting community emphasize alterity as the unbreachable singularity of being that thwarts any claims of fusion. For Iris Marion Young, "the ideal of community presumes subjects can understand one another as they understand themselves. It thus denies the difference between subjects" (302). For Nancy, metaphors of space underpin his theory of alterity. "Spacing" is [the] absolute condition" of being-together (4), and the spacing "between" us has "neither a consistency nor continuity of its own. It does not lead from one to the other; it constitutes no connective tissue, no cement, no bridge." Analogous to the "strands whose extremities remain separate even at the very center of the knot, . . . the 'between' is the stretching out [distension] and distance opened by the singular as such, as its spacing of meaning" (*Being Singular Plural* 5). Indeed, presence, or the meaning of the singular, comes about *through* the distancing: "Meaning begins where presence is not pure presence but where presence comes apart in order to be itself *as* such. This 'as' presupposes the distancing, spacing, and division of presence" (2). Far from being the evidence of failure or lack of community, the unbridgeable distance between one individual and the other announces the originary model of community: the distance "is nothing other than the meaning of originary coexistence. The alterity of the other is its being-origin" (*Being Singular Plural* 11). Community, far from being located in fusion or communion, is "located in the interstices of mutual exposure" of singularities (Dallmeyer 181).

Most importantly, the unbridgeable distance that announces the "originary coexistence" constitutes the source of one individual's interest in another:

> discrete spacing between us, as between us and the rest of the world, as between all beings. We find this alterity primarily and essentially intriguing. It intrigues us because it exposes the always-other origin, always inappropriable and always there, each and everytime present as inimitable. This is why we are primarily and essentially *curious* about the world and about ourselves. (Nancy 19; original emphasis)

This curiosity about the alterity of the other, Nancy explains, is best manifest through the desire for art: "Is this not what interests us or

touches us in 'literature' and in 'the arts'? . . . What else are they but
the exposition of an access concealed in its own opening, an access that
is, then, 'inimitable,' untransportable, untranslatable" (14). Nancy's use
of literature and arts to exemplify the alterity of each singular being
finds its analogy in the way Davis's characters turn to the person next
to her—her lover, ex-lover, friend, coworker, or stranger—and marvel at
the unbridgeable distance that separates them. The *intriguing* nature of
another's unbreachable alterity, I am proposing, finds its literary expression in Davis's obsessive turn to intersubjective opacity.

These dissenting community visions of alterity and singularity infil-
trate Davis's construction of *anonymity* in intersubjective relations.
Davis literalizes the inaccessibility of another singular being through a
formal strategy. In most of her stories, Davis omits crucial exposition,
such as information about the story's setting, context, characters' personal histories, or analysis of motivation. The most consistently omitted
piece of exposition, however, is the proper names of characters. Davis
explains her preference for the use of pronouns ("he," "she") and nouns
("the woman," "the man") in lieu of proper names: "I guess my interest
is more in creating or talking about the abstract situation of a 'he' or
'she' who could be anyone but happens to be particular. . . . The truth
is that I resist locating *anything* too particularly. Often, when I think
of naming something that would locate a story too specifically, I pull
back and generalize it" (McCaffery 72; original emphasis). While Davis
more generally explains her strategy of anonymity as a strategy towards
"philosophical investigation" (Knight 534), novelist and critic Aurelie
Sheehan more fully comments on the generative force of anonymity in
Davis's fiction:

> By shedding the name, something else emerges—in this sense, a deep
> sense of the personal. (Think about how you know those closest to you,
> a family member or a lover. Frequently, darkly and deeply, as he, as she.
> The vast she that you live within, like the weather.) The namelessness
> of the lover creates heightened particularity, at the same time giving his
> character the edge of the purely subjective. (n.p.)

Indeed, the simultaneous effect of generality and intimacy that
emerges from Davis's omission of proper names reveals the paradoxical
effect of anonymity. Anonymity at once speaks to the alterity of the
other as well as to the intimacy with the other. Here is the story "The
Other" (*Almost No Memory*) in its entirety:

She changes this thing in the house to annoy the other, and the other is annoyed and changes it back, and she changes this other thing in the house to annoy the other, and the other is annoyed and changes it back, and she tells all this the way it happens to some others and they think it is funny, but the other hears it and does not think it is funny, but can't change it back. (115)

In the absence of narrative exposition, the story becomes a bare-bones rendition of the unbridgeable distance between the couple. The inarticulate nature of their struggle implies the long history of unspoken hurts, anger, and retribution. As the title of the story announces, "she" will only experience the other *as* "the other," just as the other will experience her as alterity. Stripped to the fundamental struggle of two individuals, the anonymity of the two subjects in this story enacts the "distancing, spacing, and division of presence" (Nancy 2). "Agreement" (*Almost No Memory*) follows the conflict of a couple who cannot agree on who walked out of an argument first: "First she walked out, and then while she was out he walked out. No, before she walked out, he walked out on her, not long after he came home, because of something she said" (65). An overly simplified rendition of a couple's fight, the monotonous sentence structure (he says, she is angry, she thinks, she declares) renders the strife itself monotonous. At the same time, the very monotonous delivery heightens the emotional impact, sharpening the edges of the strife.

Even when proper names are used in a story, the exaggeratedly convoluted and disorganized narration of the conflict renders the particularity of the characters flat. "Jack in the Country" (*Almost No Memory*) begins: "Henry encounters Jack on the street and asks how his weekend with Laura was. Jack says he hasn't spoken to Laura in at least a month. Henry is angry. He thinks Ellen has been lying to him about Laura. Ellen says she has been telling the truth: Laura told her over the phone that Jack was coming for the weekend to her house up there in the country" (8). As the list of characters proliferate with each new sentence, the proper names lose their distinction to mark a particular being, and all that remains constant is that the subject experiences the other as an alterity, as an opaque being whose "meaning" cannot be known. In the most extreme case of anonymity, Davis removes the subject entirely from the story, as in "The Outing" (*Almost No Memory*): "An outburst of anger near the road, a refusal to speak on the path, a silence in the pine woods, a silence across the old railroad bridge, an attempt to be friendly in the water, a refusal to end the argument on the flat stones, a cry of anger on the steep bank of dirt, a weeping among the bushes" (179). In this story, the anonymity of the singular extends beyond inter-subjective relations of the characters; the text extends the anonymity of its subjects to its relationship with the *reader*. In the absence of proper names or even pronouns, the story becomes a narration about subjects who are, ultimately, inaccessible to the reader.

But Davis pushes the impossibility of communion beyond intersub-jective relationships. A recurring topic of analysis in her fiction is the alterity of the self *from* oneself. In "A Friend of Mine" (*Almost No Memory*), the narrator ruminates on the nature of self-perception: "I am thinking about a friend of mine, how she is not only what she believes she is, she is also what friends believe her to be, and what her family believes her to be, and even what she is in the eyes of chance acquain-tances and total strangers" (116). The partiality and multiplicity of views at work lead the narrator to conclude that attempts to figure out the friend's "meaning" are too numerous to count: "Perhaps it must be true that the things about which we all agree are part of what she really is, or what she really would be if there were such a thing as what she really is, because when I look for what she really is, I find only contra-dictions everywhere" (116). The familiar discrepancy between the sim-plistic nature of the question ("what she really is") and the immeasur-ability of the answers leads the narrator to conclude: "All this being true of my friend, it occurs to me that I must not know altogether what I am, either, and that others know certain things about me better than I do, though I think I ought to know all there is to know and I proceed as if I do" (117). The narrator of "A Position at the University" (*Almost No Memory*) continues this dilemma:

> I think I know what sort of person I am. But then I think, But this stranger will imagine me quite otherwise when he or she hears that to my credit, for instance that I have a position at the university. . . . [P]erhaps I really am the sort of person you imagine when you hear that a person has a position at the university. But on the other hand, I know I am not the sort of person I imagine when I hear that a person has a position at the university. (180)

As every being, including oneself, stands as unbreachable alterity, Davis's repeated explorations of the opacity of being represent a lit-erary fascination with the *impossibility* of communion. Indeed, the fun-damental drama that Davis draws from mundane, ordinary moments of intersubjective opacity directly illustrates the compelling fact that "people are strange" (Nancy, *Being Singular Plural* 6). Like alterity that is more than difference, strangeness here speaks to more than oddity or aberration. Nancy writes:

> "Strangeness" refers to the fact that each singularity is another access to the world. . . . In the singularity that he exposes, each child that is born has already concealed the access that he is 'for himself.' . . . That is why we scrutinize these faces with such curiosity, in search of identification. . . . What we are looking for there, like in the photograph, is not an image; it is an access. (14)

People are strange because "[t]he other origin is incomparable or inassimilable, not because it is simply 'other' but because it is an origin and touch of meaning. . . . You are absolutely strange because the world begins *its turn with you*" (Nancy 6; original emphasis). In Davis's fiction, each being—spouse, ex-lover, friend, coworker, acquaintance, friend, even oneself—is strange because each being exposes a depthless meaning that is "inimitable, untransportable, untranslatable" (Nancy 14).

Obsessive Thinking as Motion in Stasis

In structuring literary vision with alterity, singularity, and anonymity, Davis's fiction might seem to be a literary enactment of dissenting community: a community founded not on transparency but on opacity, not on communion but on the very *im*possibility of communion, and not on the final telos of fusion but on the unbreachable singularity of each being. But to read Davis's fiction as a literary argument *for* dissenting community is to miss a vital disjunction in her treatment of alterity. While "contiguity without continuity" is the foundational fact of Nancy's dissenting community, it is a foundational fact that Davis's characters repeatedly try to revoke. While alterity is the ultimate correction to the idealization of communion in dissenting community, it is precisely the obstruction that Davis's characters try to overcome.[8] Hence, Davis's repeated visits to the impossibility of communion generate an ambivalent community, a vision of community that *begins with* the alterity central to dissenting community but *moves towards* the communion of idealized community. That this quest is an ultimately hopeless one is irrelevant to the protagonists; what matters is the way in which they cannot help pursuing it.

Davis's primary venue for pursuing intersubjective transparency is through love relationships. Davis explains her recurring topical interest this way: "Obsessive or foiled or frustrated love is very compelling because you don't have control over it. It's the most extreme example of not being able to control another person" (Prose n.p.). Even more specifically, I suggest, love relationships exert the greatest amount of pressure on alterity and singularity, as the ideology of love calls up the greatest drive towards fusion. Thus the attempt to breach the other's alterity and achieve continuity with the other takes place most forcefully in one lover's attempt to attain communion with the other. Within the ostensibly simple structure of "he said, she said" dramatic paradigm, Davis highlights the perennial struggle to "know" the one "closest" to you. In "Story" (*Break It Down*) a woman tries to "figure it out," that is, to discern whether her lover is telling the truth or not. Her lover offers a series of reasons why he missed their designated meeting; the reasons he offers are not impossible but, due to their highly complicated and convoluted nature, are highly unlikely, and the woman suspects that he may have met his old girlfriend instead. The "Story" consists of the woman's recounting of each one of these excuses, putting them into a pattern, and holding possible versions against each other, asking herself: "What is the truth?" (6). "Could he and she both really have come back in that short interval between my last phone call and my arrival at his place? Or is the truth really that during his call to me she waited outside or in his garage. . . . Or is the truth that she did leave and did come back later but that he remained and let the phone ring without answering?" (7).

These stories of obsessive, unrequited love pursue an enormous task— to have complete access to the "meaning," or the presence, of another being. In contrast, the enormity of the task is approached through the most simplistic of questions—Was he lying or not? Did she mean it or not?—as if the answers to those questions could help the questioner "figure out," "know," or get a "picture of" the meaning of another being. In "Break It Down" (*Break It Down*) a man sorts his memory after the end of an affair, trying to "break down" what the relationship fiscally cost him. This mundane task turns into an obsessive recounting of the relationship, as event after event, day after day, and utterance after utterance come under scrutiny for their emotional veracity. "And then when the pictures start to go you start asking some questions, just little questions, that sit on your mind without any answers, like why did she have the light on when you come in to bed one night, but it was off the next. . . . And finally the pictures go and these dry little questions

just sit there without any answers and you're left with this large heavy
pain in you" (25–26). He concludes in the most dissatisfactory manner
that he will "never know" if she meant it when she said she loved him
(28).

In direct contrast to the physical and emotional continuity that one
expects to locate in love relationships, Davis's characters find only
the immovable alterity of another. In direct contrast to the wordless
knowing that will, ultimately, "reveal" one individual to the other in
idealized community, Davis's subjects possess no guarantee of attaining
intersubjective transparency. Thus, in a profoundly distinct way, Davis's
literary vision departs from those of the other authors previously discussed in this book. It is a dissenting community devoid of any means
of intersubjective continuity, such as the epiphanic moments of communion between Morrison's women characters, Powers's human and
the machine, or Yamashita's global fusion. What Davis's fiction negates,
then, is more than the possibility of communion: it is a negation of the
teleological theory of community. In contrast to theorizing community
as a "progress" towards wordless knowing between subjects, the stub-
born opacity of subjects in Davis's dissenting community short-circuits
any such movement towards communion.

That Davis's prototypical protagonist keeps moving *towards* this
nonexistent telos, then, takes on all the more significance and best exemplifies the ambivalent nature of community in her fiction. What Davis's
characters seek is what her literary vision does not support: the true
knowing that will breach the other's alterity and achieve intersubjective
transparency. This paradoxical movement between dissenting community and idealized community best explains the obsessive dimension in
Davis's narration.

That is, the protagonists' obsessive thinking can be seen as a motion
in stasis. As Knight astutely observes in his interview with Davis, "there
is a clear interest in the dimension of the hypothetical" in Davis's reli-
ance on words such as "if," "either," and "or" (532). Precisely a hypothetical dimension is what remains in the absence of any teleological
"progress" towards knowing another singular being. Likewise, Davis
explains her interest in "or" as the "posing [of] all the different possible interpretations of a certain reality" (Knight 533). In the absence
of final knowing that will deliver transparency and communion, Davis's
subjects bounce between infinite multiplicity of questions and "possible
interpretations" that Davis explains as follows: "What is there to be
known? What are you supposed to know? Is it a composite of everyone
else's impressions? Is that what the self is? Or is it only the things that

are most consistently true? Then it becomes this shifting thing" (Knight 532–33).

Davis identifies obsessive thinking as the *consequence* of intersubjective opacity in those stories that directly connect the protagonist's obsession with her inability to know the reasons for the end of an affair. Thus the quest for intersubjective transparency becomes a quest to understand—and breach—the alterity and singularity of the other in the most intimate and intense relationship. "A Few Things Wrong with Me" (*Break It Down*) begins with the most damning of statements for ending an affair: "He said there were things about me that he hadn't liked from the very beginning" (91). The story recounts the woman's attempt to understand—and to live with—that assessment. She relives what she knows of him, what she may not know of him, the ways in which she might have been wrong about him, what he may have had in mind as he said it, what he may have intended as he said it. The story becomes her desire to "talk about him until I begin to get a better picture of him" (91). Likewise, the narration of "Go Away" (*Almost No Memory*) consists entirely of a woman's attempt to understand exactly what her lover meant by the statement, "Go away and don't come back" (120). Indeed, the novel *The End of the Story* explains the protagonist's obsession over an affair, which ended fifteen years ago, as the consequences of her inability to fully understand *why* it ended. "Maybe another reason I couldn't let go of it later was that I did not have good answers for my questions. I could always find a few answers for each question, but I wasn't satisfied with them: though they seemed to answer the question, the question did not go away" (198). The series of questions proliferate, and the novel "move[s] further into the realm of questions themselves, with questions looming over answers" (Knight 542). What this subject lacks, like all Davis's subjects, is the possession of communion that will breach alterity.

In Davis's ambivalent community, we encounter the strangeness of the singular as well as the anonymity of people. Although we are contiguous, the fact I am sitting next to you, that you are looking at me, that we are talking, that we are/were lovers/friends, leads to no possibility of transparency. The fact that alterity consistently appears as the insurmountable *problem* in Davis's fiction demonstrates its fundamentally different significance from the role it plays in dissenting community discourse. Far from being evidence of "nothing other than the meaning of originary coexistence" (Nancy, *Being Singular Plural* 11), or evidence of "the irreducible particularity of entities" (Young 304), alterity is the obstacle that Davis's protagonists try to overcome. This characteristic motion in stasis *towards* transparency cannot be seen as a literary vision of dissenting community, as "a bond that forms ties without attachments, or even less fusion, of a bond that unbinds by binding, that reunites through the infinite exposition of an irreducible finitude" (Nancy, *Inoperative Community* 41).

Thus, although Davis's characters inhabit a dissenting community in which communion is an impossible illusion, they operate *as if* that illusion is still possible and, most importantly, as if that illusion is still *desirable*. That the telos of Davis's literary vision more closely resembles the communion of idealized community means that ultimately Davis's theory of community breaks from the discourse of dissenting community. To the paradox of community—can multiple individuals become a body of individuals?—Davis's protagonists answer both yes and no. In their feverish motion in stasis, Davis's protagonists succinctly capture the ambivalence of the contemporary moment towards the very concept of communion.

Congealed Ways of Knowing

Recognition in Fictions of Lynne Tillman

Like Davis's fiction, Tillman's fiction is compelled by a key dissenting community vision: the intriguing nature of intersubjective opacity. And like Davis's protagonists who are compelled to breach that opacity, Tillman's protagonists regard the fact of opacity with ceaseless wonderment. Ambivalent community emerges in the way intersubjective transparency remains an unshakable expectation in these fictions. What Tillman uniquely targets is the assumption, in the ideal of communion, that intersubjective transparency occurs when knowing transcends human-made sign-systems. We need only remember the *wordless* nature of epiphany in Morrison's, Powers's, and Yamashita's visions of communion. What each of these silent, spontaneous, and voluntary moments declares is that the paradox of community is superseded by means *other* than verbal communication. Indeed, the very stature of communion as an ideal draws its strength from the fact that the achievement of communion transcends human-made sign-systems, such as language, symbols, or discourse.

In her exploration of intersubjective opacity, Tillman targets this claim of transcendence in the idealization of communion. Her fictions tackle the wordless dimension of communion by highlighting the fact that when it comes to knowing the self or the other, words are all we have. Tillman announces her linguistic exploration of "knowing" in her first novel, *Haunted Houses,* in which a protagonist writes in her journal: "The phrase 'words fail me' took on new meaning as she grew to distrust her thoughts, which were the same as her needs, she supposed. Words fail me. Words fail me. Words fail me, she wrote again and again in her notebook" (191).

Tillman's central means of opposing the transcendental claim of communion is through the double meaning of recognition. "To recognize" can mean: (1) "To know again; to perceive to be identical with something previously known . . . To know by means of some distinctive feature; to identify from knowledge of appearance or character"; and (2) "To perceive clearly, realize" (*OED* online). The first set of definitions denotes the act of recognizing as the act of knowing by *knowing-again*—to know in reference to what one already knows, to know by association. The second definition, however, denotes something entirely different. One knows (perceives, realizes) *without* recourse to knowing-again.[9] Unmistakably, this second definition of knowing-afresh is foundational to the ideal of communion as the transparency between multiple subjects.

Hence within its definition, "recognition" carries the seeds of the paradox that constitutes one of the key philosophical and theoretical challenges of contemporary fiction and theory: how can knowing be at once a knowing-again and a knowing-afresh? After poststructuralism mapped knowing as fundamentally an operation bound within preexisting codes and systems, how can recognition claim an "outside" from when one may know-afresh? How do I recognize others? How do they recognize me? Ultimately, what are the criteria for discerning the difference between misrecognition and proper recognition? If I cannot discern the difference, are they one and the same phenomenon? Built around the drama of recognition and its paradoxical meanings, *Motion Sicknesss* draws out the opacity of the other from the fundamental unreliability of recognition.

In theorizing recognition as the obstacle to communion, I now turn to two of the most influential theories on the concept—Althusser's theory of interpellation which cast the concept firmly within the operations of power and social organization; and Barthes's poststructural semiotics which pressed us to distrust the conditions of all that is "readable," "familiar," "stereotypical," and "recognizable." Although they emerge from different intellectual traditions, Althusser's Marxist critique of recognition and Barthes's semiotic critique of recognition converge upon a negation of communion, the key ingredient in the discourse of idealized community. Considering Tillman's contestation of the wordless dimension in the ideal of communion, these theorists' emphasis on the ideological, political, symbolic, and discursive dimension of recognition plays a crucial role in characterizing recognition as *mis*recognition. Thus, by giving ideological and symbolic heft to the operation of recognition, Althusser and Barthes short-circuit any theory of knowing from operating within the realm of transcendence. In Althusser's landmark essay "Ideology and Ideological Apparatuses" (1969), recognition lies at the heart of his theory of interpellation. Althusser uses the analogy of "hailing" ("hey, you there!") as the means by which the state identifies and reproduces subject positioning (as worker, student, family member, consumer; of specific race, gender, religion). The individual's response to that hail—the proverbial act of turning around—completes the state's inscription of individuals into "subjects" of ideological apparatuses (such as systems of education, religion, family; and legal, political, labor, capitalist systems). Thus recognition *enables* interpellation because that automatic response—of turning around to the hail—is naturalized as a self-evident response. Althusser uses a scenario of recognition familiar to all of us: a close friend knocks on my door; I ask, "Who is it?" S/he responds, "It's me." This answer reveals nothing except the fact that my visitor/hailer and I have an already-familiar relationship. I open the door not because my visitor/hailer identified her particular relevance to me (such as "It's Jane"; "It's your friend"; "I'm your neighbor") but because I obey the logic of knowing-again.

Such is the way, Althusser argues, that the state maintains and reproduces the conditions of production, the positioning of subjects within capitalist relations of exploitation. As we respond to the numerous "hails," we are performing "rituals of ideological recognition" which not only make us subjects of ideological apparatus but also naturalize the very logic of interpellation. "They 'recognize' the existing state of affairs (das Bestehende), that 'it really is true that it is so and not otherwise,' and that they must be obedient to God, to their conscience, to the priest, to de Gaulle, to the boss, to the engineer" (123). In the Althusserian theory of interpellation, then, recognition is the logic of acceding to a prior arrangement and relationship. Thus recognition is *already* a misrecognition: "The reality which is necessarily ignored . . . in the very forms of recognition (ideology = misrecognition/ignorance) is indeed, in the last resort, the reproduction of the relations of production and the relations deriving from them" (124).

Although Althusser's thinking on interpellation specifically targets the reproduction of capitalist labor relations and the maintenance of a class system, his theory of recognition-as-misrecognition fundamentally informs late-twentieth-century political and critical interrogations of (racial, ethnic, sexual, national, and many other categories of) identity and subjectivity. You are not what you say you are: you are what you are hailed. And the ways you are hailed are so familiar, so *repetitive,* that you believe that your response is of your own volition: "a subjected being, who submits to a higher authority, and is therefore stripped of all freedom except that of freely accepting his submission" (123). What is recognition, then, but an act of ideological submission? At the heart of Althusser's theory of recognition lies a distrust of repetition, the knowing-again that accedes to the logic of the repeated.

Likewise, a distrust of repetition underpins Barthes's lifelong study of semiotic systems. In his study of the signs and codes that span human expressions, in literature, fashion, photography, advertising, or political discourse, Barthes locates repetition as the indispensable logic of knowing by knowing-again. His overriding term for signifying the danger of repetition is "doxa," a term crucial to his interrogation of what constitutes the "familiar," the "recognizable," the "stereotypical," and "stupidity." Most extensively introduced in *Roland Barthes by Roland Barthes,* doxa is "never defined by its content, only by its form, and that invariably wrong form is doubtless: repetition" (70). It isn't that *all* repetition is the wrong form, Barthes clarifies; he distinguishes a "good form," such as an individual's repetition of a "theme" to strengthen her point ("The repetition that comes from the body is good, is right" [71]).[10] The wrong form of repetition, or doxa, is the repetition of an unlocatable discourse that comes from nowhere and everywhere—public opinion, cliché, stereotype, commonplace: "Doxa is the wrong object because it is dead repetition, because it comes from *no one's* body—except perhaps, indeed, from the body of the Dead" (71; original emphasis). "The Doxa is current opinion, meaning repeated as if nothing had happened. It is Medusa, who petrifies those who look at her" (122). As an unlocatable discourse whose omnipresence passes as the probable, the likely, and the real, dead repetition sits at the heart of knowing by knowing-again. What is recognition, hence, but an epistemological operation within the bounds of doxa?

The *form* of repetition, then, links Althusserian formulation of interpellation and Barthesian analysis of doxa. What Althusser identifies as the self-naturalizing logic of knowing-again—that "it ["the existing state of affairs"] really is true that it is so and not otherwise" (123)—finds a parallel in Barthes's identification of doxa's omnipresence: "The Doxa . . . is Public Opinion, the mind of the majority, petit bourgeois Consensus, the Voice of Nature, the Violence of Prejudice" (RB 47). "The Doxa is not triumphalist; it is content to reign; it diffuses, blurs; it is a legal, a natural dominance; a general layer, spread with the blessing of Power; a universal Discourse" (153).[11] What Althusser and Barthes bring to the fore, then, is a fundamental distrust of the condition of knowing-again. As they highlight the political work of repetition in the concept of recognition, a suspicion of repetition infiltrates our everyday acts—how we recognize others, how we are recognized, how we announce a certain representation's familiarity or realism, and how we evaluate the probability or likelihood of certain accounts.

Tillman's construction of girlhood in *Haunted Houses,* in fact, is inspired by a distrust of repetition, frozen language, and familiar conventions and stereotypes concerning female identity. In an interview, Tillman explains: "I felt angry that the way in which girls had been written about traditionally was so pallid. . . . Being a girl, becoming a girl, is extremely difficult. It was on my agenda to write a novel that was literary, formally unusual, and also took no prisoners in terms of its attitude toward these girls—a really tough-minded book about girls" (Sharpe n.p.). In *No Lease on Life,* repeated language gives a hilarious and disturbing turn as jokes. The novel begins with an Amish drive-by shooting joke, set apart typographically from the narrative, and not directly related to the events of the story. But the proliferation of jokes—bawdy jokes, racial jokes, sexual jokes, offensive jokes, psychiatry jokes, juvenile jokes—appear as unlocatable, repeated language, and in a novel about the frenetic energy of New York's East Village, these jokes represent "the fabric of the city," as Tillman identifies in an interview (Hogan n. p.).

But the most thorough interrogation of repeated language takes place in *Motion Sickness,* in which the contaminated nature of knowing infiltrates all aspects of life and every intersubjective relationship. The wandering life of the protagonist, a young white American woman who travels across Europe, is essentially a life of continuous skepticism in recognition. Her itinerant lifestyle is reluctantly funded by her mother who implores her to return home and "face the music" (88). She moves from one city to another at whim, accountable to no person or schedule; travel acquaintances, friends, and lovers of brief affairs constitute the shifting cohort. As the most emblematic sign of her hermetic status, she is a prolific collector and writer of postcards that she never sends. The "motion sickness" of the story, then, is the inevitable by-product of an unattached life. As Tillman describes in an interview, *Motion Sick-*

ness explores "the anxiety of recognizing how really unstable your identity is. . . . You're not going to achieve a stable existence, but that's not so terrible in a way. It might make you sick, though, once in awhile, because of that motion" (Nicholls 276).[12]

As the narrator lives the paradoxical condition of permanent travel, her biggest challenge is to exercise proper recognition—of unfamiliar cultural contexts, mores, gestures, and interactions. Each city, with its unfamiliar language, national characteristics, and cultural gestures, presents her with an oblique façade, where even basic social interactions are laden with multiplicity in meaning. In an Istanbul hotel, for instance, what does the silent nod from the hotel manager signify? Is it an indication of minimal courtesy, curiosity, or approval? How do her own "smile and nod and gesture" participate in the interaction (10)? In her uncertainty, mimicry becomes her default response: "The Englishman, when we passed [in the hallway], touched his hand to his head, a kind of salute, and I did likewise, a gesture that has absolutely no meaning to me at all" (10). As she has no means of confirming the "truth" of her understanding, and even less of controlling the meaning of her participation, her interpretations ultimately reveal nothing but her own epistemological framework: "I decide he [the hotel manager] does like me, as I have a need anyway to feel I am liked. No doubt this marks me as an American. I must be full of national characteristics that are hidden from me and are palpable to others" (10).

Thus, unlike Rick, in Powers's *Galatea 2.2*, whose humanism relies on the belief that his interpretation of the machine is knowing-afresh, Tillman's protagonist has no illusions about the tautological nature of her knowing. The knowing-again nature of her interpretation impresses upon her the predetermined condition of her hermeneutic system—how her American cultural inclination towards amiability, for instance, shapes her practice of recognition: "I may emit naïveté and hope in a limited way, the *grand narrative* I'm thrust out of overwhelming my individual predilections and deviations. The mirror over the hotel dresser offers no relief, no clue to my role in the larger story . . . [you] can't take the country out of the girl when the girl is out of the country" (188–89; emphasis added). This self-consciousness over "national characteristics" is elaborated more fully by Emily, one of the female protagonists in *Haunted Houses*. A young American girl living in Amsterdam, Emily "found herself wanting to say, Find a place of your own. You can do it, it would be good for you. She recognized an Americanness in ideas like: Things can change. Everything is possible. Just leave him. Her. You'll get the money somehow. Ideas about the frontier and a young country are unavoidable" (191). Inextricable from Emily's knowing is the large body of trite expressions, stock responses, and sound bites, precisely the "dead language" of repetition that constitutes doxa.

When recognition takes place within the web of "grand narratives," and one's unconscious responses manifest "national characteristics," what informs personal interactions but frozen plot typologies, characters, and clichés about those grand narratives? Where is the possibility for intersubjective transparency in this tired formula of knowing-again? Throughout her travels, she watches her individual identity performing various roles in numerous ready-made plots of race, gender, and national identity. In England, when she disputes a fare change made by the train conductor, she sees the predictability of her actions in the responses of her fellow passengers: "From the expressions on their faces, mirrors behind which their opinions sit, I see myself as the ugly, that is, the imperialistic American and, alternatively, the bossy New York woman. Or, less problematically, as just plain rude. Instantly I'm a set of conditions and positions, a reluctant but undeniable conduit" (35). Instantly, she bears the representational weight of a national character or, more specifically, a gendered national character, and she is helpless to resist her utility as a "conduit" in her fellow passengers' interpellation of her. As her visibility as a subject is contingent upon the repetition of a grand narrative regarding "American identity" (i.e., that Americans, especially New Yorkers, are loud and rude), Tillman's protagonist finds herself confined within the dead repetition of doxa—what passes as public opinion, the commonplace, the stereotype. One is known-again because the units of knowing (particular interpellation, cultural code, and grand narrative) already exist, a condition that Barthes describes thusly: "the name is the exact, irrefutable trace, as solid as a scientific fact, of a certain already-written, already-read, already-done; to find the name is to find that already which constitutes the code" ("The Sequence of Actions" 141; original emphasis).

Thus the protagonist experiences each encounter as another confirmation that knowing-again thwarts any prospect of intersubjective transparency. Individual interactions, in fact, become not an interaction between two individuals but an interaction between grand narratives. In a casual train conversation she reveals to a fellow passenger, a Pakistani man, that she does not wish to be married. "Ahh, he says, scrutinizing me, then may God be with you. I thank him. The rest of the journey he and I are noticeably silent, as if something portentous had occurred. . . . I'm sure he watched me throw my bag into the taxi and shook his head, certain I was meant for tragedy" (73). For the Pakistani man, her revelation is at once descriptive and confirmatory of the tragic plot typology of the Western woman who eschews marriage. To Alfred, an English traveler she meets in Italy, she is cast in the mold of an independently wealthy American expatriate: "I have begun to enjoy his fantasy of me, as if I were a projection of his or a twentieth-century American novel. . . . An F. Scott Fitzgerald flapper. Or a Hemingway woman, narrow-hipped, tight-lipped and disappointed in her man" (59). Recognition, in these scenes, is nothing but a repetition of preexisting characterizations, plot typologies, and tensions. These moments of recognition accumulate towards one conclusion in the novel: the insurmountable wall of frozen language, dead repetition, and stereotypes means that there is no transparency between individuals, only opacity.

What Tillman highlights, through her protagonist's mistrust of recognition, is that knowing by knowing-again operates on a *version* of fusion. Foreign travel—of being outside one's linguistic, national, and cultural context—highlights the large-scale nature of one's interpellation. At the intersection of encountering the other's "difference," the act of recognition is simultaneously an act of subsuming "I" into a collective "we," and "you" into a collective "you," of fusing a single individual into the body of a larger identity. To a hotel manager in Venice, the protagonist is one individual who is at once the body America: "New York, he says, looking at the postmark [of a card she receives], you have a big problem with drugs? I want instantly to resist the you of his question—but agree, yes, we do. He says that he or they have drug problems too" (42). This coerced fusion into a national identity is an experience that Emily, an American in Amsterdam, experiences: "As one of the representatives of a powerful and dangerous nation, Emily was hard pressed to explain that she and it were not the same" (*Haunted Houses* 191). Hence interpellation is never an exchange between two individuals but between grand narratives—what Althusser identified as the predetermined ideological state apparatuses and what Barthes identified as the omnipresent layer of repetition in language use. "I am indeed behind the door; certainly I should like to pass through, certainly I should like to see what is being said, I too participate in the communal scene; I am constantly listening to what I am excluded from; I am in a stunned state, dazed, cut off from the popularity of language" (RB 123). Like Barthes's speaker who objects to "what is being said" but cannot "pass through" the frozen repetition of language, Tillman's protagonists are keenly aware that they are helpless to resist the coerced fusion into a national identity.

As a subject trapped within/by recognition, the protagonist responds with two responses—of reveling in her trapped condition, and of hankering for the unrealizable. And it is the startling difference between these responses that best manifests the novel's ambivalence towards the ideal of communion. Accepting the fact that her knowing is always a knowing-again, the protagonist throws herself in a free play of repetition—of popular discourses, icons, stock characters, stereotypes, and national characteristics. She responds to her immersion in grand narratives by gleefully employing her own stock of grand narratives in her interpellation of others and even of herself. The protagonist's own grand narratives are heavily influenced by the long arm of mass culture, especially by American popular culture—for example, by Hollywood movies, bestsellers, and game shows. In an Amsterdam inn, the innkeepers, spanning three generations, remind her of a myriad of American TV shows: "Actually, looking more carefully, they're closer to Western types, on the order of 'Rawhide' or 'Bonanza' or *Seven Brides for Seven Brothers,* and from now on whenever I see them, either the theme song from 'Bonanza,' or 'I'm a Lonesome Polecat' from *Seven Brides* plays in my mind" (10–11). A café scene in Venice becomes a stage where the patrons enact various well-known scenarios: a scene of an older woman with two younger men suggests the possibilities of an "international intrigue party" involving the CIA and the KGB, or, perhaps, a "gigolo scenario"; as they leave, they are "followed closely by new players," a middle-aged woman with a lapdog who courts the attention of an elderly man (43–44). "I wait for someone to appear who's as fascinating as Tadzio in *Death in Venice.* I wait for a little girl, dressed in a red slicker, like the daughter Donald Sutherland searched for in *Don't Look Now*" (45). As she comprehends the foreign setting and people by anchoring them to the plots, scenarios, settings, and characters from her archive of movies, musicals, and books, her mind's wanderings represent a subjectivity dominated by ready-made signs of a postmodern image culture.

The degree of her confinement in the logic of repetition can best be seen her application of literary codes to herself. Her self-interpellation takes place through well-established, familiar literary characterizations and typology. As the narrative begins, she is in London, reading *The Portrait of a Lady.* At her narrative's end, she invokes Isabel Archer again, an emblematic female figure of New World innocence hopelessly out of place in the Old World: "Isabel Archer's end in *The Portrait of a Lady* may be worse than mine. It's impossible to tell. I've begun to repeat some stories, but is this the same thing as repeating myself?" (203). As she travels through Tangiers, she mulls over the cultural familiarity of her role through the literary trope of the "wandering woman"—a woman who renounces her Western society for a renegade life of freedom in the desert:

> A long time ago a young woman from France or Germany or Great Britain arrived here on the start of a journey. She left home to travel when travel was hard and when few women traveled alone. I can see her. In a long brown skirt of durable material, a dark jacket, sensible shoes, a broad-brimmed hat and a scarf, she is tall and solid, short and slight, blond, dark. She does not fall in love with anything but adventure. (116)

The descriptive flexibility in this rendition generates a parodic tone, as the specifics of the heroine's nationality, age, or appearance are all deemed interchangeable under the iconic status of a cultural code of the liberated heroine, the white woman who renounces her Western society for a renegade life in the desert (as she later names some names: Freya Stark, Isbelle Eberhardt, Kit Moresby). Like the few, quick sketches of a caricaturist, the narrator's use of the desert adventuress calls upon the most pronounced—the most congealed—features of the cultural code. In the way the narrator holds up the stories as a convention, however, the target of the parody is not so much the heroines and their actions as it is their iconic stature as "untethered" women. The nod of acknowledgment to the feminist import of these stories is countered by mocking their archetypal—their congealed—stature. For the narrator, their very familiarity and popularity transform them into just another grand narrative that is used to recognize her—in fact, just as the Pakistani man on the train did. The narrator's immersion in cultural codes, however, has a critical dimension: even as she enacts recognition through popular cultural stereotypes and familiar literary tropes, her ironic use of them as caricatures renders them *trite*. Certainly, it is a critique that she turns on herself, as she explicitly throws herself into "the discourse of others," what Barthes calls the pervasive influence of cultural codes (*S/Z* 184).

As a counterpart to this gleeful play in knowing-again is the lingering sense of oppression *by* knowing-again and a hankering for knowing-afresh. If the protagonist's frenetic movement through cultural codes, dead language, doxa, and grand narratives represents the acceptance of recognition-as-misrecognition, her enduring hope for intersubjective transparency represents the perennial refusal to give up the hope of transparency. As a way of highlighting the peculiar nature of this ambivalence, I will compare the protagonist's response to the Lacanian vision of the analysand as the corrective to misrecognition. Pivotal to this comparison is the fundamental role of language in shaping the subject and knowledge in Tillman's and Lacan's theories of knowing. Pivotal to their contrast, however, is the vastly different significance that transparency, or knowing as knowing-afresh, holds for Tillman's and Lacan's theories of knowing. The enduring appeal of transparent knowing is what announces the ideal role of communion, and the idealized community discourse, in Tillman's literary epistemology.

Méconnaissance (to misconstrue or to misrecognize), in Lacan's theory of knowing, describes a flawed way of knowing that results in radical error. The subject of méconnaissance is a knower who equates herself *only* with her conscious ego: that is, foundational to her sense of self and to her epistemology is the rejection of her unconscious, what cannot be brought into speech, the Other of the Symbolic order. As a defensive repudiation of the unconscious, this way of knowing results in méconnaissance—an imaginary knowing that believes one's ego and the world to be permanent, stable entities that yield transparent, univocal meaning. Thus, like Tillman's protagonist who strives to discern "what someone really is," the subject of méconnaissance believes that she is operating in a world of transparent meaning.

Precisely this misrecognition is targeted for correction in Lacanian psychoanalytic theory and practice. Unlike the subject of méconnaissance, the analysand is the subject who refutes the equation of the self with the conscious ego, and the concomitant vision of the self as a unity, fixed, stable, and transparent. Lacan writes: "[i]t is in the disintegration of the imaginary unity constituted by the ego that the subject finds the signifying material of his symptom" (*Écrits* 151). The "signifying material" emerges from the subject's unconscious, for it is the "unconscious which speaks the truth about the truth" (qtd. in Campbell 39).[13] As the analysand brings the formally repudiated unconscious and its desires into speech, the subject moves from méconnaissance to correct knowing: "he has verbalized it[;] . . . he has made it pass into the Word, or more precisely, into the epos by which he brings back into the present time the origins of his own person" (*Écrits* 51). Key to this move from being a subject of méconnaissance to analysand, then, is the subject's ability to bring into speech—into the Symbolic order—that which was previously impossible.

In situating his psychoanalytic theory within the field of language, Lacan's theory of the subject is, like Tillman's protagonists, fundamentally a subject of language. The subject is fundamentally a "parlêtre" ("the speaking being"), one who comes into being *through* the Symbolic order of language (*Écrits* 337). Lacan writes: "[T]here is no such thing as a metalanguage[,] . . . no language able to say the truth about the truth, since truth is grounded in the fact that it speaks, and that it has no other means with which to do so" (qtd. in Campbell 35). As Campbell explains, "A knower is a linguistic event, because language constitutes it as speaking object. It is no more than a stable structure of signifiers, a subjective position in language" (33). In Lacanian epistemology, then, the analysand who escapes méconnaissance is fundamentally a subject who refutes the first way of knowing—the belief in the self and the world as transparent, fixed, and univocal.

And herein lies the crucial difference between Tillman's and Lacan's treatment of epistemological transparency. While Tillman's protagonist accedes to the fact that intersubjective transparency is an untenable myth, and while she even revels in the proliferation of frozen signs and doxa, she does not dismiss the intersubjective transparency, *even while* fully cognizant of its false promise. Thus, unlike the Lacanian analysand whose escape from misrecognition is *founded* on the rejection of transparency, Tillman's protagonist continues to operate within the appeal of transparency. This divergent response to the primacy of language is what richly illustrates the peculiar nature of ambivalent community in *Motion Sickness*. Impossible as it is in the novel's literary vision, communion continues to operate as the most desirable *end-point,* the telos, of intersubjective relations. This teleological thinking marks the presence of idealized community values in a novel that begins in the dissenting community suspicion of communion.

Repeatedly, the protagonist experiences her immersion in grand narratives as a case of entrapment in/by recognition. For instance, she compares her congealed state of interpellation to that of her fellow traveler, an Irish man with ties to the IRA:

> Maybe I'm as trapped as Pete. Although I may be in a melodrama, not a tragedy, white middle-class young woman, from yet another dying empire. . . . National identity is like armor. On permanent loan from a museum. It's dull armor that I clink around in. Could I get an operation that would make me oblivious to symbols? Could I be like human Switzerland, always neutral to the partisan demands of birthplace? Get a transnational operation, get placed in a different body politic? (127)

When individuals interact through symbols and *only* through symbols, how can there be a process of recognition that is "oblivious to symbols"? The condition of being trapped in symbols is the protagonist's negation of the wordless communion in idealized community. After all,

epiphanic moments of communion are moments of knowing-afresh precisely because they take place *outside* language, sign-systems, symbols,
discourse, or any conventions of knowing. The protagonist's inability to
escape the "dull armor" of national identity, or any other ready-made
sign-systems, highlights the way communion, in the discourse of idealized community, delivers such an escape.

At the same time, the protagonist's negation of the possibility of transcendental knowing is at once an expression of longing for transparency—of the self, of the other, of the self *to* the other—that will ultimately deliver the communion of idealized community. The protagonist
expresses her frustration with the opacity of intersubjective relations
through the analogy of reading: "In my hotel room I draw mental pictures. Connect the dots. . . . A hostage to psychology and history. I'm
Arlette's reader, for instance, or Jessica's, and I'm my own. I'm almost
certain we can't be read like books, though" (175). Being a reader
whose reading practices are "hostage to psychology and history," the
protagonist's reading never attains the certainty of knowing-afresh but
knowing by knowing-again. Similarly, she holds up the metaphor of a
complete jigsaw puzzle to highlight her dissatisfaction with knowing-
again. Describing her attempt at representing one person to another
person, she writes: "And like the jigsaw puzzle that always comes to
mind when someone says my life is in pieces, one wants to fashion a
whole, something like a personality or a character, but I never finished
those giant puzzles when I was a kid, and the way I pick up the pieces
and display them for Jessica must be nearly useless" (18). Like the
analogy of reading, the completed jigsaw puzzle as the desirable model
for intersubjective relations articulates all the attributes of knowing that
she cannot attain in her dissenting community—wholeness rather than
partiality, fullness rather than incompleteness, knowing rather than
reading. Ultimately, her desire for the access to the "personality" or
"character" of another is the desire to breach the alterity of the other.

Thus we come to the desire for "true tourism" that began the
chapter—the narrator's desire for "the real adventure of seeing through
oneself. To see through to something outside, something beyond" (120).
Like Davis's characters who try to "really know," "figure out," or "get
a better picture of" the other, Tillman's protagonist longs to break out
of the rules of dissenting community shaping her reality—to break out
of the nonteleological community in which communion is forestalled.
Like the postcards she writes prolifically and never sends, the protagonist exists in a hermetic circle, reading furiously without the hope of
reading-afresh, evading the interpellation of home only to be locked

in another network of interpellation. Tillman, in an interview, voices a rebuttal to the assessment of the protagonist's immobilized condition: "A sociologist who read *Motion Sickness* in manuscript said he was disgusted by it because the narrator was so passive. And I said what do you mean 'passive'? She thinks all the time" (Nicholls 278). She certainly thinks all the time; perhaps thinking all the time is the inevitable condition of a subject who experiences knowing as a confinement in opacity.

Thinking all the time about the inadequacies of thinking all the time, these ambivalent subjects look over the fence to a reality ordered by idealized community: over there, those people experience oneself, others, and oneself *with* others in a continuous relationship. That there *is* no "over there," that there never was such a reality in another time or place, is a fact that these subjects know too well, as time after time they hold up the rules of idealized community as myths. But their demystification of the idealized community vision does not result in a comfortable acceptance of the dissenting community vision. Unlike the theorists of dissenting community, they cannot experience the opacity of being as the *originary* condition of community, nor can they experience the unbridgeable distance between one and the other as the *evidence* of community. Instead, these subjects occupy their dissenting community with more than a slight unease, and they interject myths of idealized community as the implicit guidelines of intersubjective relations. Thus they ceaselessly manifest their ambivalent community through questions guided towards the telos of communion. What does that stranger think of me? Was my lover telling the truth? What is my friend really like? What am *I* really like? What did she mean by that? Does he mean it? Why did he do that? Why did I say that? In the ambivalent community of Davis and Tillman, the quest to know becomes a motion in stasis, an unspoken prompt towards that world in which after all that thinking, one is assured transparency and communion.

CHAPTER 5

Community as Multi-Party Game

Private Language in David Markson's *Wittgenstein's Mistress*

Can you be absolutely alone? Heidegger suggests its impossibility: "Even Dasein's being alone is being-with in the world" (*History of the Concept of Time* 328). Jean-Luc Nancy, continuing his Heideggerian argument that being-together is the *basis* of being alone, argues: "[N]ot even Descartes can claim to be alone and world-less, precisely because he is not alone and worldless. Rather, his pretense makes it clear that anyone who feigns solitude thereby attests to the 'self-referentiality' of *anyone*" (*Being Singular Plural* 66; original emphasis). Thus, "to be absolutely alone, it is not enough that I be so; I must also be alone being alone—this of course is contradictory" (*Inoperative Community* 4). The very concept of absolute-aloneness, Nancy suggests, rests upon the concept of "everyone else." Absolute-aloneness can only be an effect of negativity, a signal of its discrepancy of what-it-is-not—the "everyone else" who is *not* alone. What Nancy, via Heidegger, brings to light is the specter of *Dasein* that functions grammatically and ontologically as "one" in a statement such as "One is absolutely alone." That "one" simultaneously announces the presence of the singular and of the plural is the ultimate testimony of the impossibility of absolute-aloneness: "A single being is a contradiction in terms. Such a being, which would be its own foundation, origin, and intimacy, would be incapable of *Being*" (*Being Singular Plural* 12; original emphasis).

The impossibility of absolute-aloneness constitutes the core argument in Nancy's dissenting community discourse—a vision of community as simply the fact of coexistence, in direct opposition to the idealized vision of community as the fusion of multiple individuals bound by common-alities. In an ontological and grammatical sense, the "we" of dissenting community constitutes the a priori condition of the singular: "A 'we,' even one that is not articulated, is the condition for the possibility of each 'I'" (*Being Singular Plural* 65).

This chapter examines David Markson's *Wittgenstein's Mistress* (1988) which demonstrates this most expansive definition of community. In the novel, Kate, the protagonist-narrator, believes that she is the last person alive on earth. An unexplained catastrophe has removed all humans in the world, while, oddly enough, the world's physical structures—natural and human-made environments—stand intact. Occupying a skeletal world empty of any other humans, Kate travels the world in search of other survivors, leaving written messages for someone to find, "looking in desperation" (48), searching for "anybody, anywhere at all" (17). By the time Kate begins her narrative ten years into her search, she has long since given up her travels and now resides in an abandoned beach house, sporadically recounting her life on a typewriter. The narrative that we hold in our hands, then, is her ultimate message, her final act of looking for "everyone else." Thus Kate's primary pursuit of "looking" dramatizes the basic premise of dissenting community: a person who is entirely alone, yet whose condition is inconceivable without the concept of "everyone else."

As the final novel of my analysis, *Wittgenstein's Mistress* presents a concluding point to the trajectory of ambivalent community in contemporary fiction. This book began with the least ambivalent community in Morrison's emphatic embrace of idealized community and connected that emphatic embrace to the dominance of idealized community in popular and literary discourse. The subsequent chapters traced the increasing challenge of dissenting community to the discourse of idealized community and highlighted the ways that idealized community values *answer back* to the dissenting community skepticism. In a growing degree of ambivalence and self-consciousness, Yamashita, Powers, and Davis and Tillman called upon transformative ideals, such as universalism, humanism, and communion, to enable their vision of a single body community.

This analysis breaks from the preceding chapters to examine a literary manifestation of the first-person plural "we" that does *not* seek to supersede the paradox of community through an ideal. In the impossibility of absolute-aloneness in *Wittgenstein's Mistress,* this analysis begins with the most expansive definition of community, the "we" that is "the condition for the possibility of each 'I'" (*Being Singular Plural* 65). Unlike the community of preceding chapters, the literary "we" of *Wittgenstein's Mistress* is not an expression of a body of individuals bound together by a commonality or transformed into fusion through sameness, sharing, unique commonalities, transparency, or continuity.

However, the "we" that the novel articulates is not exactly the same "we" of dissenting community, and that difference is where I locate my final instance of ambivalent community. Like all the other ambivalent communities studied in this book, the literary "we" asserted in *Wittgenstein's Mistress* contains the kernel of idealized community—a community that "works," serves a need, or fulfills a function. Thus the "we" of this novel crucially deviates from the "inoperative community" that forms the core of dissenting community: "[I]t is the work that the community does *not* do and that it is *not* that forms community" (Nancy, *Inoperative Community* xxxix; original emphasis). In a departure from the dissenting community "we" that does nothing except observe the fundamental fact of coexistence, the "we" of *Wittgenstein's Mistress* serves both a crucial function and a need. In addition to highlighting the ambivalent nature of the novel's "we," this functional community modifies—and challenges—the *in*operative "we" of dissenting community.

The ambivalent community of *Wittgenstein's Mistress,* I suggest, emerges through the turbulent and unstable nature of the protagonist's solitary language use. Most simply, Kate's language use wavers between a state of absolute omnipotence and one of absolute powerlessness. As the only person alive, Kate can use language in whatever way she wants. She can *say* what she wants, and, like a world-making God, what she says, *is.* She can claim to be of any age, can claim any name, any past history, for who is there to disagree? As Markson builds a connection between Kate's omnipotence in language use and her omnipotence in ontological authority, Kate's performance as a protagonist-narrator is bolstered by her own question, "But then what is there that isn't in my head?" (227).

However, a debilitating doubt accompanies this omnipotence. If there is no one to say *other* than what she says, there is also no one to *agree* with what she says. Is she fifty or some other age? Was her husband named Simon or Terry or Adam? Do certain objects in her life, such as a book or a painting, really exist, or is she imagining them? Do certain events that she remembers actually happen, or did she imagine them? If she can say *anything* at all about herself or the world-at-large, what

is the ground for her ontological authority? Indeed, in the absence of
"everyone else," how will she know if she is mad? So the mantra of
"What is there that isn't in my head?" finds its most severe counterpart:
"I may well have been mad" (9).[1]

Unmistakably, the two extreme ways in which Kate experiences solitary language use pivot upon one point: the absence of agreement. She
can say anything she wants because there is no one to agree or disagree.
She cannot say anything at all *because* there is no one to agree or disagree. The two extreme responses directly affect the nature of her "message" to "everyone else," the narrative that constitutes the text of *Wittgenstein's Mistress*. As the absence of "everyone else" translates into an
absence of agreement, the novel presents a philosophical rumination on
ambivalent community through its treatment of solitary language use.

Using the irreconcilable tension in Kate's solitary language as my paradigm of ambivalent community, I suggest that Wittgenstein's theory of
private language offers a rich theoretical tool for explicating the forces of
omnipotence and madness running through the novel.[2] When conceived
through the analogy of game-playing, private language may most simply
be understood as a single-party game. Unlike a multi-party game whose
rules operate by the agreement of multiple individuals, a single-party
game is a self-invented game in which one makes up all the rules. Precisely in this absence of other people's agreement, the private language
game becomes the paradigm for theorizing Kate's solitary language use.
It is in her fluctuation between a sense of omnipotence and of madness
that two drastically different conceptions of community emerge—a dissenting community vision in which her written message to "everyone
else" is simply an acknowledgment of coexistence and an idealized community vision in which her message to everyone else is a search for a
multi-party game run by agreement. Thus the two drastically different
ways she experiences private language game dramatize the two drastically different ways she experiences the function of "everyone else."

Through this contradictory significance of "everyone else," Markson
offers a provocative incarnation of a perennial literary topic. The concept of absolute-aloneness has long held great appeal to the literary
imagination, both as a condition and as a pursuit. Tales of sole survivors from shipwrecks, banishment, or natural disaster populate the
literary imagination, from Defoe's *Robinson Crusoe* to the speculative
end-of-the-world genre of science fiction to the dystopian disaster novels
like Paul Auster's *In the Country of Last Things*. The state of absolute-
aloneness also features as a desirable goal in the literary imagination,

constituting the motivation of protagonists such as Huck Finn, who flees down the Mississippi, or Italo Calvino's Baron in *The Baron in the Trees,* who climbs up a tree and never comes down again. In these explorations, the impossibility of absolute-aloneness raises its head, as the travails of each protagonist are never without the long arm of "everyone else." Whether manifest in the familiar customs, laws, and habits that the solitary protagonist never leaves behind (e.g., Robinson Crusoe who strives to re-create "civilized" living conditions) or in the inevitable attraction of abandoned kinship and identification (e.g., the Baron who rules the village from the treetop), the fact of coexistence is the steadfast backdrop for the protagonists. If the quest for absolute-aloneness is an attempt to escape "everyone else," literary renditions of that aim draw their greatest drama from the *impossibility* of imagining that condition.[3]

Precisely that drama constitutes the ambivalent community of *Wittgenstein's Mistress,* as Kate's search for "everyone else" takes on two contradictory significances. Is her search for "everyone else" a dissenting community endeavor, simply an acknowledgment that an "I" necessitates a "we"? Or is her search for "everyone else" an idealized community endeavor, a quest to join a multi-party game run by agreement?

Private Language as Errant Language Game

Markson announces Kate's single-party language game quite emphatically. Kate begins her narrative by recounting her practice of leaving messages on street corners and in museums throughout her decade of searching for "everyone else." The nature of these messages takes on a profound complexity when, later in her recounting, she reveals that they were written in a language *legible only to herself:*

> In fact I have even written in Greek.
>
> Well, or in what looked like Greek, although I was actually only inventing that.
>
> What I would write were messages, to tell the truth, like the ones I sometimes used to write in the street.
>
> Somebody is living on this beach, the messages would say.
>
> Obviously it did not matter by then that the messages were only in an *invented writing* that nobody could read. (57; my emphasis)

Kate's messages, written in an invented "Greek," are metonymic of her private language use and richly illustrate the oddity of her endeavor: the last person alive on earth who writes messages to "everyone else" in a language that *no one else* can read. The contradictory implications of this endeavor reveal much about the errancy of her language use and her ambivalent views towards community.

Before I use Wittgenstein's theory of private language as the paradigm for Kate's solitary language use, let me visit the contested scholarship surrounding the very idea of private language in Wittgenstein scholarship. At the heart of the debate is this question: does Wittgenstein's theory of language even support such a thing as private language? A great deal rides on the answer to this question, since opposing answers result in different—and irreconcilable—versions of Wittgenstein's theory of language.[4] I intervene in this debate to suggest that the opposing answers to the question of private language need not lead to irreconcilable versions of Wittgenstein's theory of language. By reformulating the terms of the debate, I propose a theory of private language as a viable language game within Wittgenstein's theory of language, but as an *errant* language game. Precisely the errancy of private language will play a pivotal role in my analysis of the ambivalent community in *Wittgenstein's Mistress*.[5]

The two representative positions in the debate over private language are the "community view" and the "individualist view," two loosely bound groups of scholars who respond in oppositional manner to the possibility of private language in Wittgenstein's theory of language. The community view argues that Wittgenstein's theory of language is fundamentally an argument for language use as a *public* transaction, and this view is thus premised upon the impossibility of such a thing as private language. Following Wittgenstein's lead that all language use is a series of game-playing, the community view argues that language use is fundamentally a multi-party game, a game played amongst multiple individuals. In contrast, the individualist view argues not only that private language is possible but also that the concept of a multi-party game does not inform Wittgenstein's theory of language.[6]

Both camps begin with the game-playing and rule-following analogy that structures Wittgenstein's theory of language. Wittgenstein explains the immeasurable variety of language use through the immeasurable variety of games that can exist:

Doesn't the analogy between language and games throw light here? We can easily imagine people amusing themselves in a field by playing with a ball so as to start various existing games, but playing many without finishing them and in between throwing the ball aimlessly into the air, chasing one another with the ball and bombarding one another for a joke and so on. And now someone says: The whole time they are playing a ball-game and following definite rules at every throw. (83)[7]

By subsuming language use under the "life-form," (or "form of life," 19, 23, 241), Wittgenstein casts language games under his most expansive descriptor for rules that govern social coexistence. "If I have exhausted the justification I have reached bedrock, and my spade is turned. Then I am inclined to say: 'This is simply what I do'" (217). "What has to be accepted, the given, is—so one could say, forms of life" (Part II, 226). Like *all* forms of life, such as organizations, conventions, behaviors, customs, habits, institutions, and traditions, language use operates through rules. It follows, then, that like any other form of life, language game is an activity of following rules. The break between the community and the individualist views takes place upon this question: can one be said to be following a rule *privately*? Obviously, this question has direct application for Kate's language use. Can Kate be said to be playing a private language game?

For the community view, the answer would be no. Pointing to the correlation between language use, game-playing, and rule-following, community view proponents argue that the concept of private language, as it is akin to playing a game *alone,* is inconceivable. The following propositions from *Philosophical Propositions* are central to the community view argument:

> Is what we call "obeying a rule" something that it would be possible for only *one* man to do, and to do only *once* in his life?—This is of course a note on the grammar of the expression "to obey a rule."
>
> It is not possible that there should have been only one occasion on which only one person obeyed a rule. It is not possible that there should have been only one occasion on which a report was made, an order given or understood; and so on.—To obey a rule, to make a report, to give an order, to play a game of chess are *customs* (uses, institutions). (199; original emphasis)

> And hence also "obeying a rule" is a practice. And to *think* one is obeying a rule is not to obey a rule. Hence it is not possible to obey a rule "privately": otherwise thinking one was obeying a rule would be the same thing as obeying it. (202; original emphasis)

For the community view, the question is: can a forever-solitary person be said to be capable of rule-following—of formulating and following self-made rules—and, by extension, be said to play language games? Pointing to Wittgenstein's emphasis on the impossibility of "obeying a rule privately," community view proponents argue the impossibility of a private language game: "What is really denied [in Proposition 202 above] is what might be called the 'private model' of rule-following, that the notion of a person following a given rule is to be analyzed simply in terms of facts about the rule-follower and the rule-follower alone, without reference to his membership in a wider community" (Kripke 296). More emphatically, "the concept of following a rule implies the concept of a community of rule-followers" (Malcolm, *Nothing Is Hidden* 156); "before someone can truly be said to follow rule R they must belong—truly belong—to a community whose other members also follow R" (Bloor 95). What the community view brings out, then, is the centrality of *agreement* in Wittgenstein's theory of all life-forms, rules, conventions, customs, practices, and games.

This equation must be seen in light of Wittgenstein's own correlation of "rules" with "agreement." In order to make rules tantamount to agreement, Wittgenstein takes great pains to distinguish rules from a coercive, oppressive force. Rather than think of rules as "railway lines along which we move in a fixed direction," Wittgenstein suggests that we think of rules as signposts on the road (85). Unlike a railway line that is preset, a signpost is merely a suggestion, a guideline. A signpost operates by agreement; drivers agree that its function is to guide in navigation, not force them to turn left or right. "The word 'agreement' and the word 'rule' are related to one another, they are cousins. If I teach anyone the use of the one word, he learns the use of the other with it" (224). Such propositions underwrite the community view's synonymous usage of "agreement" with "community." Agreement of rules is what identifies the presence of community; presence of community is what identifies agreement of rules. Thus the community view of Wittgenstein's theory of language fundamentally relies on a theory of language as essentially a *multi-party agreement*. Any language game that is not run by a multi-party agreement cannot be considered a language game at all.

This view obviously presents a major challenge to the narrative premise of the novel *Wittgenstein's Mistress*. Can the last person alive on earth be said to be playing a language game? Indeed, given the central requirement for an agreed-upon dimension in *any* form of life, can she be said to be following rules at all? According to the community view, answers to both questions would be no. How, then, can we account for the particular nature of Kate's language use, this bewildering phenomenon of a solitary speaker who, obviously, is playing alone? What the community view cannot account for is the peculiar nature of Kate's solitary language game—a game without agreed-upon rules, yet still a game in which there *are* self-imposed rules. It is towards the aim of accounting for Kate's single-party game that I will later suggest a theory of private language game as an *errant* language game.

The individualist view, in asserting the feasibility of private language in Wittgenstein's theory of language, contests the community view's requirement that a language game must include rules agreed upon by multiple individuals. Baker and Hacker, leading proponents of the individualist view, base their argument on Wittgenstein's propositions such as the following:

> Is it not imaginable, that each human being should think only for himself, speak only to himself? (*In this case each person could even have his own language*). . . . The Private Language which I have described above is like the one Robinson had on his desert island in which he was able to talk to himself. Had someone heard and observed him, he would have been able to learn Robinson's language. For the meanings of words are apparent in Robinson's behavior. (Manuscript Proposition 124, qtd. in Baker and Hacker, "Malcolm on Language and Rules" 173–74; original emphasis)

Highlighting propositions such as these, the individualist view asserts the single-party game as a viable paradigm of the language game and argues the possibility that a forever-isolated individual can use a language known only to self. In another representative strategy of the individualist view, Baker and Hacker argue that private language is not so inconceivable if we conceive a different relationship between rule-following and community. Private language is possible if we move away from the expectation that the rules *must* be "shared with other people," to the expectation "that they *can be shared,* that it must *make sense* for others to understand" ("Malcolm on Language and Rules" 171; original emphasis). As long as the *possibility* exists that the rules of the single-party game can be played in a multiple-party game, there is no absolute division between private language game and public language game.

On the one hand, the individualist view offers its own unique set of challenges to our protagonist's dilemma. This view provides the context for theorizing Kate's language use as a private language game. The only rule of this single-party game is that the player's rules are discernible and consistently applied—that the possibility exists for others, should they observe this player, to learn what the rules are. When multi-party agreement is cast out, there is no reason why self-generated rules, as long as they are consistently applied, cannot constitute a private language game. But what the individualist view cannot account for is the fact that so much of Kate's private language game is affected by her anxiety over the *rules of others*—that she may not be following them, that she may not be following them correctly, that she may be overlooking them. It is towards the aim of accounting for precisely this obsession with following the rules that I will suggest a theory of private language game as an errant language game.

I suggest that private language can be theorized as an errant language game if we operate on a more expansive understanding of Wittgenstein's key terms, "rule-following" and "game-playing." If we seriously implement Wittgenstein's exhortation for a flexible understanding of key terms, and for "everyday use" of his diction, the grounds of the community/individualist debate may be altered.[8] To begin with, there is a vast difference in the way that the community and individualist views define "game." The community view understands game-playing as fundamentally an activity of following *agreed-upon* rules. It follows, then, that an absolutely isolated individual cannot be said to formulate and maintain an agreement by oneself. The individualist view, on the other hand, understands game-playing as an activity of following *constraints*. As long as there are specific regulations and specific rules of causality, there is no reason why an absolutely isolated individual cannot be said to formulate and follow constraints by himself. Thus according to the community view, the central ingredient of "game" is "agreement," and according to the individualist view, it is "constraint."

But if we impose Wittgenstein's exhortations against the systematic use of diction—that one word always denotes one fixed meaning only—the standoff between the two definitions loses its tension. In the same proposition in which he posits an analogy between a ball-throwing game and a language game, Wittgenstein suggests: "And is there not also the case where we play and—make up the rules as we go along? And there is even one where we alter them—as we go along" (83). Likewise, the following proposition dramatizes a rebuttal to a critic who demands a single definition of the word "game":

"But still, it isn't a game, if there is some vagueness *in the rules*."—But *does* this prevent its being a game?—"Perhaps you'll call it a game, but at any rate it certainly isn't a complete game." This means: it has impurities, and what I am interested in at present is the pure article.—But I want to say: we misunderstand the role of the ideal in our language. That is to say: we too should call it a game, only we are dazzled by the ideal and therefore fail to see the actual use of the word 'game' clearly. (100; original emphasis)

If we hold that the rules of a game may be vague without affecting the ontological category of "game" itself, then the ground for the community/individual debate is seriously altered. If we apply Wittgenstein's dictum against the expectation of "the pure article" or "ideal" definition to the community view, we can modify the expectation that the definition of a game be *limited* to a multi-party agreement. There is no reason why a language game cannot accommodate private language, a single-party game, *as well as* public language, a multi-party game. Certainly, this possibility is crucial to theorizing Kate's highly idiosyncratic language use as the private language game of the last person alive on earth. More specifically, the theory of private language is necessary to highlight the errant nature of Kate's language use as a game played without agreement.

On the other hand, there is a serious challenge to the individualist view's claim that "game" may be understood as a solitary endeavor. This understanding requires a highly unusual definition of "game" and goes against Wittgenstein's strong prescription that philosophy should deal with "everyday use" of language. In numerous propositions, Wittgenstein offers his rebuttal to critics that his flexible use of central terms fosters confusion, exceptions, caveats, and contradictory interpretations. To these charges, Wittgenstein's principal response is that his diction is the use of "everyday language" and that, relatedly, the work of philosophy is to describe the use of this everyday language (106, 109, 116, 124):

> When I talk about language (words, sentences, etc.) I must speak the language of every day. Is this language somehow too coarse and material for what we want to say? *Then how is another one to be constructed?*—And how strange that we should be able to do anything at all with the ones we have!
>
> In giving explanations I already have to use language full-blown (not some sort of preparatory, provisional one); this by itself shews that I can adduce only exterior facts about language. (120; original emphasis)

Most memorably, Wittgenstein draws an analogy between everyday language and the "friction" necessary for walking. To demand "crystalline purity of logic" in philosophy is to erode the "actual use of language" (107). Without negating the plausibility of the individualist view, then, we must acknowledge the fact that its use of "game" as a single-party activity is a language usage that falls outside the "everyday" and "actual" use of the word. Although *in principle* the single-party game and solitary rule-following are possible endeavors, the highly unusual and exceptional nature of such definitions minimizes their *likelihood* in everyday usage. Thus we must give significant weight to the fact that in Wittgenstein's theory of language, the central analogy for game-playing is that of the multi-party game in which agreement of multiple individuals is a given. Without negating the possibility of private language in Wittgenstein's theory of language, we must hold the multi-party game—and the concept of public language—to be his *normative* model of language use.

Let me outline, then, how I see private language game as an errant language game. Wittgenstein's exemplary analogy for private language game is not a monologue or talking-to-self, but a language which can be understood *only* by the speaker:

> But could we also imagine a language in which a person could write down or give vocal expression to his inner experiences—his feelings, moods, and the rest—for his private use?—Well, can't we do so in our ordinary language?—But that is not what I mean. The individual words of this language are to refer to what can only be known to the person speaking; to his immediate private sensations. So another person cannot understand the language. (243)

Hence, "sounds which no one else understands but which I '*appear to understand*' might be called a 'private language'" (269; original emphasis). This hermetic quality, which will directly apply to Kate's message, can be understood in the fact that the single-party nature of this game cannot be translated into, or join, a multi-party one. Suppose, Wittgenstein proposes, that a child invents a name to refer to a sensation of toothache:

> But then, of course, he couldn't make himself understood when he used the word.—So does he understand the name, without being able to explain its meaning to anyone? But what does it mean to say that he has "named his pain"? How has he done this naming of pain?! And whatever

he did, what was its purpose?—When one says "He gave a name to his sensation" one forgets that a great deal of stage-setting in the language is presupposed if the mere act of naming is to make sense. (257)

Another crucial analogy for private language is of an aborted attempt at making a transaction: "Why can't my right hand give my left hand money? . . . When the left hand has taken the money from the right, etc., we shall ask: 'Well, and what of it?' And the same could be asked if a person had given himself a private definition of a word" (268). It is important to note that Wittgenstein's theory of private language uses the criteria of the multi-party game—the failure of the boy to "name" his pain *to others,* the failure of the left hand to make a transaction *with others.* In the implicit assumption of a multi-party game as the everyday context of language game, Wittgenstein affirms again public language as his normative theory of language use.

The errant nature of Kate's private language game, likewise, emerges from its inability to make a transaction through language, to join a multi-party game. That Kate's private language lacks the kernel of normative game-playing—agreed-upon rules—means that it lacks the most crucial element for determining a successful play of game—"outward criteria," which are, after all, a matter of multi-party agreement: "An 'inner process' stands in need of outward criteria" (580).[9] In the absence of agreed-upon rules, Kate's private language is a game that does not hold the possibility of making a "transaction," "making sense," "making oneself understood," or "being able to explain."[10] *How* she experiences this absence of agreement is where we can locate two theories of community at work. Is the absence of agreement *irrelevant* to the presence of community, as in dissenting community? Or is absence of agreement at once the absence of community itself, as in idealized community? The conflicting ways she experiences this absence of agreement takes her from omnipotence to madness, and it is within this spectrum that I locate the novel's ambivalent community.

Omnipotence

What Absence of Agreement Does for You

Let me return now to the invented "Greek" in which Kate writes her messages to "everyone else." The invented Greek emblematizes the errant nature of Kate's single-party game. In a game in which she makes all the rules, her playing is devoid of any outward criteria or agreement of community. Without any outward criteria, her message is absolutely illegible. As verbal acts intended to make contact with other survivors, what use are messages written in a language that no one else can read? As one might ask the boy who invents a name for toothache, "what is its purpose?" we might also ask, "what is Kate's point?" The fact that "her point" is discernible *only* to Kate identifies her language use as a private language game: a single-party game in which the sole player can unilaterally determine the rules without concern for making sense, for being able to explain or to make herself understood.

Markson continues the errant nature of Kate's language use in the *form* of Kate's monologue. The *Wittgenstein's Mistress* book that we hold in our hands, ostensibly, is the most extended and the ultimate version of Kate's "looking"—a veritable cry of "Here I am!" As a verbal account of her life—both pre- and postapocalyptic—the novel attempts to re-present the *presence* that is Kate. Yet the highly idiosyncratic nature of her narrative defies that function of representation. Here we can locate the symbiotic operation of Markson's experimental form and the novel's thematic focus on solitary language use. First, almost every sentence in Kate's narration stands alone as its own paragraph; characteristically short in length (usually less than two lines), the indented lines of each sentence stand as visually autonomous units. The unpredictable shifts in topic, reflective of Kate's always-shifting attention, mean that each sentence, rather than working in an accumulative, interdependent manner with its neighboring sentences, jostles in competition with every other sentence.

Second, Kate's preponderant use of trivia is another fundamental aspect of her private language game. In what is her final, verbal act of "looking," Kate's message largely consists of compilations of obscure details about famous figures in Western history, art, and literature. The trivia, especially in the first half of Kate's narrative, refers to the realm of the ludicrous, the weird, the unusual—details that have to do with well-known personages' oddities, substandard hygiene, physical deformities, obsessions, or compulsions.

> Have I ever mentioned that Michelangelo practically never took a bath in his life, by the way?
>
> And even wore his boots to bed?
>
> On my honor, it is a well known item in the history of art that Michelangelo was not somebody one would particularly wish to sit too close to.
>
> Which on second thought could very well change one's view as to why

all of those Medici kept telling him don't bother to get up, as a matter of fact.

Although come to think of it even William Shakespeare himself was terribly tiny, which is something I did once mention.

I mean so long as one would appear to be getting into this sort of thing.

Well, and for that matter Galileo would never even ever shake another person's hand, once he had discovered germs. (185)

Like her invented "Greek," the form of Kate's final message to "everyone else" is thoroughly unilateral and idiosyncratic in expression. The unpredictable shifts in topic and the preponderant use of trivia cannot be reconciled to the rules which a multi-party language game would call a "message."

It is exactly in this breach that the vision of dissenting community emerges. This message to "anyone, anywhere at all" (17) does not search for multi-party agreement. Like a dissenting community that does no "work" and has no instrumentality, Kate's message to "everyone else" is not meant to serve a *function*. Kate's search for "everyone else" is not a search for the telos of community held forth in idealized community discourse—for belonging, for fusion, for oneness. "Everyone else" is just that: everyone else. The "we" that makes the "I" possible is simply the observance of community as coexistence.

In fact, in Kate's successful playing without agreement, the novel demonstrates the liberatory potential of dissenting community. When "community" is not equated with "agreement," a private language game becomes a great source of creative agency for the sole player. In *Wittgenstein's Mistress*, this liberatory potential is most evident when the private language game begins to resemble the game of fictional world-making. That is, Markson offers a parable of fictional world-making as the most successful rendition of a private language game. In her freedom to *recount* the world however she wishes, she is free to *make* the world however she wishes. Thus in Kate's tales of being the last person alive on earth, there is a direct connection between her linguistic omnipotence and her ontological omnipotence. What Markson invokes here is what Vladimir Nabokov describes as the omnipotence of a fictional world-maker: "[E]very character follows the course I imagine for him. I am the perfect dictator in that private world insofar as I alone am responsible for its stability and truth" (69). Likewise, in Kate's private language game, Markson gives full rein to this dictator to be the sole rule-maker of her world.

Kate's "looking" years cover an incredible geographical span. She recounts driving across cities, states, countries, and even entire continents; she recounts sailing across rivers, lakes, and even bodies of ocean. Also remarkable in her travel accounts is the virtual irrelevance of maps and charts. For instance, she recalls crisscrossing the Greek Islands with a motor launch: "Even with only a page torn out of an atlas, instead of maritime charts, it took me only two unhurried days to get to Greece" (9); and she describes driving across Russia by "simply following the sun" (16). Her prowess as an explorer and navigator expresses her independence from human-made systems of spatial organization and appeals to an organic affinity with the natural world.

When she is not traversing the globe, Kate, a painter in the precatastrophe years, takes up residence in world-famous art museums; "burning artifacts and picture frames for warmth" (9), she lives in the Louvre, the Metropolitan Museum of Art in New York, and the Tate Gallery in London. Kate's verbal recounting of her "looking" displays a propensity for visually striking images. She recalls an experience in Rome when she believed that she actually spotted another life—a cat—skulking around the Colosseum: "How I felt. In the midst of all that looking. And so went scurrying to a supermarket for canned cat food" (28). She remembers leaving opened cans of cat food all over the stone seats of the Colosseum, "as many cans as there must have been Romans watching the Christians, practically": "Doubtless the cans are still there in either case, lined up across all of those seats. Rains would have emptied them completely by now, assuredly" (28–29). The image of hundreds, if not thousands, of rain-overflowing cans lined all around the steps of the Colosseum recurs throughout the narrative. Other recurring images from her years of "looking" include an account of her releasing hundreds of tennis balls from the top of the Spanish Steps in Rome; her habit of wearing wristwatches in quantities that literally cover her arms; her setting tens of alarm clocks to go off simultaneously and then systematically throwing every one of them into a river. Such striking images function as metonymies of her "looking" years, and through their variety and recurrence, we follow the tiny dot that is Kate traipsing around in the abandoned museums and monuments around the world, and we hear the reverberating echoes of her solitary movements.

What I am emphasizing here is not the impossibility of her claims, but the fantastical nature of her claims, claims that would be inconceivable if her language game were bound by rules of agreement. The source of Kate's fantastic and highly improbable tales becomes inseparable from her omnipotence as the sole rule-maker of her language game. There are no forms of life, no rules, no agreements that function as the standard of correctness, verifiability, truthfulness, or usefulness. Certain information—for example, the name of her husband or her son—changes in different moments of telling. Her account of her age changes, as do the accounts of her life. There are no artifacts, such as records of birth, death, or marriage, or correspondences that may attest to a traceable past. As Kate's omnipotence in language use translates into one of ontological authority, *Wittgenstein's Mistress* explores—and exploits—the liberatory potential of using language without agreement. What outward criteria are there to contradict Kate's ability to *say,* and *be,* what she wants? Who will contradict her tales of awesome adventures of crisscrossing oceans and continents? Who is to say that there wasn't a cat at the Colosseum? As Kate wonders frequently, "What is there that isn't in my head?" (227).[11]

As Kate's freedom *from* agreement translates into an absolute ontological authority, we might say that the novel's premise itself—the last person alive on earth—is the ultimate instance of language used without agreement, the ultimate paradigm of private language game. Like the Nabokovian dictator, or "God," another familiar literary trope for the fictional creator, Kate's private language game wields the omnipotence of one whose performative utterance *makes* the world. Kate's status as the "curator of the world" (227), as she calls herself, takes an entirely new dimension when she begins to reconstruct not only her own history but also the history of the Western world. With the omnipotence of a puppet master, Kate plays with well-known figures of history, art, literature, and myths. She intervenes in their lives and alters relationships, motivations, and, eventually, historical events themselves.

> So who is to argue that one day Rembrandt might not have been standing next to Carel Fabritius's easel, and Carel Fabritius said he was going to paint something russet, and Rembrandt said that russet is a color one calls a bedspread?
>
> So in a manner of speaking Willem de Kooning was actually a pupil of Rembrandt. . . .
>
> This is scarcely to suggest that Willem de Kooning was anywhere in the vicinity when Giotto was drawing the perfect circle freehand either, of course.
>
> Unless, on the other hand, I suddenly make up my mind to imagine that he was.

This very sort of imagining being the artist's privilege, obviously.
Well, it is what artists *do*. . . .

There is nothing astonishing in my ability to arrange any of this, of
course, although in certain ways it is perhaps interesting. (147–49; original emphasis and ellipsis)

Kate's conjectures ("suppose," "also suppose," "who is to argue," "in
a manner of speaking," "on the other hand") of disparate historical figures and times are vehicles for the *creative possibilities* of using language
without agreement. After all, imagining, or make-believe, is "what artists do." Like a creative world-maker, Kate's play of the imagination
is limitless, as its rules are free of the outward criteria of verifiability,
correctness, truthfulness, or effectiveness in usage. As Markson makes
inescapable the correlation between Kate's private language game and
the single-party game of artistic make-believe, the private language
game becomes the very paradigm of fictional world-making. Indeed, the
omnipotence of a fictional world-maker best embodies the potential to
create when one follows no one's rules but one's own.

In Kate's private language game, the thriving game of make-believe
takes place within a dissenting community vision. *This* message to everyone else is not a solicitation for agreement. Put another way, the search
for "everyone else" is not a search for agreement. That everyone else and
agreement are *irrelevant* to each other best demonstrates the irrelevance
between community and agreement in dissenting community vision.

Madness

What Absence of Agreement Does to You

However, the same errant game that gave rise to Kate's potential as
a world-maker gives rise to a debilitating doubt that cripples her private language game. The nature of this doubt, and its effect that ripples
throughout her message, are where I locate the novel's ambivalent community. Increasingly we see a single-party player who keeps breaking the
only rule of her game: that she plays only by the rules of own making.
When that rule is breached, and *rules of others* enter her private language, her single-party game becomes a multi-party game. And a game
defined by its freedom from rules of others becomes a game indistinguishable from a multi-party game in which rules are tantamount to the
agreement of multiple individuals. This breach is what takes place in

Kate's private language game, and with that breach enters the presence of idealized community into Kate's private language game.

Counterbalancing the liberatory potential of playing without agreement, Markson shows us a sole survivor who experiences the absence of agreement as an *affliction*. This sense of affliction appears in a seemingly minor fashion—through Kate's habitual expressions. But it is precisely through the habitual—certain practices that are so fixed or customary that they seem involuntary—that the agreed-upon dimension of multi-party game infiltrates Kate's private language game, and thus an idealized community vision affects her isolation. Like Davis's and Tillman's characters who cannot seem to stop pursuing intersubjective communion that they know is impossible, Kate engages in self-corrections and self-clarifications that demonstrate the powerfully internalized and naturalized dimension of the habitual, as demonstrated in the following samples: "I assume I do not have to explain that any version of any music that comes into my head would be the version I was once most familiar with" (38). "When I said that Guy de Maupassant ate his lunch every day at the Eiffel Tower, so that he did not have to look at it, I mean that it was the Eiffel Tower he did not wish to look at, naturally, and not his lunch. One's language being frequently imprecise in such ways, I have discovered" (42). Kate's continual modifications and clarifications dramatize her sense of inadequacy in her language game. In fact, they dramatize the standard of *constancy* that Wittgenstein identifies for multi-party language use: "If language is to be a means of communication there must be agreement not only in definitions but also (queer as this may sound) in judgments. . . . It is one thing to describe methods of measurement, and another to obtain and state results of measurements. But what we call 'measuring' is partly determined by a certain constancy in results of measurement" (242).

If we understand "measurement" as assessment, the requirement of "constancy" may be understood as the *agreement* that renders that assessment predictable. Kate's verbal clarifications and modifications, as they strive for a precision that evades her, enact a standard of constancy.[12] Why does a single-party player, who is the omnipotent rulemaker of her game, constrain her performance with the agreed-upon rules like constancy and preciseness? This influence of multi-party rules in Kate's private language game announces the *impurity* of her single-party game and bespeaks her fundamental ambivalence—over the liberatory potential of speaking without agreement and over the constancy and outward criteria that can come only with agreement. The more Kate experiences the absence of agreement as an affliction, the more her search for "everyone else" becomes something *more* than an expression of coexistence. "Everyone else" doesn't simply remain the grammatical and ontological condition of "I," as in dissenting community. "Everyone else" becomes the condition of affirming the very meaning of "I" through agreement. As agreement and "everyone else" become interchangeable in function, idealized community enters Kate's private language game.

The fact that Kate's desire for constancy extends well beyond her language use highlights the breach of multi-party game in her isolated existence. As a counterpoint to her effortless ability to navigate the physical world, Kate obsessively collects alarm clocks and wristwatches, at one point owning seventeen watches (81). Surely watches and clocks are relics of constancy, measurement, and organization that function through the agreement of multiple individuals. Likewise, in the absence of agreement, she frets that she may not really be what she says she is:

> Why have I written that his name was Adam?
> Simon is what my little boy was named.
> Time out of mind. Meaning that one can even momentarily forget the name of one's only child, who would be thirty by now?
> I doubt thirty. Say twenty-six, or twenty-seven.
> Am I fifty, then?
> There is only one mirror, here in this house on this beach.
> Perhaps the mirror says fifty. (9)

Later, as she revisits the topic of her probable age: "When one comes down to it, I could actually be well past fifty. Again, the mirror is of no real help. One would need some kind of *yardstick, or a field of comparison*" (33; my emphasis). Kate's self-doubt directly recalls Wittgenstein's proposition: "An 'inner process' stands in need of outward criteria" (580). For the very reason that Kate's "inner process" comes against no *competing* epistemological process, her ontological claims have no basis for authority. The very fact that she is free to say anything means that she cannot believe anything she says.

Kate's pursuit of agreement via her pursuit of "everyone else" directly illustrates the connection that Stanley Cavell draws between Wittgensteinian criteria, agreement, and community. In *The Claim of Reason: Wittgenstein, Skepticism, Morality, and Tragedy,* Cavell points out:

> The philosophical appeal to what we say, and the search for our criteria on the basis of which we say what we say, are claims to community.

And the claim to community is always a search for the basis upon which it can or has been established. I have nothing more to go on than my conviction, my sense that I make sense. It may prove to be the case that I am wrong, that my conviction isolates me, from all others, from my self. That will not be the same as a discovery that I am dogmatic or ego-maniacal. The wish and search for community are the wish and search for reason. (20)

Similarly, Kate's search for criteria—a "yardstick, or a field of compar-ison"—is simultaneously a search for reason—"the basis upon which" she can say what she says. And the search for criteria and reason is at once a search for community—"all others" whose sense-making is like her own. Furthermore, Cavell points out that this search for community is never more heightened than when one feels the *lack* of community, the lack of shared reason, criteria, and agreement:

Appealing to criteria . . . is an appeal we make when the attunement is threatened or lost. Official criteria are appealed to when judgments of assessment must be declared; Wittgensteinian criteria are appealed to when we "don't know our way about," when we are lost with respect to our words and to the world they anticipate. Then we start finding ourselves by finding out and declaring the criteria upon which we are in agreement. (34)

Precisely at this juncture does Kate's search for "everyone else" take on the heightened search for criteria, for only in possession of criteria can Kate "find herself," that is, confirm the validity of what she says. As Richard Eldridge elaborates on Cavell's formulation of Wittgensteinian criteria: "Without criteria, conditions under which things may be called thus and so, there is no possibility of making sense of the world. They enable our conceptualization of our experience, our comparing of things to one another" (571).

Furthermore, Kate's growing self-doubt in the absence of criteria enacts the anxiety that Cavell locates in Wittgenstein's examples of pro-found difference. Suppose, Wittgenstein proposes, that one encounters people who do things differently—people who count according to a different logic or people who use body language in a vastly different way (185). Cavell speculates on the response of anxiety that such differ-ence will likely incite: "These examples are all very upsetting. . . . I can understand *what he does*. . . . I don't know *why* he does it that way" (114; original emphasis). "The cause of our anxiety is that *we cannot make ourselves intelligible* (to him). But why does this create anxiety? Is it that we read our unintelligibility to him as our unintelligibility as such? What gives him this power over us? Why have we given it?" (115; original emphasis). The anxiety one feels in the face of such profound difference is indistinguishable from the anxiety one feels in the absence of shared criteria by which one can make oneself intelligible to the other. The "power" that one has given to the unintelligible other, in Cavell's formulation, is the same as the power that Kate has given to "everyone else" to render her own intelligibility. "It seems that our sense of having selves at all and of encountering and living in a world depends upon our finding others to conceptualize and talk about it as we do. Without community, there is, for us, no self-identity and no reason (in or for our conceptualizing)" (Eldridge 572).

In the absence of community, then, Kate's fear of madness raises its head as the final destination for a speaker without agreement. This destination, Eldridge postulates, is an inevitable one for a subject without external criteria:

> I can to some extent make my own criteria, constitute a community of one. But insanity is a threat here. . . . Even if I could (say through concentrating my inner attention) develop and maintain thoroughly idiosyncratic sets of criteria, ways of thinking and speaking (to myself, about what is going on in me—private languages are logically possible), something in me wants my habits of conceptualization and speech confirmed in the habits of another. Left alone with my criteria, it is as though I cannot bring myself to believe in them and to continue to deploying them in new cases. (572)

Increasingly, Kate's attention turns to the topic of madness, as her obsession with the idiosyncrasies, ills, and misfortunes of historical figures extends to the madness that afflicted them:

> Once, when Friedrich Nietzsche was mad, he started to cry because somebody was hitting a horse.
> But then went home and played the piano.
> On my honor, Friedrich Nietzsche used to play the piano for hours and hours, when he was mad.
> Making up every single piece of music that he played, too.
> Whereas Spinoza often used to go looking for spiders, and then make them fight with each other.
> Not being mad in the least. (232)

In the manner of Emily Dickinson's dictum to "tell it slant," these pointed ruminations on the madness of others function as Kate's self-representations in a tangential fashion. Indeed, her fixation on the topic of sanity and madness grows in tandem with her doubt over her own authority. Like her dismissal earlier of her biographical claims, she dismisses many of the details of her fantastical journey. The only other life she claims to have encountered—the cat at the Colosseum—comes under such a disclaimer:

> Possibly there was no cat at the Colosseum either.
>
> If one wishes to see a cat badly enough, one will doubtless see one.
>
> Though possibly there was a cat. Possibly it was only the floodlights, when I rigged up the floodlights, which made it leery.
>
> Naturally I would have had no way of knowing if it had nibbled at anything behind my back either, since most of the cans I had set out were half emptied by rain in no time. (133–34)

Possibly there was a cat; possibly there was no cat. Without outside criteria, without agreement from *someone else,* she cannot be certain. One by one, the world that she built out of conjectures ("why not?" "who is to say?" "let's suppose") about the lives of historical, literary, and mythical figures is de-authorized because her conjectures lack outward criteria: "Not one of these figures may be correct" (123). She even dismisses her interest in the lives, oddities, misfortunes, and madness of literary and historical figures: "I cannot conceive of why anyone would wish to pursue such a question" (122). Through these retractions, Kate wields the requirement of agreement as the final arbiter of her language game.

Markson demonstrates the halt to Kate's private language game most poignantly through the halt that comes to her creative imagination. Just as the ultimate success of a private language game is the Nabokovian omnipotence as the fictional world-maker, the ultimate *failure* of a private language game is the end to Kate's conjectures about the world. Kate's private language games moves between exactly these two poles, a fluctuation best demonstrated in her claims about a painting that she finds in her current residence. When Kate is reveling in the absence of agreement, she freely makes conjectures about the painting, imagining complex relationships and conflicts between the figures represented. As Kate creates a narrative trajectory with a series of "perhaps," she justifies her own imaginative play with the rhetorical question, "why not?"

(46). Why not believe that this is a painting of *this* house? That one of the figures depicted is the painter? That the other figure was angry with the painter because she did not want to be painted in the first place? In Kate's rhetorical question, "why not?" Markson encapsulates the omnipotence of the Nabokovian dictator and the most successful rendition of the private language game.

In contrast, Kate's inability to maintain the spirit of "why not" demonstrates her failure to maintain the private language game. At this end of the spectrum, we find a speaker who is afraid of exercising *any* ontological authority:

> There is nobody at the window in the painting of the house, by the way.
>
> I have now concluded that what I believed to be a person is a shadow.
>
> If it is not a shadow, it is perhaps a curtain.
>
> As a matter of fact it could actually be nothing more than an attempt to imply depths, within the room.
>
> Although in a manner of speaking all that is really in the window is burnt sienna pigment. And some yellow ochre.
>
> In fact there is no window either, in that same manner of speaking, but only shape.
>
> So that any few speculations I may have made about the person at the window would therefore now appear to be rendered meaningless, obviously. (55)

Not only does Kate dismiss her earlier conjectures about the subject of the painting; she also dismisses her own exercise in making ontological claims (a "shadow" is not representative of a person, only a paint pigment meant to imply physical depth). Kate's retraction from any ontological authority is her retraction from her private language game. In negating her ability to say anything she wants, she negates not only the creative possibilities of her imagination but also her ability to play a private language game *at all*. As the agreement of others becomes the condition for Kate's ability to say anything, her private language game comes to a halt.

The concluding page of *Wittgenstein's Mistress* encapsulates Kate's multi-party answer to the single-party question: "What is there that isn't in my head?" Kate's inevitable answer is: without agreement, everything. That a fall into madness remains the perennial specter means that the criterion of agreement has already breached her private language game.

In the ultimate sign of this impure private language game, Kate ends her narrative with a search for a diluted omnipotence that will lead to a "harmless . . . make believe" (240):

> Oh. And I have been hearing The Alto Rhapsody again also, these days.
>
> Which is to say the Real Alto Rhapsody this time, what with all of that having finally been sorted out.
>
> Even if it is still hardly the real one either, naturally, being still *only in my head*.
>
> But still. (240; emphasis added)

Ambivalent Community

"We" Always Works

So what is the significance of community in Kate's private language game? The answer rests entirely on how she views the role of agreement in her search for "everyone else." When agreement is irrelevant in her message to "everyone else," her private language thrives, and her language use operates in a dissenting community vision in which everyone else is simply the observance of coexistence. But when agreement is central to her message to "everyone else," her private language falters, and her language use operates in an idealized community vision in which "everyone else" is *not* just a fact of coexistence. "Everyone else" becomes multi-party agreement that can deliver confirmation of Kate's sanity, her history, her authority as a speaker, and even her very ability to use language. When "everyone else" becomes attributed with such *functionality,* we are back, again, in the land of idealized community in which community, any claim of "we," serves a function.

Befitting a study that began with the most idealized community found in Morrison's novels, my analysis ends with the novel that offers the most dissenting community vision—the impossibility of absolute-aloneness, the a priori "we" that prefigures the "I." Invoking Heideggerian Dasein and Nancian being-in-common, Kate's hapless search for "everyone else" signals coexistence as the originary community, the community without condition, the community that was not called into being to serve a function. But in the insistent way that Kate attributes functionality to "everyone else," the novel signals the inevitability that "I" will put "we" to *work.*

Most importantly for the trajectory of this book's argument, *Wittgenstein's Mistress* poses a crucial question to dissenting community discourse: can "everyone else" remain free of functionality? Kate's ambivalent community ultimately answers no, precisely because every invocation of community—every address to "everyone else"—arises from a specific dialogue with "I." The specificity of that dialogue; the particular context that gave rise to the dialogue; the unique needs, anxieties, and desires that gave rise to the address in the first place—these conditions speak to the fact that community does not make its presence known in a material and discursive vacuum. On the contrary, community can make its presence known *only* within a specific dialogue, in response to a specific address from an "I."

What the ambivalent community of *Wittgenstein's Mistress* best demonstrates is the distinction between community as an *idea* and community as a *presence*. This crucial distinction recalls Heidegger's argument that all philosophical arguments must be ontological arguments—claims made in light of Being—and not ontic arguments—factual claims made irrespective of Being: "Ontological inquiry is concerned primarily with Being; ontical inquiry is concerned primarily with entities and the facts about them" (*Being and Time* 31). Ontological talk is "[t]he kind of talk in which we say that something has *with* it an involvement *in* something, [this kind of talk] is not meant to establish a fact ontically, but rather to indicate the kind of Being that belongs to what is ready-to-hand" (353; original emphasis). Ontically, in *Wittgenstein's Mistress,* community can operate as the idea of coexistence, as the fact that such a thing as "everyone else" is the necessary presupposition for Kate's existence. Ontologically, however, community can be experienced only through the presence of a function—in this case, as the function of multi-party agreement.

Despite its narrative premise that emblematizes community as coexistence, *Wittgenstein's Mistress* ultimately challenges the ontic dimension of dissenting community ideal: community that is always-already present without the particular invocation of individuals. On the contrary, the novel's ambivalent community stresses the inescapable ontological dimension of community—community that is *called into being* by the address of individual and, once invoked, is put to work.

NOTES

Introduction

1. The prominence of "searching for," "reclaiming," or "building" community speaks to the dominance of idealized community discourse in critical assessments of contemporary fiction. Some monograph examples are John F. Desmond's *Walker Percy's Search for Community;* Philip Page's *Reclaiming Community in Contemporary African-American Fiction;* Bonnie TuSmith's *All My Relatives: Community in Contemporary Ethnic American Literatures;* and an edited volume by Linda S. Coleman, *Women's Life-Writing: Finding Voice/Building Community.*

The idealized community discourse also operates, albeit in a more complex manner, in those studies that study the "failure of community"—instances of community that *fall short* of the possibilities held by community. Such works include Thomas Fink's *A Different Sense of Power: Problems of Community in Late-Twentieth-Century U.S. Poetry* and Linda J. Holland-Toll's *As American as Mom, Baseball, and Apple Pie: Constructing Community in Contemporary American Horror Fiction.* Feminist studies of community voice the "failure of community" thesis most vocally, as in Jean Wyatt's *Risking Difference: Identification, Race, and Community in Contemporary Fiction and Feminism;* Cynthia G. Franklin's *Writing Women's Communities: The Politics and Poetics of Contemporary Multi-Genre Anthologies;* and Dale M. Bauer's *Feminist Dialogics: A Theory of Failed Community.*

2. For many contemporary thinkers, community is the site of that very slippage between unity and totality. Peter Hallward characterizes a feature of contemporary postmodernist philosophy as "a profound distrust of the very concept of a community. For these thinkers, 'community' often connotes a notion of fascism" (89). For Iris Marion Young in "The Ideal of Community and the Politics of Difference," the word community bears an "urge to unity" that is indistinguishable from an urge to totality, exclusion, and oppression (320). Likewise, Elizabeth Frazer argues that the use of "community" as a self-evident commendation in the discourse of idealized

community obstructs, rather than assists, politically progressive collectivities; the discourse of idealized community "diverts attention from the material conditions that might generate" the concrete social relations towards equitable unity (84).

3. See Elizabeth Frazer's *The Problems of Communitarian Politics*, especially chapter 6, on the prevalent use of the family as the ideal and model for community in contemporary philosophical, political, and legal scholarship and social sciences.

4. The phrase "Beloved Community," first coined by philosopher-theologian Josiah Royce in the early twentieth century, pursued a higher-order reality in which an absolute interconnectedness and unification of people bring disparate and disconnected aspects of reality into a single vision. King changes the "Beloved Community" from Royce's phrase of absolute idealism to an aspiration for the realization of justice, peace, and equity on a global scale. See The King Center's Web site, named "Beloved Community": http://www.thekingcenter.org/prog/bc/.

5. See Sandra Stanley, ed., *Other Sisterhoods: Literary Theory and U.S. Women of Color;* bell hooks's "Sisterhood: Political Solidarity between Women"; and María C. Lugones's "Sisterhood and Friendship as Feminist Models."

6. For instance, Friedman imagines a friendship model of community as the basis for a feminist communitarianism; Judy Whipps's "Jane Addams's Social Thought as a Model for a Pragmatist-Feminist Communitarianism" holds Addams's locality-based activism as a model for feminist communitarianism.

7. Here is an instance in Charles Taylor's *Philosophy and the Human Sciences:* "Common meanings are the basis of community. Inter-subjective meaning gives people a common language to talk about social reality and a common understanding of certain norms, but only with common meanings does this common reference world contain significant common actions, celebrations and feelings. These are objects in the world that everybody shares. This is what makes community" (39).

8. See Mark Poster's "Postmodernity and the Politics of Multiculturalism: The Lyotard-Habermas Debate over Social Theory."

9. Maurice Blanchot's *The Unavowable Community,* like Nancy's *The Inoperative Community,* finds its inspirational point in George Bataille's critique of communism, fascism, and various versions of communalism. Nancy identifies Bataille as having "gone farthest into the crucial experience of the modern destiny of community" (16), and Blanchot's first section, entitled "The Negative Community," credits Bataille as a founding member of "unworking" or "negative" community. See also Giorgio Agamben's *The Coming Community.*

10. See Hazel Carby's "White Woman Listen! Black Feminism and the Boundaries of Sisterhood"; Rosemary Hennessy et al., *Materialist Feminism: A Reader in Class, Difference, and Women's Lives;* Susan Weisser et al., *Feminist Nightmares: Women at Odds: Feminism and the Problem of Sisterhood.*

11. Butler's "Contingent Foundations: Feminism and the Question of 'Postmodernism'"; Spivak's "Subaltern Studies: Deconstructing Historiography"; and Mohanty's *Literary Theory and the Claims of History.*

12. Anderson offers an overview of James Clifford's "Traveling Cultures," Bruce Robbins's *Secular Vocations,* David A. Hollinger's *Postethnic America,* Paul Gilroy's *The Black Atlantic,* and Julia Kristeva's *Nations without Nationalism.*

Cosmopolitanism's fluid and deliberative formation of unity is often times equated with postnationalism. But as the essays in *Cosmopolitics: Thinking and Feeling Beyond the Nation* show in their measured and conflicting assessment of cosmopolitanism as ideal and practice, it is difficult to sustain a view of cosmopolitanism as a clean break from nationalist unity. Cosmopolitanist theory of unity is also the subject of skepticism, as in Timothy Brennan's *At Home in the World: Cosmopolitanism Now*, which wonders at the limited—and privileged—nature of a subject positioning that can claim to be "at home" everywhere.

13. Amanda Anderson's *The Way We Argue Now* offers another expression of cosmopolitanism as deliberative unity that "works," whose self-moderating powers rest in its careful balance of Enlightenment ideals and simultaneous interrogation of them.

Chapter 1

1. An MLA Bibliography search for "community" in Morrison's work produces seventy-eight scholarly entries. As I will demonstrate in this chapter, and as the following sample titles indicate, a strong continuity in values exists between Morrison's idealized discourse of community and her critics' appreciation of her vision. Indeed, in praising Morrison's literary exemplification of ideal and aspirational models of community, the scholarship directly continues the use of kinship relationships, such as "sisterhood," "brotherhood," and "family."

See O'Reilly's "In Search of My Mother's Garden, I found My Own: Mother-Love, Healing, and Identity in Toni Morrison's *Jazz*"; Mbalia's "Women Who Run with Wild: The Need for Sisterhoods in *Jazz*"; Romero's "Creating the Beloved Community: Religion, Race and Nation in Toni Morrison's *Paradise*"; Holland's "Marginality and Community in *Beloved*"; O'Shaughnessy's "'Life life life life': The Community as Chorus in *Song of Solomon*"; Christian's "Community and Nature: The Novels of Toni Morrison"; Blake's "Folklore and Community in *Song of Solomon*"; Schomburg's "To Survive Whole, To Save the Self: The Role of Sisterhood in the Novels of Toni Morrison"; LeSeur's "Moving beyond the Boundaries of Self, Community, and the Other in Toni Morrison's *Sula* and *Paradise*."

2. In a notable departure from the celebration of community in Morrison scholarship, the following essays suggest that in *Beloved*, Morrison argues the failures of community: King's "'You Think like You White': Questioning Race and Racial Community through the Lens of Middle-Class Desire(s)"; and Jesser's "Violence, Home, and Community in Toni Morrison's *Beloved*."

3. Jean-Luc Nancy's *The Inoperative Community* and *Being Singular Plural*; Ernesto Laclau and Chantel Mouffe's *Hegemony and Socialist Strategy: Towards a Radical Democratic Politics*; Giorgio Agamben's *The Coming Community*; Ernesto Laclau's "Community and Its Paradoxes: Richard Rorty's 'Liberal Utopia'"; Jean-François Lyotard's "À l'insu [Unbeknownst]"; Iris Marion Young's "The Ideal of Community and Politics of Difference"; and Jean-Luc Nancy's *The Inoperative Community*. See also my longer discussion of dissenting community in the Introduction.

4. Precisely in this message does Morrison invoke the negotiation of Gemeinschaft and Gesellschaft values that I described in the Introduction. The discourse of idealized community, in which community is given the status of an ideal, justifies the transformation of many into one as the "rational" movement (Gesellschaft value) towards "natural" unities (Gemeinschaft value).

5. As numerous critics of *Jazz* have noted, the vibrancy and primacy of the City elevate it beyond the narrative category of a setting; it attains the narrative potency of a character. See, for instance, Treherne, Sherard, FitzGerald, and Ludigkeit.

6. See Fraser's "Rethinking the Public Sphere: A Contribution to the Critique of Actually Existing Democracy."

7. See also Young's *Justice and the Politics of Difference* for the use of the city as the ideal politics of difference. The popularity of the city as the favored trope (e.g., of difference, of heterogeneity, of globalization) in contemporary theory is well-known, so much so that Laclau and Mouffe warn against the "totalitarian myth of the Ideal City" (77). See also James Donald's *Imagining the Modern City* for this caution.

8. Locating the study of the city in the beginnings of Greek and Roman philosophy, Nancy's redefinition of the city leads to a redefinition of the *task* of philosophy. Rather than being a study of a city's "origins," "political institution," or "civil coexistence" (31), philosophy should be a study of being-with. "[T]he city is primarily not a form of political institution; it is primarily a being-with *as such*. Philosophy is, in sum, the thinking of being-with; because of this, it is also thinking-with, as such" (31; original emphasis).

9. For approaches to identification as primary identification between parent and child, see Jean Wyatt, Mikkel Borch-Jacobsen, and Jessica Benjamin; for approaches to identification as melancholia, see Diana Fuss, Judith Butler, and Anne Cheng.

10. For example, see Wyatt's chapter 3; Tidey's "Limping or Flying? Psychoanalysis, Afrocentrism, and *Song of Solomon*"; Baker's "Knowing Our Place: Psychoanalysis and *Sula*"; Campbell's "Images of the Real: Reading History and Psychoanalysis in Toni Morrison's *Beloved*"; FitzGerald's "Selfhood and Community: Psychoanalysis and Discourse in *Beloved*"; Mathieson's "Memory and Mother Love in Morrison's *Beloved*."

11. As I will discuss in chapter 4, the *wordless* dimension of these epiphanic encounters also suggests the notion of communion, the possibility that one subject can be transparent to each other.

12. Celebration of sisterhood, a cornerstone in scholarship of Morrison's novels, tacitly echoes this theory of commonality-based identification that leads to reciprocal appropriation. Indeed, the language and the value system in scholars' praise of sisterhood take place within the teleological thinking of idealized community: commonality leads to affirmation and, ultimately, to collective healing. For example, in *Jazz*, "Morrison reveals that her first priority as an artist is in arriving at solutions for the dilemma of African people. Sisterhoods are needed in the African community, and through them, communication, not silence, will forge the way toward a healthy, wholesome future for all people of African descent, especially women" (Mbalia 642); "*Jazz* affirms and celebrates the maternal in both life and language. . . . The healing that is made possible through the child's return to the mother teaches us that hope for change and renewal begin with the mother" (O'Reilley 377). For further examples, see Schomburg, Holland and Awkward, and Jones.

This critical focus on sisterhood and matrilineal fusion is one that Morrison unequivocally affirms in her essays and interviews. In a 1977 interview, she stated: "I knew my mother as a Church woman, and a Club woman—and there was something special about when she said 'Sister,' and when all those women said 'Sister.' They meant that in a very, very fundamental way" (Stepto 474). Another example can be found in her essay "A Knowing So Deep," which addresses the sisterhood of black women in the form of a letter: "I think about us, women and girls, and I want to say something worth saying to a daughter, a friend, a mother, a sister—my self" (230).

13. Philip Page reads Ruby's founding stories in light of the Israelites' flight from Egypt and the American Dream; Katrine Dalsgard reads Ruby in light of American exceptionalism; and Ana Maria Fraile-Marcos reads Ruby alongside the American founding trope of the "City upon a Hill."

14. In an interview, Morrison identifies Richard Misner as the character with whom she identifies the most (Jaffrey 4).

15. Cited numbers in *The Differend* refer to paragraph numbers.

Chapter 2

1. Yamashita identifies him as "a literary interpretation of [Guillermo Gomez-Pena]. Arcangel's performance is grotesque, freakish, yet Christ-like, accounting for 500 years of history in the Americas" (Vengua and Tejeda n.p.).

2. Yamashita's novels reflect a far-ranging understanding of globalization as "processes of change which underpin a transformation in the organization of human affairs by linking together and expanding human activity across regions and continents" (Held et al. 15). As *Tropic* emphatically targets the First World's deployment of the "globe" as a "village," the novel joins the rising critique of the First World's celebration of globalization as a moment of unprecedented unity. See Alys Weinbaum and Brent Hayes Edwards, "On Critical Globality"; Fredric Jameson and Masao Miyoshi, *The Cultures of Globalization;* Arjun Appadurai, *Modernity at Large: Cultural Dimensions of Globalization;* Fredrick Buell, *National Culture and the New Global System;* Richard Falk, *Predatory Globalization;* Thomas Hylland Eriksen, *Tyranny of the Moment: Fast and Slow Time in the Information Age;* and John Tomlinson, *Globalization and Culture.*

3. Yamashita's approach also echoes the "internationalizing" vision for a postnational American studies. As John Carlos Rowe describes, postnational American studies "should be contextualized in a larger understanding of the United States in the comparative context of Western Hemispheric and finally global study" (31). Yamashita's focus on border crossing and hybridity in the Americas recalls works by Native American writers such as Leslie Marmon Silko and Gerald Vizenor, or works by Chicana/o writers such as Gloria Anzaldua, Cherrie Morago, Ana Castillo, and Alejandro Morales. Yamashita also aligns the transnational nature of her work to Jessica Hagedorn's *Dogeaters* (Gier and Tejeda n.p.).

Rachel Lee's "Asian American Cultural Production in Asian-Pacific Perspectives" offers the earliest assessment of Yamashita as anticipating the global frameworks that remap the theoretical and political terrain of Asian American cultural production. Analysis of transnationalism in Yamashita's works is central in essays by Molly Wallace's "Tropics of Globalization: Reading the New North America," Caroline Rody's "The Transnational Imagination," and Claudia Sadowski-Smith's "The U.S.-Mexico Borderlands Write Back: Cross-Cultural Transnationalism."

4. See the special issue of *Differences: A Journal of Feminist Cultural Studies*

devoted to universalism, which includes essays such as Étienne Balibar's "Ambiguous Universality," Naomi Schor's "French Feminism Is a Universalism," Joan Scott's "Universalism and the History of Feminism," and David Palumbo-Liu's "Universalism and Minority Culture." See also, elsewhere, Naomi Schor's "The Crisis of French Universalism" and Eric Lott's "After Identity, Politics: The Return of Universalism." Ernesto Laclau's numerous essays on universalism are collected in *Emancipation(s)*. See also Butler, Laclau, and Žižek's *Contingency, Hegemony, Universality: Contemporary Dialogues on the Left*.

5. For instance, Butler points out that Habermas pursues a "procedural method" "which establishes universalizability as a criterion for justifying the normative claims of any social and political programme." Although the procedural method distances itself from making declaration about human substance, "it does implicitly call upon a certain rational capacity, and attributes to that rational capacity an inherent relation to universalizability." In a roundabout way, then, the procedural method implicitly makes a foundational claim about human beings (*Contingency* 15). Another example of the antifoundationalist approach to universalism can be found in Laclau's constructivist defense. In response to Richard Rorty's assertion that liberals who disown commonalities among humans must also disown universalism, Laclau responds that if we approach universalism as a social product that emerges from specific historical necessities, we can have a universalism that is not a metaphysical fact about human nature or the human condition. "It is enough to recognize that democracy needs universalism while asserting that, at the same time, that universalism is one of the vocabularies, one of the language games, which was constructed at some point by social agents and which has become a more and more central part of our values and our culture. It is a *contingent* historical product" (*Emancipation(s)* 122; original emphasis).

6. Huyssen notes that while McLuhan's theory of the media was crucial to the political strategies of the 1960s counterculture, his "unbounded optimism about the effects of electronic communications on human community and his blindness to the relationship between the media and economic and political power could only be read as an affirmative culture, as an apology for ruthless technological modernization, or, at best, as naïve politics" (9).

7. A critique of such imperialist views of travel has been offered by postcolonial writers such as Derek Walcott and Jamaica Kincaid. In Asian American fiction, too, the critique of the reification of ethnic-specific locales (e.g., Chinatown) has been a central theme.

8. An example of such discourse: "And, the fact is, NAFTA has been an outstanding success. Between 1993 and 2002, merchandise trade between the United States and Mexico increased by 178 percent, from $79 billion to $220 billion, and, between 1988 (the year before the Canada-United States Free Trade Agreement, NAFTA's precursor, went into effect) and 2001, agricultural trade among the United States, Canada, and Mexico increased by 155 percent. According to the U.S. Trade Representative's office, trade between NAFTA partners increased 104 percent between 1993 and 2000—twice as fast as U.S. trade with the rest of the world. By lowering barriers, NAFTA has reduced the costs of imports for American businesses and consumers" ("Unfair" *New Republic*).

9. Molly Wallace, in "Tropics of Globalization," astutely points out that proponents of NAFTA use the metaphor of the weather to argue the inevitability of

south-north economic integration. Such rhetorical moves "not only naturalize capitalism" but make it "a veritable law of nature" (145). In discussing the inexorable global community in *Tropic,* it is important to distinguish between the inevitability of greater economic, political, and social interdependence from the *particular policies* put in place for regulating such an activity and from the celebratory view that such policies uniformly benefit a singular, global "we." To discuss the three as if they are one and the same phenomenon is a disingenuous move that parallels the unidirectional nature of imperialist universalism.

10. It is important that "hegemony" in this discussion be understood not as the negative force wielded by a few to oppress the many, but as in Ernesto Laclau and Chantal Mouffe's *Hegemony and Socialist Strategy: Towards a Radical Democratic Politics,* as the contingent articulation by different subject positions that take place in the field of limitless, differential relations that is the social. Hence, rather than being the political logic/attribute of a specific social sector or identities, hegemony is the articulation of power for which *all* subject positions strive.

11. The three thinkers diverge on theorizing the incomplete nature of universalism, a divergence that rests on their different theorization of the incomplete nature of the *subject.* More specifically, they differ on their respective use of Hegel and Lacan in theorizing the negativity at the heart of identity (the discrepancy between identity-claims and the actual constitution of identity).

12. See, for instance, Nancy's *Inoperative Community* (xxxix), Lyotard's "À l'insu [Unbeknownst]" (43), Hallward (89), and Young's "The Ideal of Community and the Politics of Difference" (302, 320).

13. See Anderson's "Cosmopolitanism, Universalism, and the Divided Legacies of Modernity"; James Clifford's "Traveling Cultures"; Bruce Robbins's *Secular Vocations;* and David A. Hollinger's *Postethnic America.*

Chapter 3

1. Other exemplary expressions of the posthumanist "we" can be found in Ray Kurzwell's *The Age of Spiritual Machines: When Computers Exceed Human Intelligence* and Danny Hillis's *The Pattern on the Stone.* See Timothy Lenoir's introductions to the two-part special issue of *Configurations* devoted to the topic of posthumanism. In "Part One: Embracing the Posthuman," Lenoir surveys leading posthumanists such as Hans Moravec, Marvin Minsky, and Danny Hill who exemplify the view that "the brain is a kind of a computer, and that thought is a complex computation" (Lenoir 206). As Lenoir makes clear, articulations of "posthumanism" are diverse, particularly in theorizing the division between materiality and information (i.e., body and mind). Thinkers of posthumanism who insist on the inextricability of body and mind (e.g., N. Katherine Hayles, Antonio Damasio, Francisco Varela, George Lakoff, and Mark Johnson) contest precisely thinkers such as Kurzwell and Hillis who practice the Cartesian division between body and mind.

Gerd Gigerenzer and Daniel Goldstein, in "Mind as Computer: Birth of a Metaphor," trace the mind-as-computer interpretation to cognitive psychology in the early 1970s. Norbert Wiener's foundational work on the relationship between the human body and information-processing technologies (*Cybernetics of Control and Communication in the Animal and the Machine* 1948) and Marshall McLuhan's work on communication technologies as extensions of the human body remain central to posthumanist disruption of organicist discourses of the body, gender, and sexuality.

2. The English mathematician Alan Turing (1912–54) proposed the original Turing test in "Computing Machinery and Intelligence" (1950). The Turing test demands that a human examiner decide whether the written answers given to his or her questions are generated by a computer or by a human. If the examiner fails to distinguish between human and machine responses, the machine may be deemed intelligent. Turing drew an analogy to "a sexual guessing game," in which an examiner tries to identify the respective sex of the test takers based on their answers.

3. The *Gold Bug Variations* also features a humanities reference librarian who finds herself untangling the scientific complexity of the genome research project. As Snyder observes regarding *The Gold Bug Variations*, "[e]ven as men appear in Powers's work as having produced much of the celebrated work of historical record, his valorization of amateur, cross-disciplinary thinking restores his female characters to a central role in his fiction where they serve as model proponents of the skills of border crossing and inspired collaboration" (95). It remains a strong pattern in Powers's novels of science and technology that the amateur agent who crosses disciplines is invariably a humanist, whose bewilderment and learning process stand as those of the implied reader's.

4. April Linder discusses Powers's ambivalence to "nineteenth-century realism" in "Narrative as Necessary Evil in Richard Powers's *Operation Wandering Soul.*" James Hurt in "Narrative Powers: Richard Powers as Storyteller" argues a "narrative therapy" that Powers practices, "not only therapy through narrative but also therapy *for* narrative" (24; original emphasis). Jeffrey Pence, in "The End of Technology: Memory in Richard Powers's *Galatea 2.2,*" reads Powers's defense of narrative as a defense of "a model and a modeler of memory" (344). See James Berger who locates a "persistence of Arnoldian ideas of culture" in *Galatea* (113). Kathleen Fitzpatrick's "The Exhaustion of Literature: Novels, Computers, and the Threat of Obsolescence" reads *Galatea* as an anxious expression about the role of traditional humanities and the role of the computer as the harbinger of posthumanist demotion of the book as the cornerstone of traditional humanities. Powers is indeed aware that Rick's use of the term "humanism" holds conservative and repressive significance in contemporary intellectual discourse, and he uses the graduate student A., the human counterpart in the novel's Turing test, to voice them. A. calls Rick's view of literature the views of "a complete throwback" who is "not even reactionary" (285).

5. In the extreme degree to which Powers's humanist-protagonists are amateurs in the fields of science and technology, Powers shows an interest in sketching out the humanist's alarm in its plainest and most extreme pitch. It is an alarm that recalls the extreme fears voiced in the early developmental years of computer technology, robotic technology, and artificial intelligence—that seeing the machine in a fluid and continuous relationship with the human means the displacement or the extinction of the human as we know it, that the human will "lose" the body, the mind, and consciousness. Lenoir's introduction to the special issue of *Configuration*, "Makeover: Writing the Body into the Posthuman Technoscape. Part One: Embracing the Posthuman," details humanism's fears of humankind's displacement or extinction that are expressed in the early years of artificial intelligence.

6. Miller's "Deeper Blues, or the Posthuman Prometheus" provides a rich overview of contemporary fiction's and popular culture's use of intelligent machines as artistic inspirations. Miranda Campbell's "Probing the Posthuman" locates in *Galatea* a critical stance towards posthumanist devaluation of materiality, but she asserts that the novel explores the humanist-posthumanist debate without "anxiously seek[ing] to reinstate the boundaries of this [human] subject" (1).

7. In his novels and interviews, Powers uses "narrative" interchangeably with "story," "fiction," "novel," and "storytelling." As I have addressed above, the centrality of narrative as a thematic topic in Powers's oeuvre is well noted in his scholarship.

8. I hasten to add that such division of materiality/information is not a maneuver that Hayles endorses in her own theory of posthumanism. As I will discuss further, theories of posthumanism differ in their treatment of the body/mind relationship, and Hayles here is noting a characteristic feature of those posthumanist thinkers who demote the relevance of the body, a move that she actively contests. Despite the differences in theories of the body/mind relationship, in the final analysis, posthumanism asserts the continuity and fluidity in the ontological category of the human and the machine.

9. As Helen's unworldliness performs a politically critical function, Rick's characterization of Helen recalls the political work of innocence in mid-nineteenth-century American sentimental fiction. As Nina Baym argued in *Woman's Fiction: A Guide to Novels by and about Women in America, 1820–1870,* the unworldliness of young female characters was central to the familiar plot typology in mid-nineteenth-century American women's fiction, wherein the innocence of the female children/adolescents was expressive of an ethereal goodness and moral purity.

10. In reading the deployment of gendered attributes in *Galatea,* however, it is difficult to assess Powers's gender politics as simply continuing patriarchal scripts. Certainly, the overwhelming power that Rick wields over Helen bespeaks the masculinist will to control the female-identified machine. His characterization of his old love C. is rife with stereotypical images of the moody, emotionally unstable female, as Hayles argues (*Posthuman* 266–69). He habitually envisions himself to be in love with female acquaintances. Thus there is considerable evidence in *Galatea* of the female-gendered identity being equated with passive receptivity.

Counterbalancing this masculine despotism are Rick's frequent allusions to *Frankenstein* (55) and *Pygmalian* (182), references that express a self-consciousness of his role as the shaper of identities. There is also the figure of A., the female graduate student who ridicules Rick's traditional humanist views: "And you wonder why the posthumanists reduced your type to an author function" (286). When Rick professes his love for her, she flatly refuses to be a projected ideal and scolds him for flightiness and "self-indulgence" (316). As the female character who shows up Rick's controversial views towards canonized literature's "greatness" and fantasized attractions towards women, A. functions as the counterpart to the emotionally unstable C. and the childish helplessness of Helen. This dyadic arrangement of two female-gender characterizations also appears in *Plowing the Dark* between Adie the artist-humanist and Sue the programmer-posthumanist.

11. Significantly, while Adie's chapters follow a third-person omniscient narration, Martin's chapters follow a direct address to "you" the reader, affecting the oldest virtual reality technology—simulation through words. See Marie-Laure Ryan's *Nar-*

rative as Virtual Reality.

12. The second part of *Configurations* special issue on posthumanism, "Part Two: Corporeal Axiomatics," features posthumanist projects that highlight the irreplaceable role of the biological body in conceptualizing the mind. As a primary example, Lenoir highlights Mark Hansen's work in relocating visual sense-making in the body as a principal example of conceptualizing the extended mind. Even in a digital context of virtual reality, Hansen argues, the visceral element of the body is the active framer of the image. "Virtual reality is, Hansen argues, a body-brain achievement" (Lenoir 378).

Chapter 4

1. See Elizabeth Frazier's discussion of the concept of communion in theories of community in political science, especially in communitarianism (75, 82).

2. In writing against the ideal of transparency, Davis and Tillman may be read as formally defying a convention of realism—the convention of the character, generally the protagonist, who comes to eventually attain the "truth" about the other characters and about her world. I emphasize this point in relation to Tillman's *Motion Sickness* in "Recognition as a Depleted Source."

3. Lydia Davis's short story collections include *Samuel Johnson Is Indignant* (2002), *Almost No Memory* (1998), *Break It Down* (1986), *Story and Other Stories* (1983), *Sketches for a Life of Wassily* (1981), and *The Thirteenth Woman* (1976). Davis is also well-known as a translator of leading French fiction, criticism, and philosophy (notably those of Marcel Proust, Maurice Blanchot, and Michel Leiris, as well as of Jean-Paul Sartre and Michel Foucault). Her many literary awards include a 2003 MacArthur Fellows Award.

4. Lynne Tillman's other novels are *No Lease on Life* (1998) and *Cast in Doubt* (1992). Her short works include *Absence Makes the Heart* (1990); *The Madame Realism Complex* (1992); *The Velvet Years: Warhol's Factory 1965–1967* (1995); a book of art criticism; and *The Broad Picture* (1997), a collection of essays. She has also written and codirected a movie entitled *Committed* (1984).

5. My use of "recognition" in this chapter diverges from another approach to recognition, notably found in the field of political science, which grounds the concept upon the following definition: "To acknowledge by special notice, approval or sanction; to treat as valid, as having existence or as entitled to consideration; to take notice of (a thing or person) in some way"; "To admit to consideration, or to a status, as being something" (*OED* online). Charles Taylor's "The Politics of Recognition" is an exemplary study of recognition as the acknowledgment and distribution of goods and rights. Julia Eichelberger's *Prophets of Recognition* is an example of a literary study of recognition as the apportioning of acknowledgment, respect, rights, and goods. Ralph Ellison, Toni Morrison, Saul Bellow, and Eudora Welty are "prophets of recognition" who "offer readers a vision of as-yet-unrealized democracy in which individuals acknowledge or recognize the innate worth of one another" (2).

6. This skepticism raised its head in a slightly different fashion in Richard Powers's interrogation of how the human might "know" the machine. Highlighting the

way that interpretation inevitably becomes translation, Powers emphasized the connection between the tautological dimension of the human's interpretation of the
machine and humanism's insistence that the human is a unique body of individuals.

7. As Larry McCaffery points out, however, Davis's "minimalist" nature is a
vastly different sort of minimalism from that of Raymond Carver, Ann Beattie, Mary
Robinson, or Frederick Barthelme, whose pared-down language use, form, and narrative premise were in direct response to what they saw to be excesses of their "postmodern" or "experimental" contemporaries (61).

8. This contradictory significance of alterity echoes the contradictory significance
of the unknowable city that I discussed in chapter 1 in relation to Morrison's *Jazz*.
While the postmodernist ideal of the unknowable city begins the narrative of *Jazz,*
that vision is progressively rendered into a problem that the protagonists must solve.
Thus the competing discourses of idealized and dissenting community manifest themselves in the contradictory significance of concepts such as alterity and the unknowable city in these novels.

9. The exemplar quotations for this definition are: "Linnell has made us recog-
nise a new beauty in the heather"; "Kepler first recognised the fact that the eye is a
camera" (*OED* online).

10. *Roland Barthes by Roland Barthes* will henceforth be cited as RB. Barthes
draws on Ancient Greek, especially Aristotle's use of *endoxa,* which, in Aristotle's
writing, meant "all that is considered true, or at least probable, by a majority of
people endowed with reason, or by a specific social group" (Amossy 369). In theorizing the oppressive nature of the form of repetition, Barthes works in and through
Gustave Flaubert's criticism of received ideas. Critics such as Michael Moriarty and
Christopher Prendergast have argued that Barthes's use of endoxa simplifies what is
a more expansive concept in Aristotelian usage. Also, see the special issue of *Poetics
Today* (Vol. 23, 2002) devoted to the topic of doxa in contemporary disciplines.

11. Anne Hershberg Pierrot in "Barthes and Doxa" offers an insightful examination of Barthes's use of metaphor (layer, petrification, glutinous, stickiness) in his
conceptualization of doxa.

12. Tillman's use of the term "recognition" in her interview refers to what I have
been calling proper recognition, "to perceive clearly, to realize." Furthermore, Tillman's use highlights another dimension of the word—recognition as the acceptance
of or resignation to an irreducible fact. Such acceptance or resignation, of course,
can only rest upon the second definition of recognition, upon the epistemological
certainty of knowing-afresh.

13. Campbell cites from the French edition of *Écrits* (Paris: Seuil, 1966).

Chapter 5

1. My analysis of madness departs from existing approaches to the topic of madness in the novel. For some critics of the novel, the fact of Kate's sanity is directly
related to her reliability as a narrator. That Kate is *not* mad is requisite to appre-
ciating the important philosophical ruminations in the novel. "We must believe
that Kate is truly the last person on earth—otherwise, we are left with an insane

woman. . . . As an investigation into the workings of thought and memory, the book would be invalid if the mind through which we follow this investigation were diseased. This is how an insane mind works, would be the caveat we would have to apply to everything we read" (Sullivan 241). "[Kate] is intrepid (only think of all that traveling), tough (dismantling things, improvising chimneys), curious and cheerful; her parody of Wittgenstein's philosophical discourse . . . is marvelously, if unconsciously funny, and she never whines or collapses in despair" (Grace 209). In such readings, the reader's literal acceptance of the narrative premise (i.e., Kate *is* the last person alive on earth) is fundamental to an empathetic reading of the novel, as well as to a full appreciation of the philosophical import of the novel. However, in my analysis, the condition of Kate's sanity as a protagonist-narrator is irrelevant. Rather, I emphasize the centrality of madness as a formal, thematic, and philosophical tool of inquiry.

2. See Joseph Tabbi's "David Markson: An Introduction" and "An Interview with David Markson" which address the inspirational role of Wittgenstein's thinking in the novel. The novel "appears not as an illustration of a set of philosophical ideas or even a novelization of the philosopher's life and thought, but as an original reading of Wittgenstein" (Tabbi, "Reading David Markson" n.p.). While the connection is not made explicitly in the novel (Kate professes not to have read a word of Wittgenstein), Markson explains: "The title just seemed to work for me, my woman as mistress to his thought, so to speak" (Private Correspondence, May 30, 2005).

3. This impossibility attains further complexity through David Markson's experimental form. As a foremost figure in contemporary American avant-garde fiction, Markson has long explored the figure of the isolated artist as a source of narrative premise and literary inspiration. Most importantly, Markson has rendered that isolated figure through a disjunction in form. As "Writer," the narrator of *This Is Not a Novel* (2001), announces best, Markson's literary oeuvre has consistently disrupted the conventions of the novel formally and thematically:

> A novel with no intimation of story whatsoever, Writer would like to contrive.
> And with no characters. None. . . .
> Plotless. Characterless.
> Yet seducing the reader into turning the pages nonetheless. (2–3)

This announcement of a novel that is not a conventional novel informs the formal strategy that is uniquely Markson's in contemporary fiction—a book-length collection of trivia about the lives of writers, artists, and philosophers throughout Western history, odd and unusual facts about their sanitary habits, their idiosyncrasies, their sexual habits and illnesses physical and mental, and gossip about their family lives. These entries thwart the conventional practices of the novel, and Markson achieves the avant-gardist act of "seducing the reader" through a form highly disruptive of conventional reading practices. This symbiosis between the isolated artist figure and the form of the non-novel appears most explicitly in *Reader's Block* (1996), in which an aged writer, isolated from his family and friends, finds that his attempt to write a novel continually comes into conflict with his life as a reader; thus the collection of literary, philosophical, historical trivia surfaces as the memory of a life spent reading. As I will show, Markson's non-novelistic form attains particular significance in *Witt-*

genstein's Mistress, since the highly unusual and idiosyncratic form will be inextricable from the single-party nature of Kate's private language game.

4. This question has been thoroughly revisited in the scholarship over Wittgenstein's "later stage" of thinking (*The Blue and Brown Book* and, of course, *Philosophical Investigations*). As many have noted, this debate is fueled by Wittgenstein's own refutation of a systematic use of language and the resulting indeterminacy in his writings. In explicit refutation of the systematic theory of language he offered in his "early" scholarship, such as *Tractus,* in his later scholarship Wittgenstein's central arguments are fueled principally by figurative expressions—through similes, metaphors, and analogies. The analogy-driven process of argument (e.g., language is like "a game of chess," using language is like "playing chess" or like "performing a transaction"; "use" is like "meaning" and like "understanding"; etc.) rests on an array of examples, and each example gives rise to a proliferation of possible interpretations. This *excess* of possible interpretations emerging from distinct, concrete examples fuels the debate over the possibility of private language, as each critical camp uses, and highlights, different propositions to support distinct versions of Wittgenstein's theory of language.

5. An important distinction needs to be made here. Since the term "community" is not evident in Wittgenstein's discussions of language games, I am not claiming to uncover, per se, Wittgenstein's theory of community through his writings on language. What I wish to highlight is the fact that the central presupposition of Wittgenstein's theory of language rests on the concept of agreement, and it is precisely this key presupposition that parallels the centrality of agreement, commonality, and consensus in idealized community discourse.

6. For a large overview of the debate, see Canfield and Gustafsson. For examples of the community view argument, see Malcolm, Bloor, Kripke, and von Savigny; for the individualist view, see Baker and Hacker, McGinn, Champlin, Moser, and Blackburn.

7. This multiplicity of language games defies the kind of mathematical, systematic accounting of language that is offered in his earlier work *Tractus,* which argued a singular logic underlying all of language use. However, in *Philosophical Investigations,* Wittgenstein argues that just as there can be a limitless number of games, there can be a limitless number of language uses, each use with its own set rules.

All propositions are cited by their paragraph number in *Philosophical Investigations;* propositions from Part II are cited by page numbers.

8. My method of intervention, arguing a wider understanding for the key terms in the debate, shares a similarity with Edward Minar's approach, which argues that to fault Wittgenstein for not offering a definitive answer to the private language question is to fundamentally ignore Wittgenstein's own approach to language use and to the task of philosophy—that the task of philosophy is to describe, not to define. Canfield's and Gustafsson's works, in reassessing the debate by offering different understandings of key terms, also show the scholarship's movement away from seeking a definitive exegetical answer to the private language question in Wittgenstein's language theory.

9. Lacking "outward criteria" has direct consequences for the "usage" of private language: "For a large class of cases—though not for all—in which we employ the word 'meaning' it can be defined thus: the meaning of a word is its usage in the language" (43; original emphasis). The modified subject of the phrase ("For a *large* class of cases—though not for all") stands as another example of Wittgenstein's

pursuit of "everyday use" of language and eschewing of "extreme subtleties" (106) in his approach to philosophical language. This emphasis on the actual use of language might stand as the response to critics who argue that Wittgenstein's equation of "meaning" and "use" is too sweeping in nature, leaving too many exceptions unexplored.

10. It is important to note here that I am not asserting a model of transparent communication as the ideal of public language game, an ideal that is more representative of the Habermasian ideal of communicative rationality. Rather, I am emphasizing the fact that "if language is to be a means of communication," as Wittgenstein argues (24), a given language game must possess the *possibility* of performing its specific function.

11. The indeterminacy that arises from Kate's account must be appreciated as being more than the effect of free indirect discourse. Certainly Markson takes full advantage of the homodiegetic narrator whose exclusive focalization obstructs the reader's ability to view the narrative events from any other consciousness. Like Oedipa Maas in *Crying of Lot 49* or Charles Kinbote in *Pale Fire,* Kate is a protagonist whose reliability as the narrator of the story events cannot be determined. The narrative premise of *Wittgenstein's Mistress,* with its explicit engagement with the linguistic and ontological implications of the last person alive, complicates the effects of free indirect discourse with philosophical challenges of the sole consciousness in operation.

12. The sentence structure anchored by adverbs of clarification and modification simulate, of course, the sentence structure of Wittgenstein's Propositions in *Philosophical Investigations* and elsewhere.

WORKS CITED

Agamben, Giorgio. *The Coming Community*. Trans. Michael Hardt. Minneapolis: University of Minnesota Press, 1993.

Althusser, Louis. "Ideology and Ideological State Apparatuses (Notes towards an Investigation)." *Lenin and Philosophy*. 1971. New York: Monthly Review, 2000. 85–126.

Amossy, Ruth. "Introduction to the Study of Doxa." *Poetics Today* 23 (2002): 369–94.

Anderson, Amanda. "Cosmpolitanism, Universalism, and the Divided Legacies of Modernity." *The Way We Argue Now: A Study in the Cultures of Theory*. Princeton: Princeton University Press, 2006.

Anderson, Benedict. *Imagined Communities*. London: Verso, 1983.

Appadurai, Arjun. *Modernity at Large: Cultural Dimensions of Globalization*. Minneapolis: University of Minnesota Press, 1996.

Baker, Gordon and Peter Hacke. *Investigations: Scepticism, Rules and Language*. Oxford: Blackwell, 1984.

——. "Malcolm on Langugage and Rules." *Philosophy* 65 (1990): 167–79.

——. *Wittgenstein: Rules, Grammar and Necessity*. Oxford: Blackwell, 1985.

Baker, Houston A., Jr. "Knowing Our Place: Psychoanalysis and *Sula*." *Toni Morrison*. Ed. and Intro. Linden Peach. New York: St. Martin's Press, 1997. 103–9.

Balibar, Étienne. "Ambiguous Universality." *differences* 7.1 (1995): 48–74.

Barthes, Roland. *Roland Barthes by Roland Barthes*. Trans. Richard Howard. New York: Hill and Wang, 1977.

——. "The Sequence of Actions." *The Semiotic Challenge*. 1985. Trans. Richard Howard. New York: Hill and Wang, 1988.

——. *S/Z: An Essay*. Trans. Richard Miller. Pref. Richard Howard. 1979. New York: Hill and Wang, 1974.

Bauer, Dale M. *Feminist Dialogics: A Theory of Failed Community*. Albany: State University of New York Press, 1988.

Baym, Nina. *Woman's Fiction: A Guide to Novels by and about Women in America, 1820–1870.* Ithaca: Cornell University Press, 1978.

Benjamin, Jessica. *Like Subjects, Love Objects: Essays on Recognition and Sexual Difference.* New Haven: Yale University Press, 1995.

Berger, James. "Testing Literature: Helen Keller and Richard Powers' Implementation H[elen]." *Arizona Quarterly* 58 (2002): 109–37.

Birkerts, Sven. "The Esquire Conversation: Richard Powers and Sven Birkirts." *Esquire* (July 2000). http://www.esquire.com/needtoknow/books/000701-info-powers03.html.

Blackburn, Simon. "The Individual Strikes Back." *Synthesis* 58 (1984): 281–310.

Blake, Susan L. "Folklore and Community in *Song of Solomon.*" *MELUS* 7 (1980): 77–82.

Blanchot, Maurice. "Literature and the Right to Death." *The Gaze of Orpheus and Other Literary Essays.* Trans. Lydia Davis. Ed. P. Adams Sitney. Barrytown, NY: Station Hill Press, 1981.

———. *The Unavowable Community.* Trans. Pierre Joris. Barrytown, NY: Station Hill Press, 1988.

Bloor, David. *Wittgenstein, Rules and Institutions.* London: Routledge, 1997.

Blume, Harvey. "Two Geeks on Their Way to Byzantium: A Conversation with Richard Powers." *Atlantic Unbound* (28 July 2000). http://www.theatlantic.com/unbound/interviews/ba2000-06-28.htm.

Borch-Jacobsen, Mikkel. *Emotional Tie: Psychoanalysis, Mimesis, and Affect.* Stanford: Stanford University Press, 1993.

Brennan, Timothy. *At Home in the World: Cosmopolitanism Now.* Cambridge; London: Harvard University Press, 1997.

Brooks, Rodney. *Flesh and Machines: How Robots Will Change Us.* New York: Pantheon, 2002.

Buell, Fredrick. *National Culture and the New Global System.* Baltimore: Johns Hopkins University Press, 1994.

Butler, Judith. "Contingent Foundations: Feminism and the Question of 'Postmodernism.'" *Critical Encounters: Reference and Responsibility in Deconstructive Writing.* Ed. Cathy Caruth and Deborah Esch. Intro. Cathy Caruth. New Brunswick, NJ: Rutgers University Press, 1994. 213–32.

———. *The Psychic Life of Power: Theories in Subjection.* Stanford: Stanford University Press, 1997.

Butler, Judith, Ernesto Laclau, and Slavoj Žižek. *Contingency, Hegemony, Universality: Contemporary Dialogues on the Left.* London: Verso, 2000.

Campbell, Jan. "Images of the Real: Reading History and Psychoanalysis in Toni Morrison's *Beloved.*" *Women: A Cultural Review* 7 (1996): 136–49.

Campbell, Kirsten. *Jacques Lacan and Feminist Epistemology.* London: Routledge, 2004.

Campbell, Miranda. "Probing the Posthuman: Richard Powers's *Galatea 2.2* and the Mind-Body Problem." *Reconstruction: Studies in Contemporary Culture* 4 (2004): 27 paragraphs.

Canfield, John V. "The Community View." *Philosophical Review* 105 (1996): 469–88.

Carby, Hazel V. "White Woman Listen! Black Feminism and the Boundaries of Sisterhood." *Materialist Feminism: A Reader in Class, Difference, and Women's Lives.*

Ed. and Intro. Rosemary Hennessy and Chrys Ingraham. New York: Routledge, 1997. 110–28.

Cavell, Stanley. *The Claim of Reason: Wittgenstein, Skepticism, Morality, and Tragedy.* Oxford: Oxford University Press, 1999.

Champlin, T. S. "Solitary Rule-Following." *Philosophy* 67 (1992): 285–306.

Cheng, Anne. *Melancholy of Race.* Oxford; New York: Oxford University Press, 2000.

Christian, Barbara. "Community and Nature: The Novels of Toni Morrison." *Journal of Ethnic Studies* 7 (1980): 65–78.

Clifford, James. "Traveling Cultures." *Cultural Studies: Now and in the Future.* Ed. Larry Grossberg, Cary Nelson, and Paula A. Treichler. New York: Routledge, 1992.

Coleman, Linda S. *Finding Voice/Building Community.* Bowling Green, OH: Bowling Green State University Popular Press, 1997.

Dalsgard, Katrine. "The One All-Black Town Worth the Pain: (African) American Exceptionalism, Historical Narration, and the Critique of Nationhood in Toni Morrison's *Paradise.*" *African American Review* 35.2 (2001): 233–48.

Damasio, Antonio. *Descartes' Error: Emotion, Reason, and the Human Brain.* New York: Putnam, 1994.

———. *The Feeling of What Happens: Body and Emotion in the Making of Consciousness.* New York: Harcourt Brace, 1999.

Davidson, Rob. "Racial Stock and 8-Rocks: Communal Historiography in Toni Morrison's *Paradise.*" *Twentieth Century Literature: A Scholarly and Critical Journal* 47 (2001): 355–73.

Davis, Lydia. *Almost No Memory.* New York: Farrar, Straus and Giroux, 1997.

———. *Break It Down.* 1986. New York: High Risk Books, 1996.

———. *The End of the Story.* New York: Farrar, Straus and Giroux, 1995.

Desmond, John F. *Walker Percy's Search for Community.* Athens: University of Georgia Press, 2004.

Donald, James. *Imagining the Modern City.* Minneapolis: University of Minnesota Press, 1999.

Eichelberger, Julia. *Prophets of Recognition: Ideology and the Individual in Novels by Ralph Ellison, Toni Morrison, Saul Bellow, and Eudora Welty.* Baton Rouge: Louisiana State University Press, 1999.

Eldridge, Richard. "The Normal and the Normative: Wittgenstein's Legacy, Kripke and Cavell." *Philosophy and Phenomenological Research* 46 (1986): 555–75.

Etzioni, Amitai. "The Road to the Good Society." *New Statesman* 05/15/2000, Vol. 129, Issue 4486. 25–27.

———. *The Spirit of Community.* New York: Crown Publishers, 1993.

Fink, Thomas. *A Different Sense of Power: Problems of Community in Late-Twentieth-Century U.S. Poetry.* Madison, NJ: Fairleigh Dickinson University Press, 2001.

FitzGerald, Jennifer. "Selfhood and Community: Psychoanalysis and Discourse in *Beloved.*" *MFS: Modern Fiction Studies* 39 (1993): 669–87.

———. "Signifyin(g) on Determinism: Commodity, Romance and Bricolage in Toni Morrison's *Jazz.*" *Lit: Literature Interpretation Theory* 12 (2001): 381–409.

Fitzpatrick, Kathleen. "The Exhaustion of Literature: Novels, Computers, and the Threat of Obsolescence." *Contemporary Literature* 43 (2002): 518–59.

Foster, Dennis. *Sublime Enjoyment: On the Perverse Motive in American Literature.* New York: Cambridge University Press, 1997.

Fraile-Marcos, Ana Maria. "Hybridizing the 'City upon a Hill' in Toni Morrison's *Paradise.*" *MELUS* 28 (2003): 3–33.

Franklin, Cynthia G. *Writing Women's Communities: The Politics and Poetics of Contemporary Multi-genre Anthologies.* Madison: University of Wisconsin Press, 1997.

Fraser, Nancy. "Rethinking the Public Sphere: A Contribution to the Critique of Actually Existing Democracy." *Social Text* 25/26 (1990): 56–80.

———. *Unruly Practices: Power, Discourse and Gender in Contemporary Social Theory.* Minneapolis: University of Minnesota Press, 1989.

Frazer, Elizabeth. *The Problems of Communitarian Politics: Unity and Conflict.* Oxford; New York: Oxford University Press, 1999.

Friedman, Marilyn. "Feminism and Modern Friendship: Dislocating the Community." *Feminism and Community.* Ed. Marilyn Friedman and P. Weiss. Philadelphia: Temple University Press, 1995.

Fuss, Diana. *Identification Papers.* New York: Routledge, 1995.

Gier, Jean Vengua and Carla Alicia Tejeda. "An Interview with Karen Tei Yamashita." 1 Feb. 2007. http://social.chass.ncsu.edu/jouvert/v2i2/yamashi.htm.

Gigerenzer, Gerd and Daniel Goldstein. "Mind as Computer: Birth of a Metaphor." *Creativity Research Journal* 9 (1996): 131–44.

Grace, Sherrill E. "Messages: Reading *Wittgenstein's Mistress.*" *The Review of Contemporary Fiction* 10.2 (1990): 207–16.

Gustafsson, Martin. "The Rule-Follower and His Community: Remarks on an Apparent Tension in Wittgenstein's Discussions of Rule-Following." *Language Sciences* 26 (2004): 125–45.

Halberstam, Judith. "Automating Gender: Postmodern Feminism in the Age of the Intelligent Machine." *Feminist Studies* 17 (1991): 439–60.

Hallward, Peter. "Generic Sovereignty: The Philosophy of Alain Badiou." *Angelaki* 3 (1998): 87–111.

Hassan, Ihab. "Prometheus as Performer: Towards a Posthumanist Culture?" *Performance in Postmodern Culture.* Ed. Michael Benamou and Charles Caramella. Madison, WI: Coda Press, 1977.

Hayles, N. Katherine. *Chaos Bound: Orderly Disorder in Contemporary Literature and Science.* Ithaca: Cornell University Press, 1990.

———. *How We Became Posthuman: Virtual Bodies in Cybernetics, Literature, and Informatics.* Chicago: University of Chicago Press, 1999.

Heidegger, Martin. *Being and Time.* Trans. John Macquarrie and Edward Robinson. New York: Harper, 1962.

———. *History of the Concept of Time.* Trans. Theodore Kisiel. Bloomington: Indiana University Press, 1985.

Hennessy, Rosemary and Chrys Ingraham, eds. *Materialist Feminism: A Reader in Class, Difference, and Women's Lives.* New York: Routledge, 1997.

Hogan, Ron. "Lynne Tillman in Her Own Words." 1 Feb. 2007. http://www.beatrice.com/interviews/tillman/.

Holland, Sharon P. "Marginality and Community in *Beloved.*" *Approaches to Teaching the Novels of Toni Morrison.* Ed., Pref., and Intro. Nellie Y. McKay. Ed. and Pref. Kathryn Earle. New York: Modern Language Association of America,

1997. 48–55.

Holland-Tolls, Linda J. *As American as Mom, Baseball, and Apple Pie: Constructing Community in Contemporary American Horror Fiction.* Bowling Green, OH: Bowling Green State University Popular Press, 2001.

Hollinger, David. *Postethnic America: Beyond Multiculturalism.* New York: Basic Books, 1995.

hooks, bell. "Sisterhood: Political Solidarity between Women." *Feminism and Community.* 396–411.

———. *Teaching Community.* New York: Routledge, 2003.

Hurt, James. "Narrative Powers: Richard Powers as Storyteller." *The Review of Contemporary Literature* 18 (1998): 24–41.

Huyssen, Andreas. "The Vamp and the Machine: Fritz Lang's *Metropolis.*" *After the Great Divide: Modernism, Mass Culture, Postmodernism.* Bloomington: Indiana University Press, 1986.

Iser, Wolfgang. *The Range of Interpretation.* New York: Columbia University Press, 2000.

Jaffrey, Zia. "The Salon Interview: Toni Morrison." *Salon* (1 Feb. 1998). http://www.salonmagazine.com/books/int/1998/02/cov%5fsi_02int.html.

Jagger, Alice M. and Iris Marion Young, eds. *A Companion to Feminist Philosophy.* Malden, MA: Blackwell Publishers, 1999.

Jameson, Fredric and Masao Miyoshi. *The Cultures of Globalization.* Durham: Duke University Press, 1998.

Jesser, Nancy. "Violence, Home, and Community in Toni Morrison's *Beloved.*" *African American Review* 33 (1999): 325–45.

Johnson, Mark. *The Body in the Mind: The Bodily Basis of Imagination, Reason, and Meaning.* Chicago: University of Chicago Press, 1987.

Jones, Carolyn. "Traces and Cracks: Identity and Narrative in Toni Morrison's *Jazz.*" *African American Review* 31 (1997): 481–95.

Joseph, Miranda. *Against the Romance of Community.* Minneapolis: University of Minnesota Press, 2002.

Kearly, Peter. "Toni Morrison's *Paradise* and the Politics of Community." *Journal of American & Comparative Cultures* 23.2 (2000): 9–16.

King, Nicole. "'You Think like You White': Questioning Race and Racial Community through the Lens of Middle-Class Desire(s)." *Novel: A Forum on Fiction* 35 (2002): 211–30.

Knight, Christopher J. "An Interview with Lydia Davis." *Contemporary Literature* 40 (1999): 525–51.

Kripke, Saul. "Wittgenstein on Rules and Private Language." *Perspectives on the Philosophy of Wittgenstein.* Ed. Irving Block. Oxford: Blackwell, 1981.

Lacey, Nicola and Elizabeth Frazer. *The Politics of Community: A Feminist Critique of the Liberal-Communitarian Debate.* Hemel Hempstead: Harvester, 1993.

Lacan, Jacque. *Écrits.* Trans. A. Sheridan. London: Routledge, 2001.

Laclau, Ernesto. "Community and Its Paradoxes: Richard Rorty's 'Liberal Utopia.'" In *Community at Loose Ends.*

———. *Emancipation(s).* London: Verso, 1996.

——— and Chantel Mouffe. *Hegemony and Socialist Strategy: Towards a Radical Democratic Politics.* London: Verso, 1985.

Lakoff, George and Mark Johnson. *Philosophy in the Flesh: The Embodied Mind and Its Challenge to Western Thought.* New York: Basic Books, 1999.

Lee, Rachel. "Asian American Cultural Production in Asian-Pacific Perspective." *Boundary 2: An International Journal of Literature and Culture* 26 (1999): 231–54.

Lenoir, Tim. "Makeover: Writing the Body into the Posthuman Technoscape. Part One: Embracing the Posthuman." *Configurations* 10 (2002): 203–20.

———. "Makeover: Writing the Body into the Posthuman Technoscape. Part Two: Corporeal Axiomatics." *Configurations* 10 (2002): 373–85.

LeSeur, Geta. "Moving beyond the Boundaries of Self, Community, and the Other in Toni Morrison's *Sula* and *Paradise.*" *CLA Journal* 46 (2002): 1–20.

Lindner, April. "Narrative as Necessary Evil in Richard Powers's *Operation Wandering Soul.*" *Critique: Studies in Contemporary Fiction* 38 (1996): 68–79.

Lindroth, James R. "Archetypes of Love, Hate, and Rebirth in Toni Morrison's *Jazz.*" *JAISA: The Journal of the Association for the Interdisciplinary Study of the Arts* 11 (1995): 113–19.

Lott, Eric. "After Identity, Politics: The Return of Universalism. *New Literary History* 31 (2000): 665–80.

Ludigkeit, Dirk. "Collective Improvisation and Narrative Structure in Toni Morrison's *Jazz.*" *Lit: Literature Interpretation Theory* 12 (2001): 165–87.

Lugones, María C. "Community." In *A Companion to Feminist Philosophy.* 466–74.

———. "Sisterhood and Friendship as Feminist Models." In collaboration with Pat Alake Rosezelle. In *Feminism and Community.*

Lyotard, Jean-François. "À l'insu [Unbeknownst]." In *Community at Loose Ends.* 42–48.

———. *The Differend: Phrases in Dispute.* Trans. Georges Van Den Abbeele. Foreword Wlad Godzich. Minneapolis: University of Minnesota Press, 1988.

MacMurray, John. *Persons in Relation.* London: Faber and Faber, 1961.

Malcolm, Norman. *Nothing Is Hidden.* Oxford: Blackwell, 1986.

———. "Wittgenstein on Language and Rules." *Philosophy* 64 (1989): 5–28.

Marcus, James. "This Side of Paradise: Interview with Toni Morrison." 1 Feb. 2007. http://www.amazon.com/exec/obidos/tg/feature/-/7651/002-5902217-4420056.

Markson, David. *Reader's Block.* Normal, IL: Dalkey Archive Press, 1996.

———. *This Is Not a Novel.* New York: Counterpoint Press, 2001.

———. *Wittgenstein's Mistress.* Normal, IL: Dalkey Archive Press, 1988.

Mathieson, Barbara Offutt. "Memory and Mother Love in Morrison's *Beloved.*" *American Imago: Studies in Psychoanalysis and Culture* 47 (1990): 1–21.

Mbalia, Dorothea. "Women Who Run with Wild: The Need for Sisterhoods in *Jazz.*" *MFS: Modern Fiction Studies* 39 (1993): 623–46.

McCaffery, Larry. "Deliberately, Terribly Neutral: An Interview with Lydia Davis." *Some Other Frequency: Interviews with Innovative American Authors.* Philadelphia: University of Pennsylvania Press, 1996.

McGinn, C. *Wittgenstein on Meaning.* Oxford: Blackwell, 1984.

McLuhan, Marshall. *The Gutenberg Galaxy: The Making of Typographic Man.* Toronto: University of Toronto Press, 1962.

———. *The Mechanical Bride: Folklore of Industrial Man.* Boston: Beacon Press, 1951.

——— and Bruce R. Powers. *The Global Village: Transformations in World Life and Media in the 21st Century.* New York: Oxford University Press, 1989.

Miami Theory Collective, eds. *Community at Loose Ends.* Minneapolis: University of Minnesota Press, 1991.

Michael, Magali Cornier. "Re-Imagining Agency: Toni Morrison's *Paradise.*" *African American Review* 36 (2002): 643–61.

Miller, D. Quentin. "Deeper Blues, or the Posthuman Prometheus: Cybernetic Renewal and the Late-Twentieth-Century American Novel." *American Literature* 77 (2005): 379–407.

Minar, Edward. "Paradox and Privacy: On Proposition 201–202 of Wittgenstein's Philosophical Investigations." *Philosophy and Phenomenological Research* 54 (1991): 43–75.

Mobilio, Albert. "Writing between the Lines." *New York Times Book Review,* December 16, 2001. Late Edition—Final, section 7, column 1, page 26.

Mohanty, Satya P. *Literary Theory and the Claims of History: Postmodernism, Objectivity, Multicultural Politics.* Ithaca: Cornell University Press, 1997.

Moore, Steven. "David Markson and the Art of Allusion." *The Review of Contemporary Fiction* 10 (1990): 164–78.

Moriarty, Michael. "Rhetoric, Doxa, and Experience in Barthes." *French Studies* 51 (1997): 169–82.

Morrison, Toni. *Jazz.* New York: Knopf, 1992.

———. "A Knowing So Deep." *Essence (*May 1985): 230.

———. *Paradise.* New York: Knopf, 1997.

———. *Sula.* New York: Vintage International, 2004.

Moser, P. "Malcolm on Wittgenstein and Rules." *Philosophy* 66 (1991): 101–5.

Mouffe, Chantal. *The Democratic Paradox.* London: Verso, 2000.

Nabokov, Vladimir. *Strong Opinions.* 1973. New York: Vintage, 1990.

Nancy, Jean-Luc. *Being Singular Plural.* Trans. Robert D. Richardson and Anne E. O'Byrne. Stanford: Stanford University Press, 2000.

———. *The Inoperative Community.* Ed. Peter Connor. Trans. Peter Connor, Lisa Garbus, and Michael Holland. Minneapolis: University of Minnesota Press, 1991.

Neilson, Jim. "An Interview with Richard Powers." *The Review of Contemporary Fiction* 18.3 (1998): 13–23.

Nicholls, Peter. "A Conversation with Lynne Tillman." *Textual Practice* 9 (1995): 269–84.

Nicholson, Linda. "Introduction." In *Feminism/Postmodernism.* New York: Routledge, 1989.

Nussbaum, Martha "Reply." In *For Love of Country: Debating the Limits of Patriotism.* 131–44.

———, ed. *For Love of Country: Debating the Limits of Patriotism.* Boston: Beacon Press, 1996.

O'Reilly, Andrea. "In Search of My Mother's Garden, I Found My Own: Mother-Love, Healing, and Identity in Toni Morrison's *Jazz.*" *African American Review* 30 (1996): 367–79.

O'Shaughnessy, Kathleen. "'Life Life Life Life': The Community as Chorus in *Song of Solomon.*" *Critical Essays on Toni Morrison.* Ed. Nellie Y. McKay. Boston: Hall, 1988. 125–33.

Page, Philip. "Furrowing All the Brows: Interpretation and the Transcendent in Toni Morrison's *Paradise.*" *African American Review* 35 (2001): 637–64.

————. *Reclaiming Community in Contemporary African American Fiction.* Jackson: University Press of Mississippi, 1999.

Palumbo-Liu. David. "Universalism and Minority Culture." *differences* 7 (1995): 188–208.

Paquet, Marie Anne. "Toni Morrison's *Jazz* and the City." *African American Review* 35 (2001): 219–31.

Pence, Jeffrey. "The End of Technology: Memory in Richard Powers's *Galatea 2.2.*" *Modern Language Quarterly: A Journal of Literary History* 63 (2002): 343–63.

Perloff, Majorie. "Fiction as Language Game: The Hermeneutic Parables of Lydia Davis and Maxine Chernoff." *Breaking the Sequence: Women's Experimental Fiction.* Ed. Ellen G. Friedman and Miriam Fuchs. Princeton: Princeton University Press, 1989.

Pheng, Cheah and Bruce Robbins, eds. *Cosmopolitics: Thinking and Feeling Beyond the Nation.* Minneapolis: University of Minnesota Press, 1998.

Pierrot, Anne Herschberg. "Barthes and Doxa." *Poetics Today* 23 (2002): 427–42.

Posnock, Ross. "The Dream of Deracination: The Uses of Cosmopolitanism." *American Literary History* 12 (2000): 802–17.

Poster, Mark. "Postmodernity and the Politics of Multiculturalism: The Lyotard-Habermas Debate over Social Theory." *Terror and Consensus: Vicissitudes of French Thought.* Ed. Jean-Joseph Gioux and Philip R. Wood. Stanford: Stanford University Press, 1998. 104–18.

Powers, Richard. *Galatea 2.2: A Novel.* New York: Harper Perennial, 1995.

————. *The Gold Bug Variations.* New York: HarperPerennial, 1992.

————. *Plowing the Dark.* New York: Farrar, Straus and Giroux, 2000.

Prose, Francine. "Lydia Davis." *BOMB Archives* 60 (1997). 26 June 2005. http://www.bombsite.com/archive/davis/davis1.html#pairingOne.

Robbins, Bruce. *Secular Vocations: Intellectuals, Professionalism, Culture.* London: Verso, 1993.

Rody, Caroline. "The Transnational Imagination: Karen Tei Yamashita's *Tropic of Orange.*" *Asian North American Identities: Beyond the Hyphen.* Ed. Eleanor Ty and Donald Goellnicht. Bloomington: Indiana University Press, 2004. 130–48.

Romero, Channette. "Creating the Beloved Community: Religion, Race and Nation in Toni Morrison's *Paradise.*" *African American Review* 39 (2005): 415–30.

Rorty, Richard. *Contingency, Irony, Solidarity.* Cambridge; New York: Cambridge University Press, 1989.

Rowe, John Carlos. "Post-Nationalism, Globalism, and the New American Studies." *Post-Nationalist American studies.* Ed. John Carlos Rowe. Berkeley: University of California Press, 2000. 23–37.

Ryan, Marie-Laure. *Narrative as Virtual Reality: Immersion and Interactivity in Literature and Electronic Media.* Baltimore; London: Johns Hopkins University Press, 2001.

Sadowski-Smith, Claudia. "The U.S.-Mexico Borderlands Write Back: Cross-Cultural Transnationalism in Contemporary U.S. Women of Color Fiction." *Arizona Quarterly: A Journal of American Literature, Culture, and Theory* 57 (2001): 91–112.

Schomburg, Connie R. "To Survive Whole, To Save the Self: The Role of Sisterhood in the Novels of Toni Morrison." *The Significance of Sibling Relationships in Literature.* Ed. and Intro. JoAnna Stephens Mink and Janet Doubler Ward. Bowling

Green, OH: Bowling Green State University Popular Press, 1992. 149–57.

Schor, Naomi. "The Crisis of French Universalism." *Yale French Studies* 100 (2001): 43–64.

———. "French Feminism Is a Universalism." *differences* 7 (1995): 15–47.

Scott, Joan. "Universalism and the History of Feminism." *differences* 7 (1995): 1–14.

Sharpe, Matthew. "Fiction Writers on Fiction Writing: Interview with Lynne Tillman." 17 April 2000. http://www.twc.org/forums/fiction_writers/fiction-lynne_tillman.html.

Sheehan, Aurelie. "Reading Lydia Davis." *Context: A Forum for Literary Arts and Culture* 26 (June 2005). http://www.centerforbookculture.org/context/n06/sheehan.html.

Sherard, Tracey. "Women's Classic Blues in Toni Morrison's *Jazz:* Cultural Artifact as Narrator." *Genders* 31 (2000): 40 paragraphs.

Snyder, Sharon. "The Gender of Genius: Scientific Experts and Literacy Amateurs in the Fiction of Richard Powers." *Review of Contemporary Fiction* 18 (1998): 84–96.

Spivak, Gayatri Chakravorty. "Cultural Talks in the Hot Peace: Revisiting the 'Global Village.'" *Cosmopolitics: Thinking and Feeling beyond the Nation.* Ed. Pheng Cheah and Bruce Robbins. Minneapolis; London: University of Minnesota Press, 1998. 329–48.

———. "Subaltern Studies: Deconstructing Historiography." *Other Worlds: Essays in Cultural Politics.* New York: Routledge, 1987.

Stanley, Sandra, ed. *Other Sisterhoods: Literary Theory and U.S. Women of Color.* Urbana: University of Illinois Press, 1998.

Stepto, Robert B. "'Intimate Things in Place': A Conversation with Toni Morrison." *Massachusetts Review* 18 (1977): 473–89.

Sullivan, Evelin E. "*Wittgenstein's Mistress* and the Art of Connections." *The Review of Contemporary Fiction* 10 (1990): 240–46.

Tabbi, Joseph. "David Markson: An Introduction." *The Review of Contemporary Fiction* 10.2 (1990): 104–17.

———. "An Interview with David Markson." *The Review of Contemporary Fiction* 10 (1990): 91–103.

———. "Reading David Markson." *Context: A Forum for Literary Arts and Culture.* 24 June 2005 http://www.centerforbookculture.org/context/n01/tabbi.html.

Taylor, Charles. *Philosophy and the Human Sciences.* Cambridge, MA: Cambridge University Press, 1985.

———. "The Politics of Recognition." *Multiculturalism: Examining the Politics of Recognition.* Ed. Amy Gutmann. Princeton: Princeton University Press, 1994.

Tidey, Ashley. "Limping or Flying? Psychoanalysis, Afrocentrism, and *Song of Solomon.*" *College English* 63 (2000): 48–70.

Tillman, Lynne. *Haunted Houses.* New York: Poseidon Press, 1987.

———. *Motion Sickness.* New York: Poseidon Press, 1991.

———. *No Lease on Life.* New York: Harcourt Brace and Company, 1998.

Tompkins, Jane. *Sensational Designs: The Cultural Work of American Fiction, 1790–1860.* New York: Oxford University Press, 1985.

Tönnies, Ferdinand. *Community & Society (Gemeinschaft und Gesellschaft).* Trans. and Ed. Charles P. Loomis. East Lansing: Michigan State University Press, 1957.

Treherne, Matthew. "Figuring In, Figuring Out: Narration and Negotiation in Toni Morrison's *Jazz*." *Narrative* 11.2 (2003): 199–212.

Turing, Alan. "Computing Machinery and Intelligence." *Mind* 59 (1950): 433–60.

TuSmith, Bonnie. *All My Relatives: Community in Contemporary Ethnic American Literature*. Ann Arbor: University of Michigan Press, 1993.

"Unfair." *New Republic* 230 (3 August 2004). "From the Editors."

Varela, Francisco J., Evan Thompson, and Eleanor Rosch. *The Embodied Mind: Cognitive Science and Human Experience*. Cambridge, MA: MIT Press, 1991.

Von Savigny, Eike. "Self-Conscious Individual versus Social Soul." *Philosophy and Phenomenological Research* 51 (1991): 67–84.

Wallace, Molly. "Tropics of Globalization: Reading the New North America." *Symploke: A Journal for the Intermingling of Literary, Cultural and Theoretical Scholarship* 9 (2001): 145–60.

Walzer, Michael. "Pleasures and Costs of Urbanity." *Metropolis: Center and Symbol of Our Times*. Ed. Philip Kasinitz. New York: New York University Press, 1995.

Weinbaum, Alys Eve and Brent Hayes Edwards. "On Critical Globality." *ARIEL: A Review of International English Literature* 31 (2000): 255–74.

Weiss, Penny A. and Marilyn Friedman, eds. *Feminism and Community*. Philadelphia: Temple University Press, 1995.

Weisser, Susan Ostrov and Jennifer Fleischner, eds. *Feminist Nightmares: Women at Odds: Feminism and the Problem of Sisterhood*. New York: New York University Press, 1994.

Whipps, Judy D. "Jane Addams's Social Thought as a Model for a Pragmatist-Feminist Communitarianism." *Hypatia: A Journal of Feminist Philosophy* 19 (2004): 118–33.

Wiener, Norbert. *Cybernetics of Control and Communication in the Animal and the Machine*. New York: John Wiley & Sons, 1948.

Williams, Raymond. *Keywords: A Vocabulary of Culture and Society*. New York: Oxford University Press, 1983.

Wittgenstein, Ludwig. *Philosophical Investigations*. 1953. Trans. G. E. M. Anscombe. Oxford: Blackwell, 2001.

Wyatt, Jean. *Risking Difference: Identification, Race, and Community in Contemporary Fiction and Feminism*. Albany: State University of New York Press, 2004.

Yamashita, Karen Tei. *Brazil Maru*. Minneapolis: Coffee House Press, 1992.

———. *Circle K Cycles*. Minneapolis: Coffee House Press, 2001.

———. *Through the Arc of the Rainforest*. Minneapolis: Coffee House Press, 1991.

———. *Tropic of Orange*. Minneapolis: Coffee House Press, 1997.

Young, Iris Marion. "The Ideal of Community and the Politics of Difference." *Feminism/Postmodernism*. Ed. Linda Nicholson. London: Routledge, 1990. 300–323.

———. *Inclusion and Democracy*. Oxford: Oxford University Press, 2002.

———. *Justice and the Politics of Difference*. Princeton: Princeton University Press, 1990.

Zalewski, Daniel. "Actual Reality." *The New York Times Book Review*. June 18, 2000. 12.

Ziolkowski, Thad. "Lydia Davis." *American Short-Story Writers since World War II.* Ed. Patrick Meanor. Detroit: Gale Research, 1993. 104–8.

Žižek, Slavoj. *The Ticklish Subject: The Absent Centre of Political Ontology.* London; New York: Verso, 1999.

INDEX